SOCIAL THEORY PERSPECTIVES ON ADULT EDUCATION

KV-501-381

SOCIAL THEORY PERSPECTIVES ON ADULT EDUCATION

BARRY ELSEY

Department of Adult Education, University of Nottingham

✓ **ISBN** 1-85041-013-5

Printed in Malta by Interprint Limited

ACKNOWLEDGEMENTS

As always, the sources of inspiration for writing a book are numerous and among these must be the many students on adult education courses who have responded to earlier try-outs of this material. My thanks to them. But two of my Nottingham colleagues stand out in my mind for sustained support and guidance and enduring friendship – Professors Michael Stephens and Teddy Thomas. In recent years I have received a great stimulus from Australian friends and colleagues in Adelaide, Armidale and the little paradise of Coffs Harbour. Above all, I wish to acknowledge my great debt to Heidi Kliche for fantastic support and some high speed typing on an Apple computer. All the errors are my own doing.

PART ONE

CHAPTER ONE

INTRODUCTION

The purpose of this book is to provide a straightforward guide to various social theories and perspectives that comprise a background to policies and practices in adult education. The book is mostly intended for students and practitioners in the diverse range of agencies and activities that are brought together under the wide umbrella of adult education. My assumption is that both students and practitioners in adult education, and they are sometimes studying and working at the same time, have a need, even a duty, to become reasonably familiar with the considerable variety of ideas that lie behind policy making and practice in adult education. This assumption is somewhat idealistic, as are several others that follow, but a book of this kind is allowed the luxury of expressing ideas as if in an ideal world.

The value of theory in adult education is a matter of some debate. It is not uncommon to hear adult education workers of all kinds express the opinion that the job is so practical that there is little call for the abstract generalisations of theory. This is, in my view, another way of claiming that ignorance is bliss and that adult education is better left to pragmatic decision making and practical action. However, I do share the view that sometimes theory building is so unrelated to policy and practice as to be useless. Theory should relate to practice if only because it provides scope for intelligent discussion about purposes, efficiency and effectiveness in the delivery of adult education. My assumption is that theory can inform the choice of policy options and practice, at least in a general way. At best theory provides a stimulating insight into everyday practice, even if the variety of perspectives that are embraced causes some confusion and uncertainty at times. Finally, in a book geared to the needs of students of adult education theory perspectives are a way of enhancing professionalism and keeping abreast of ideas. The point about ideas is that they ventilate thought and without that adult education becomes dull and lifeless. What I do know is that adult education is rich with ideas and both generates its own theoretical perspectives as well as uses the ideas in related fields, such as community development and social welfare, and the theories and concepts drawn from sociological perspectives.

Another realisation is that it is important to have a clear idea of the social theory perspectives that relate adult education to the social context of political economy, culture and the institutional and ideological frameworks of society as a whole. This provides depth to understanding ideas, policy and practice in adult education. In addition, it provides both intellectual stimulus and a basis for rational thought, which are essential ingredients for decision makers and the serious study of adult education as an intellectual and academic discipline.

It is worth stressing at this point that this book is not designed to tender any personally favoured school of thought. It is best to declare bias although by no means do I believe in everything I once thought. Nor am I against pragmatism. I favour the view that it is intelligent to try different ideas in a practical way to see if they work rather than operate exclusively from a fixed theoretical perspective. My personal experience is that people who insist, for example, on a radical perspective on adult education sometimes allow their prejudices, dogma and intolerance to get the better of the need of work with all kinds of people and points of view.

With these preliminary introductions over it is appropriate to proceed with a more specific account of the book. The starting point is a review of purposes and values in adult education, set within a brief descriptive profile of its historical evolution and current meanings. The main aim is to present the different perspectives or schools of thought in adult education which reflect interpretations about its role in society.

The next chapter, then, deals with the various schools of thought or ideological standpoints in adult education. Thereafter the following chapters focus on different areas of social theory perspectives as they relate to some of the main concerns of adult education. The purpose is twofold, first to explain the various social theories and the different perspectives they contain, and second, to relate these concepts and standpoints, at least in a tentative way, to ideological positions in adult education. Thus chapter three deals with concepts and models of social welfare as a background to the problem of making provision for disadvantaged adults and the question of public expenditure on the adult education service. In exploring the relationship between adult education and social welfare, through the connecting link of provision for the disadvantaged, the focus is more on theoretical ideas rather than institutional and practical details. It is sufficient to observe that adult education policy and practice with regard to the disadvantaged and deprived communities overlaps with many agencies and activities in social welfare provision. It would take too much space to detail these connections. The important point is to forge theoretical connections to explore different schools of thought or 'ideal-type' models in adult education and social welfare.

This is related quite naturally to an outline of various kinds of innovative provision in adult education centred around the problem of non-participation and the needs of disadvantaged groups, particularly the urban working classes, and using ideas and practices derived from community development. It is in this realm of adult education with a social dimension that many of the theory perspectives and concepts drawn from sociology and social policy can be introduced and applied. For example, much of the innovative forms of provision relates both directly and sometimes indirectly to theories and concepts of poverty, disadvantage, social equality, social class and sub-cultures and the meanings of terms, such as community, community development and social participation. The idea of the book, therefore, is to introduce and relate these ideas, expressed in the form of theories, different perspectives and concepts, to live issues and concerns in the policy making and practice of adult education without going into detail as to how the latter is or should be conducted.

From these theoretical perspectives in adult education, social welfare and related concepts and ideas it is then possible to move to wider sociological theory dealing with two models of society. This very general and abstract sociological model of society not only provides the ultimate theoretical framework but also distinctive ways of interpreting the nature and causes of the social problems dealt with by adult education and social welfare agencies. In addition sociology provides several theoretical perspectives and conceptual tools for a better understanding of issues and problems in adult education. Hence chapter seven introduces sociology as an intellectual discipline and provides the foundation upon which the earlier topics have been approached. For example, the 'systems' or 'holistic' theory approaches in sociology is very useful in the analysis of the relationship between adult education and society. This permits a more detailed appraisal of the ideas of various sociological writers and those who have attempted to apply their theories to practice in the context of adult education and community development with disadvantaged groups and the usually non-participating urban working class.

To give the purpose of this book even more concrete meaning a specific example may be given. Underpinning many of the expressions of purpose affecting policy and practice in adult education is the idea of social change. Whereas it is possible to use the idea of social change as an unexamined assumption the serious study of adult education requires that the concept be understood. Thus it is relevant to introduce the concept of social change by defining its meaning and outlining different classical theories and modern treatments. As this book is intended as an introductory text it is not possible to delve in great detail. Instead emphasis is placed on clarifying meanings and outlining the different theoretical perspectives applied to the concept of social change, especially where it relates to adult education. This topic runs through several sections of the book wherever it is most appropriately relevant.

The earlier chapters of the book use broad sociological and social welfare/policy theory in order to introduce the variety of perspectives and concepts that can be applied to issues and problems in adult education, which represent the focal points for policy and practice. These broad theories are especially useful in understanding the overall relationship between adult education and social context. Their limitations show up in dealing with more specific topics where another sociological perspective, the 'social action' one has greater applicability. For instance, in developing the idea of the 'second chance', a central theme in adult education, use can be made of micro-sociological theories. These deal with the specific experiences of adults undertaking education as returners to learning or mature students. Thus sociological theories of roles, status passage and marginality all have something to contribute as insights and frameworks of thought relevant to the processes of becoming an adult student and taking account of their social, educational and inter-personal experiences.

It should be clear what this book is about and how its content is generally organised. Two more things remain to be dealt with in this introduction. First there is a need to clarify my meaning of the terms 'theoretical perspectives', which has already been used several times, and 'social theory'. Both are very broad terms and can easily be overlooked in the effort to

3

explain more particular theories and concepts relating to adult education. The second task is to outline some key issues in adult education which warrant the application of social theory and various concepts.

My understanding of social theory is based on a dictionary definition which emphasises the ideas of speculative thought and the explanation of the main ideas, principles and concepts of a discipline. This accords well with the discipline of sociology. The really important point to make is that sociology has several theories of society and social behaviour, hence the emphasis upon different perspectives. Thus theory perspectives refers to the several ways of interpreting a social problem or issue. This applies as much to the study of adult education as with any other subject of sociological interest and analysis. There is a choice to be made, for instance, between 'consensus' and 'conflict' theory perspectives in sociology in the analysis of the relationship between adult education and society or, more particularly, the appraisal and approach to social issues by different schools of thought in the service. Similarly, in the analysis of the experiences of adult students sociologists can adopt several different ways of examining a problem within the social action theory framework. Social theory, then, is another of those umbrella terms comprising several different perspectives on social behaviour. I repeat that it is not my intention to advocate any one perspective but simply and plainly introduce several theories which have something to contribute towards the serious study of adult education and its relationship to society.

The book should be viewed as a companion to the several excellent texts dealing with the study of adult education from historical, philosophical, organisational, psychological and policy advocating perspectives [1]. It appears that the contribution of sociological theory is a latecomer to the study of adult education. There has always been a distinctive sociological contribution, though, through descriptive social surveys of students, volunteers and professional workers in adult education [2].

Finally it is useful to set some kind of scene of adult education issues and problems which invite the contribution of social theory perspectives. The choice of issues and problems is invariably selective but hopefully representative of some major concerns in adult education.

Adult educators, like most other workers, have views about the main issues and problems confronting them. Views differ but there is a generally agreed agenda of issues and problems. A principal one is the problem of marginality, in relation to the rest of the education system and in terms of under-resourcing, minority participation and little political support. The main symptom of marginality in adult education is the smallness of its budget granted by government. The whole issue of the funding of adult education can be understood, not just in terms of pragmatic government policy, but also as a consequence of a philosophical standpoint on the role of government in the funding of social welfare. The issue of marginality, therefore, runs through the chapter dealing with theories of social welfare and rather more implicitly in the chapters dealing with non-participation and the ideas of community development in partnership with innovative programmes in adult education.

A number of related issues and problems in adult education emerge as themes, such as democratic participation in decision making, the idea of second chance education and the issue of middle class bias. These matters can be related to theories of equality, community, social class sub-cultures and participation. The issue of whether adult education should be regarded as a public service with legitimate claims on the welfare system and the related links with community based services, is controversial within adult education circles. The various positions or points of view can be better understood by outlining the schools of thought on the nature and purpose of adult education. These positions when related to theories of welfare and of society illuminate the different perspectives and provide intellectual links between everyday issues and theory.

Another and final illustration centres on the role of adult education as a means of social change. Again there are different viewpoints and they are given more depth when related to theories of social change. These theories encapsulate very different interpretations and best expresses the spirit as well as the form in which this book is written. My ultimate aim is to present various social theories and perspectives in a clear and orderly way so that students of adult education may understand the intellectual links between speculative thought, disciplined thought and policy and practice. It is an open question whether such knowledge improves policy making and practice but it is surely better than ignorance.

CHAPTER TWO
IDEOLOGICAL MODELS OF ADULT EDUCATION

This chapter deals with the ideas about meaning and purpose in adult education. This approach reveals that there are several interpretations on the nature of adult education, all offering a different way of dealing with the broad questions about meaning and purpose as well as specific issues of policy and practice.

To get to the heart of this chapter it is useful to approach it by two stages. The first stage deals with the question of what is meant by the term adult education. This question is the subject of many of the reports, textbooks and commentaries on adult education [1]. It is not my intention to work through detailed definitions of adult education again as that has already been done very thoroughly by others. Nonetheless brief reference to the meaning of adult education is important because it does embrace so many different kinds of workers in such a diverse field. I shall return to this point shortly.

The second stage is to summarise the main lines of development of adult education from a broad historical perspective. I have found an understanding of the dynamics of adult education, which have arisen from its long historical evolution, more important as a way of appreciating its several interpretations about meaning and purpose than extended discussions about definitions. My choice of the term 'dynamic' reflects an image of adult education as a movement of ideas and activities, embracing a diversity of educational forms, organisations and policies. In tandem with the diversity of adult education it is possible to identify a broad movement which gathered momentum and took shape in the last century. Looking closer it is very apparent that adult education comprises several different perspectives about meaning and purpose with regard to its relationship to society. These perspectives are the subject of this chapter.

Sometimes the obsession with defining terms in adult education becomes a tedious business enjoyed only by pedants. Yet it is difficult to deny the sense of defining adult education for it is so diverse and admits to no easy classification. Any subject of serious study should be based upon some reasonably clear notion of the field and scope of the subject matter. It is part of being rational in thought and providing a useful framework of ideas for others to understand and follow.

The issues of definition centre around three topics of discussion – the subject matter or curriculum of adult education; the meaning of adult; and the nature and organisation of the learning process. These topics seem to arise quite normally in the minds of people working in adult education, judging from selection interviews for various kinds of training courses. What the workers are saying in their different ways is that what they do is meaningful to them as adult education. These workers come from varied branches of adult education – as employees of local education authorities; youth and community workers;

school teachers with a part time responsibility for community education; workers in leisure and recreation departments; neighbourhood and community workers; managers of day-centres for the elderly and disabled; workers in the various specialisms of the social services; clergy, health workers in different branches of hospital, health centre and community based caring; trainers in industry; media workers and several other occupational groups. They all share the view that what they do is adult education insofar as they regard themselves as teachers of adults or as organisers of learning opportunities for adults. They emphasise the business of providing for adult learning and make no particular distinctions between a primary or secondary commitment through their jobs to provide education. Essentially they regard themselves as communicators concerned to help adults learn knowledge and skills related to their self perceived needs and interests. They embrace all kinds of learning processes from the very formal to the informal. There appears to be no particular meaning of adult except for being above the minimum school leaving age or the age of majority. Nor is there a limit to the curriculum or subject matter of adult learning activities.

What I am claiming is that adult education is being defined and often redefined by the workers who find their way into training courses. What is interesting is that so many kinds of workers in statutory, commercial and voluntary agencies regard themselves in the business of adult education. There is no fixed view of adult education but there are some commonly agreed properties and these can be briefly presented.

The most important is that the meaning of adult education is essentially elastic, a recognition also made by the committee which produced the famous 1919 Report. They deliberately favoured an elastic interpretation of the meaning of adult education in order to embrace a wide range of learning activities, processes and agencies to reflect the many ways in which adults seek knowledge for a variety of purposes. Like many workers in adult education today the 1919 Report avoided placing a tight boundary of meaning. Indeed it is reasonable to assert that modern day adult educators start from the premise that education is a seamless process and permeates human life wherever learning occurs. As living and learning are indivisible processes adult education has no beginning or end but is continuous.

For the more immediate and practical requirements of most employers or sponsers adult education workers understandably focus their attention on deliberate intents to learn by adults. This approach covers a wide range of situations where learning may take place for its own sake, such as the pursuit of leisure time intellectual, artistic and recreational interests or through the performance of social and economic roles at the workplace, in home and family settings or in conjunction with personal needs associated with health, welfare, spiritual needs and so forth.

Thus in support of an elastic and wide interpretation of the meaning of adult education there is an emphasis upon learning as continuous throughout life, occurring in a range of settings arising from social interaction as well as instructional situations. These learning situations can be formally organised by educational bodies or through non-formal bodies with some emphasis on educational objectives or arise in an informal way as a result of learning from others or learning by doing or by the efforts of self directed learning. The conceptual problem of defining adult education gets more difficult with each attempt to encapsulate all the varieties of forms and processes whereby people learn. What is required is an imagination alive enough to comprehend the full extent of the scope of adult education, without ignoring or devaluing its wide range of subject matter and types of learning activities, participants, educational providers and philosophical outlooks. This is the clear message that emerges from the practitioners and offers a better working definition of adult education than one too tightly bound by semantics.

This more expansive approach to the meaning of adult education has certainly affected the nature of training courses, in order to reflect more fairly the wide cross section of workers in the field. In a general sense the recognition of the diversity of adult education and the arrival of new workers regarding themselves as adult educators reflects wider social changes. These need to be recognised as a new addition to the historical evolution of adult education. As the 1919 Report acknowledged adult education must be seen and re-interpreted in the light of a changing social context. The increasing impact of science and technology, higher levels of disposable income, more leisure, higher levels of unemployment and greater complexity in everyday living and more concern with self development, for example, has resulted in a need for more knowledge and skills to cope with change. Education is like a new religion, without too many dogmas, that is required to provide know-how in a widening range of subjects, mediated through a variety of forms and employing several different approaches to learning.

The impact of social changes on the meaning and nature of adult education has been most considerable in learning activities with a social dimension. That is why this book focusses so much attention on social theory perspectives, as will be shown in subsequent chapters. This theme of social relevance has a long history in adult education and has manifested itself in three related ways; through the ideas of education for citizenship, for social well being and social welfare. The range of these activities with a social dimension encapsulates community projects with an emphasis on citizen participation and self-help; political education; matters dealing with health and welfare; parent education; consumer affairs and environmental education; interpersonal relations and personal awareness; and educational work with various kinds of disadvantaged groups, including the mentally ill and disabled, hearing and sight impaired, the elderly, those requiring basic education and other groups in need of a combination of economic, social welfare and educational services. It is in these areas of activity where the borderline between education and health, welfare and other kinds of personal social services meet that a new professionalism in adult education is emerging. These new groups, and others not identified by name in this chapter, are extending the meaning of adult education shaping its recent history, providing the students for training courses and creating a climate for exploring the links between social theory and the practical business of providing educational services for adults.

Returning to the images of adult eduation as a movement with several dynamic strands of thought and action a brief historical perspective underlines these points. It also reinforces the view that the nature of adult education is essentially changing as new ideas and purposes are grafted onto existing lines of evolution and development. These general images also support the elastic and wider interpretations of the meaning of adult education.

The history of adult education is well documented with detailed studies based on developments in regions, communities and specific institutions, as well as through biographies of significant contributors as teachers, scholars, organisers, visionaries and political leaders[2]. These are all important contributions to knowledge but for the purposes of this book all that is required is a synoptic overview to chart the main lines of thought and action in the development of adult education.

One approach is to relate the development of adult education to social change, particularly in the unfolding of distinctive lines of thought and emphasis regarding the purposes behind the provision of different kinds of learning opportunities. This approach is accomplished by several writers. Kelly in a lucid paper outlines successive lines of development beginning with education for salvation, with a strong link forged between religion and literacy, and proceeding through to education for vocational purposes, for civilisation, participation and recreation[3]. Vocational education for adults was originally intended to provide the rudiments of scientific knowledge to working men in industries requiring higher levels of technical skill. This idea became tarnished with too many competing motives and patronising interest groups but laid the foundations for a comprehensive system of technical and commercial colleges at the latter end of the nineteenth century.

Education for civilisation represents the idea that learning should be about matters concerning the imagination and the values and basic purposes of life. These ideas are embodied and expressed through liberal education and the study of the humanities and other subjects for the love of knowledge for its own sake. Like the earlier forms of adult education, outlined above, provision was strongly motivated by an almost missionary zeal. Commitment to the values underpinning the different purposes and forms of adult education has always been one of its distinctive hallmarks.

This is also true of education for participation, which refers to various attempts to provide a knowledge base relevant to the growing political awareness and power of the working class, through the trade union movement and the formation of political parties representing labour interests. Educational leaders, such as Tawney and Mansbridge, the founder of the Workers' Educational Association, were fired by a passion for social improvement, usually combined with Christian and socialist idealism and service to the community. For them education in a liberal manner was a source of power and a means of extending the principles and practices of democracy.

At each stage of development in adult education a range of institutions were established, each with their distinctive styles of organisation and approaches to learning, sharing a broad primary commitment to either spiritual, economic, political or social values giving a coherence and purpose to their activities. These various stages were like strands of ideas and institutions co-existing and overlapping with each other rather than replacing one form of adult education with another.

Bringing the overview to recent times mention is made of adult education for recreation. This view is enshrined in the 1944 Education Act reflecting a number of social changes, such as an increase in leisure time, disposable income and the extension of the network of statutory and voluntary social welfare services. The latter develoments supported the view that recreational activities were justifiably regarded as educational in the broadest sense and were an integral part of social well-being for which the State had assumed some responsibility.

Another major historian of adult education also identifies a number of strands of thought reflecting different ideas and practices in the evolution of the movement from early times to the affluent years of the 1960s. The theme of social change is more consciously employed to express the idea that adult education has been used to help people adjust to changing circumstances in their lives, deriving from increased economic and employment specialisation, greater complexity of human relations and other forces creating a demand for new knowledge, skills and attitudes towards a multitude of social issues. At earlier stages of the development of adult education its nature and purpose was characterised by social elitism and social control, through the spreading of an emerging middle class ideology and self-help values. This reformist purpose combined with an emphasis on remedial education through literacy provision and, very gradually, an independent liberal education service, related more directly to the perceived needs of a more powerful and politically aware working class.

The reformist and social amelioration developments in the history of adult education emerges as a very strong purpose even though its advocates have operated from different motives, ranging from social control to radical change in political economy and the distribution of power. This dynamic appears to have been of a cyclical nature ebbing and flowing especially around the major reports on adult education that have issued from time to time as well as in response to wider social changes.

The 1919 Report, for instance, advocated adult education as a national necessity during the reconstruction period after the 1914-18 World War. Liberal education was seen as a means of enhancing a democratic citizenship. The service was expected to adopt a missionary approach and create a demand for education among the culturally impoverished by forming a closer link between labour and learning. The economic recessions of the inter-war years made most of the idealism of the 1919 Report appear over-confident and out of touch with the problem of mounting a universal scheme of lifelong learning on meagre resources and flimsy institutional structure.

The 1944 Act by emphasising the recreative aspects of learning contributed towards the broadening of adult education and laid the foundations for a more secure professional base through the increased role of the local education authorities. But the emphasis on recreation and leisure time learning, while possibly popularising education for adults, also devalued it by making it appear undemanding. More significantly, adult education lost its thrust as a means of confronting social issues and the identification and meeting of personal needs extending beyond the partly diversionary nature of recreation. Of equal importance is the possibility that the association of adult education with recreation and leisure gave the service a trivial label and low status image. This placed it at a lower estimate of value in the minds of politicians compared with work related education. Thereby adult education was seen as marginal to the central concerns of the educational system.

The relative absence of a social purpose in adult education in the affluent years of the 1950s and early 1960s more or less reflected the mood of the times. But with the rediscovery of poverty and inequality in the welfare state adult education caught the changing mood of the more disillusioned late 1960s and early 1970s and the deepening of economic problems in society. During these times there was an upsurge of social protest taking an extra-parliamentary form. This was often through community based 'grass roots' political action centred around issues of urban renewal, unemployment, racial and other forms of discrimination on the basis of class, gender and age.

By the time of the Russell Report in 1973 the nature of adult education was beginning to modify itself and was actively seeking new avenues of activity with a wider and more relevant social purpose [4]. The Russell Report reaffirmed many of the values and practices of recreation, leisure time learning and liberal adult education. It also had appeal as a low cost and practical guide to steady growth in mainstream work undertaken by the Local Education Authorities (LEAs), responsible bodies and other voluntary, non-formal kinds of adult education. At the same time as affirming the principle of responding to expressed demands from the educationally interested adult public the Russell Report also advocated the expansion of provision for the 'disadvantaged adult', through the detection of unmet and felt needs leading to programmes of special and compensatory education. Similarly the Alexander Report on adult education in Scotland moved in the same direction and officially popularised the growing use of the term community adult education to encompass a wider range of learning activities and social purposes [5].

Economic and political events have since overtaken the community and welfare services orientations of both the Russell and Alexander Reports, not so much in form but more in terms of dynamic thrust as the centre of gravity in education and employment policy-making shifted towards work training [6]. The impact of the Manpower Services Commission on ideas and practices in adult education has been considerable. The MSC has operated from an enormous budget and with strong central government direction as the political parties struggled to find policies to deal with growing levels of unemployment that would give some semblance of hope by offering work training and redeployment opportunities.

Finally, in outlining the historical development of adult education reference must be made to the search for a more unifying concept which brings together all sectors of the educational system into a comprehensive and integrated whole. Various terms have been used to express the idea that education should be regarded as a lifelong and continuous process, permanent with life and designed to enable people to perform in a variety of social

11

and economic roles in a society characterised by rapid change. The specific impetus for a comprehensive system of continuing education, to use the British term, arises mostly from a need to increase the supply of skilled and adaptable manpower to an economy shaped by science and technology and needing to become more competitive in a changing world economy. Continuing education is not only about work related training, for recognition is given to the impact of increased leisure, but even in that context the arguments stem from changing productive methods and its consequent effect on the occupational structure through the distribution of employment requirements and opportunities. In other chapters these ideas will be more fully explored. At this point it is only necessary to suggest its significance as a set of ideas affecting the future course of the education of adults.

These various lines of development both in thought and organisation of adult education strongly suggests distinct ideologies regarding meaning and social purpose. These ideologies, and the term is used to express different views and beliefs about the nature of adult education and its relationship to society in general and selected issues in particular, represent a kind of sub-structure of values and perspectives. These values, in an ideal sense, are the basis of policy and practice, assuming that theory is seriously applied to practice whenever questions of meaning and social purpose are discussed.

Before attempting to outline the different schools of thought, or working philosophies or ideological perspectives in adult education two points must be made. The first is that these different schools of thought are more distinct in theory than they appear to be in practice. The business of doing adult education is more complex than bookish theory or abstract reasoning because real life situations are made by individual personalities, prevailing and changing political, economic, cultural and social conditions. Hence the value of pragmatism in adult education. Nonetheless theoretical perspectives provide a general direction to thought and action and these should be broadly understood as a basis of relating theory to practice.

The second point, and the more important one, is that adult education as well as having different theoretical perspectives and ideologies deriving from different schools of thought, is held together in a general sense by some broadly agreed ideas about social purpose. Attention now turns to these, both as a way of summarising the previous sections and as a final section to this chapter. It should be added, though, that my views about commonly held ideas in adult education considerably stretches its meaning and, above all, is controversial for others have argued that there is no single unifying purpose [7].

The overriding characteristic, historically and in a contemporary context, is the search for social relevance which provides a rationale of purpose for adult education in society. The nature of social purpose is not static but a dynamic force and subject to re-definition in the light of changes in society. This idea is highlighted by most general histories of adult education. More particularly, adult education has traditionally adopted a social problem focus. Adult education has addressed itself in thought and action to some of the main social problems of the day – illiteracy, lack of job knowledge and skills, cultural impoverishment, lack of political awareness, democratic principles and practices, the constructive use of leisure, welfare rights and a growing list of community issues related to housing, health care, unemployment, discrimination and so forth. This view of adult education locates it firmly as a branch of social welfare and an adjunct to economic, policial and social action working to improve social conditions and enhance the well-being of society and its individual members. As will be shown later this benign view of adult education is simplistic. At the core of adult education though there has always been a simple commitment to welfare through learning. Taken together this idea represents adult education as a community service bridging the gap between education and social welfare which over the past one hundred years and more has developed a wide network of services based on the needs of society and individuals.

Adult education within this context has made use of three central ideas of social organisation − liberty, equality and fraternity, which can be freely translated into ideas of individuation and personal development, democratic citizenship, social amelioration and fairness, 'second chances', and the notion of community. All these ideas are so embracing as to be criticised for romantic idealism and inadvertent falsity. Yet it is this idealism which lies at the heart of adult education as a movement of ideas, fired by a voluntary spirit and a liberal, open-minded approach to learning. It also incorporates a wide range of educational activities, organisations and educators, many of whom are only partially engaged with adult learning.

Maybe the diversity of adult education, expressed through different forms, contents and approaches to learning, cannot be contained within simple and unifying ideas, no matter how much appeal they have as underlying values related to social purpose. It is also stretching the point too far if it is claimed that all forms of adult education, such as the functions of the MSC in work training or the activities of non-formal agencies, such as voluntary associations, were given equal footing alongside the historic role of University Extension, the WEA, Adult Colleges and LEA provision for community education and disadvantaged groups. Some forms of adult education have other priorities than those with a cultural bias through liberal studies or leisure time learning through recreational activities or education with a social welfare dimension or those activities addressed to issues of political economy and power in society. Yet in rather more specific and limited ways many kinds of adult education are characterised by a seeking after social purpose and relevance, if only because much of adult learning relates to individual and social interests. It is conceptually more difficult to deny the social purpose behind much that goes on in adult education than it is to emphasise some kind of connection between adult learning, individual interests and needs and the functioning of society culturally, economically and politically.

This brings the discussion to the point of outlining different theoretical perspectives within adult education. A number of writers have attempted to outline the different perspectives and these are selectively summarised [8].

In surveying the broad and diverse field of adult education and including a historical perspective four main perspectives emerge. The first is the recreational model which emphasises leisure time learning and has a limited commitment to wider social purposes. The second model concerns itself more with work training, with a primary commitment to economic purposes. Together these two models represent what may be termed the conventional provision perspective. The third model has been called the liberal progressive and has the longest history of commitment to social purposes. The liberal progressive perspective encompasses many forms of adult education provision ranging from the formal and traditional to newer forms of community based and informal learning. The fourth model offers a radical appoach and a strong prescriptive alternative set of ideas about the nature of adult education in society, especially its role as a means of social change. Like the liberal progressive model the radical approach to adult education ranges across different forms of provision. Hence the real differences are of outlook and interpretation and derive from separate intellectual origins. These intellectual differences find expression through ideas in the related field of social welfare and sociological theories which offer quite distinct interpretations about cultural, economic and political issues in society.

These four models of adult education chiefly reflect interpretations regarding social purpose. It is also reasonable to highlight some differences in approach to knowledge and curriculum, learning and teaching, organisation and the role of public expenditure in supporting adult education. These will be dealt with shortly.

Before then it is necessary to add that these four models are of general types only and there is some overlap with respect to certain practical and ideological features of theory perspectives. Given that many writers in adult education have attempted to summarise meaning and purpose, structure and function, and underpinning values some semantic complication is bound to exist. Moreover there are several approaches to interpreting the purposes of adult education varying from the personal standpoints and dispositions of individual theorists, to the use of different academic disciplines, whether primarily historical, psychological or sociological. Within each discipline there are also different schools of thought such as progressivism or existentialism in philosophy and systems or social action theories in sociology. There is also a strong strand of atheoretical, pragmatic thought in adult education which deals more with the practice of adult education mediated through the roles of prefessional workers. Nor should it be expected that each model is neutral and free from bias. Adult education is as much involved in the articulation and transmission of social values and political interests as any other sector of the educational system and social welfare.

A selective framework identifying the various features of different models of adult education referring mostly to goals and social purposes is presented in summary form.

MODELS OF ADULT EDUCATION

MODEL 1 – THE RECREATION-LEISURE MODEL

1.   Commitment to social purpose mostly restricted to the ideas of social well-being through the constructive use of leisure for recreative purposes and offsetting boredom and loneliness through social mixing with like minded people.

2.   Knowledge and curriculum usually approached in terms of systematic organisation even in many kinds of voluntary associations specialising in hobbies, cultural, sporting and social interests, etc. [9].

3.   Learning and teaching usually formal and didactic with some emphasis on practical learning and application. Teaching and learning valued as activities in their own right.

4.   Provision usually through statutory and voluntary bodies with a high level of public expenditure commitment under the 1944 Education Act in the statutory sector with student fees bearing a relatively small part of the real economic costs of provision. Mostly self-financed provision in the voluntary sector.

5.   Commitment to a 'needs meeting ideology' through responding to the felt and expressed needs of adults as well as the normatively defined needs of professional workers in the statutory sectors of adult education as well as youth and community and leisure-recreation services, etc.

MODEL 2 – THE WORK TRAINING MODEL

1.   Commitment to social purpose mostly interpreted in terms of vocational preparation and work skill training – economic purposes of education and training predominate over life skills and social awareness education.

2.   Knowledge and curriculum approached in formal terms with an overriding emphasis on utilitarian purposes.

3.   Learning and teaching formal and didactic with an emphasis on competency performance in practical work settings as a real test of learning.

4.   Organisation predominantly sponsored and financed by central government in accordance with economic and employment policies.

5.   Commitment to 'needs meeting' ideology almost exclusively defined by experts, prevailing economic-job market conditions and political contingency.

MODEL 3 – THE LIBERAL-PROGRESSIVE MODEL

This model embraces a number of standpoints regarding the nature and purpose of adult education in its social context. A number of points may be made -

1.   The aim of education is to hand down knowledge that is regarded as worthwhile for its own sake. Knowledge is of intrinsic value in itself for its cognitive content presents to inquiring minds learning material that deepens understanding and critical judgement. In this view the curriculum of adult education need not be about learning for any extrinsic purpose, such as personal happiness, vocational or practical ends, social reform or change in society. This traditional view of adult education tends to favour a teacher centred approach to learning, as the responsible authority for transmitting knowledge in a formal manner. Learning by discussion certainly occurs but is usually directed by and through the teacher in a classroom setting.

2.   A second view is that the content and methods of adult education should be addressed to social purposes for it represents through the power of knowledge and learning an important means of bringing about a better world. There is more than one route to a better world in the eyes of advocates of the liberal progressive perspective. One route is through the process of individuation or self actualisation. Both terms are intended to express the idea of achieving personal growth, intellectually and as a mature person, through learning. Furthermore implicit in these ideas is the belief in education as a means of individual achievement – through a strengthened self-image or personal confidence and enhanced opportunities for higher levels of education, occupational and social mobility. Views differ as to how far to extend the meaning of individuation. Advocates of the 'Great Tradition', which represents the traditional aspirations and values of liberal adult education, tend to play down the significance of learning for career related purposes and emphasise instead learning as a means of personal satisfaction and the development of an informed and critically aware citizenship for a democratic society [10].

3.   The idea of liberal education as an arm of democracy derives some historical impetus from the threats to free speech and political liberty arising from two major world wars. It also reflects a contemporary concern with threats to democracy arising from the power of multi-national enterprises and the large scale bureaucratic organisations of government and industry. These are often secretive and unaccountable to public opinion. These fears have played some part in the popularisation of the community participation theme in representative democracy, social planning, and the day to day public relations of education, health and welfare agencies, planning and environmental agencies.

4.   Another important dimension of the liberal progressive model is the belief in achieving social progress, hence the progressive tag. This implies a commitment to social progress, which really amounts to bringing about various measures of social reform in the political, economic, welfare and cultural areas of society. In this approach various deprivations and needs are perceived to exist by experts and commentators on social values and conditions. The fundamental belief is that education is a vehicle for social progress for it is in people's minds that ideas for social change begin. The duty of liberal education is to initiate changes of thought through academic scholarship, a relaxed manner of teaching and friendly, adult relationships with students. Informed minds and a responsible concern for social issues lie at the heart of the reformist approach in liberal adult education.

5.   Related to this belief in social advancement are ideas of democratic citizenship and participation, and the longer term goals of fostering a pluralistic society which contributes towards the achievement of a broad consensus about the directions of social change. Associated with these major ideas are the more immediate policy goals of remedial, 'second chance' and compensatory forms of adult education provision. The ideas of community based adult education derives in part from these general ideas about the role of liberal education in a context where various social problems are high on the agenda in discussing and prescribing social changes. The origins of these ideas go back to developments in adult education during the last century where it struggled to act as a remedial and second chance service based on the philanthropic concerns of the intellectual middle class.

6.   Running through the ideas of individuation and social advancement the liberal education ethos has been characterised by an emphasis on maintaining standards of excellence. In the content of the curriculum in teaching and small group learning and the predigrees of the providing bodies adult education has been expected to provide standards of academic work consistent with the best in intra-mural university education.

These ideas also stem from the last century with its gentlemen ideal of the all-round educated person. This ideal reflected the interests of dominant social groups and it was regarded as in the highest traditions to seek to transmit these values and bodies of worthwhile knowledge downwards and through the class structure of society. This process also reinforced the cultural superiority of those in a position to determine what knowledge should be transmitted and incorporated through adult education.

7.   Altogether the liberal-progressive model of adult education harnesses a range of ideals —expanding knowledge to cope with the demands of adult life, relating knowledge to experience through problem solving and critical appraisal, personal growth and change, participation in a democratic society, social advancement through applying knowledge to social problems and so on. Three ideas are being expressed. The first is a romantic ideal with learning as a key to creative personal and social change. The second is the ideal of educating the whole person through the transmission of culturally valued knowledge. The third is the ideal of social betterment and progress. All these ideas are the subject of criticism by the radical perspective on adult education.

MODEL 4 – THE RADICAL MODEL

1.   The starting point for the radical perspective on adult education is to challenge established assumptions regarding the role of education and its relationship to economic, political and cultural ideas and structures in society. The radical perspective asserts that it is insufficient to seek reform, which is the characteristic liberal adult education ethos, but necessary to seek revolutionary social change.

2.   This approach is based on the view that education is not a neutral activity. Education incorporates several kinds of bias reflecting the interests and values of those in possession of social, economic and political power. Education in general is regarded as a system designed purposefully to reflect and reproduce the economic, status and power hierarchies in society. Adult education, partly consciously and partly through inadvertent and misguided bias simply reinforces the inequalities reproduced by the educational system.

3.   Much of the radical questioning of society refers to the role of education in general. Thus Freire, for instance, criticises the banking concept of education where emphasis is laid upon storing up large amounts of knowledge and reproducing it at specified times [11]. The result of knowledge tests is then used to determine life chances through educational, occupational and social selection. Another radical view is that the compulsory nature of education is oppressive and incompatible with the idea of learning for freedom of thought and personal independence.

4.   Above all, the radical perspective is based on commitment to action or praxis, rather than being content either to simply point out problems in society or exhort others to action on moral grounds. Education is seen as an active ingredient in bringing about change in society and accompanies two other key processes – organisation and agitation.

5.   The idea of praxis can be organised into a number of related stages, according to Freire, who is one of the leading exponents of the radical perspective in adult education [12]. Freire identifies four stages in the development of a radical consciousness. The culture of silence, where the oppressed and dispossessed are too pre-occupied with immediate needs, often of survival, to examine the source of their oppression is the first stage. The second stage represents an awareness of how they are regarded by their oppressors. This reinforces dependency through the effects of a persistent negative image where the dispossessed are told that they are to blame for their own condition. The third stage begins an awareness of how the dispossessed have some degree of personal control over their fate through their own actions. The fourth stage is characterised by acting upon their perceptions of reality – praxis – arising from a critical consciousness, self confidence and know-how. The application of the praxis concept to specific examples in adult education will appear in another chapter.

6.   Returning to the critical side of the radical perspective several writers have pointed out the failures of the liberal adult education perspective. At one level liberal adult education is associated with the failure of Keynesian economy theory and over-reliance on education

as an effective means of social engineering in significantly redistributing power and redressing inequalities between the social classes. In this analysis liberal adult education is part of the problem in perpetuating social injustice and inequality, through its benign social control functions. Social control in this respect alludes to activities and agencies which contribute in various ways to maintaining the social order in its existing forms.

7.   More specifically the radical perspective makes several criticisms of some of the main tenets of liberal and recreative adult education. One criticism is that too much attention to educational matters has narrowed its purpose and relevance to ordinary people. Therein lies the attack on the middle class bias of conventional adult education provision. Hence the curriculum in leisure time, recreational classes is regarded as biased towards middle class groups with higher levels of disposable income in pursuit of socially trivial knowledge. Furthermore the values underpinning the curriculum reflect traditional ideas of contented domesticity and the passive citizen, rather than alerting people to the need for critical thought and political action in opposition to various and subtle forms of class, racial and gender repression in society. The radical view argues for a curriculum geared to a wider social awareness which is partisan but debatable, immediate and relevant in its appeal to more people, leading to a wider framework of conceptual analysis and stressing the value of learning by doing.

8.   The notion of excellence is also open to challenge on the grounds that there is no objective means of defining meaning, criteria and measurement of educational standards. In voluntary learning, which is a main feature of much of adult education, the expectations and motives of adults and their tutors are so diverse as to defy standardising and forming a basis for notions of excellence. Existing notions of excellence simply reflect the middle class values of sponsors and tutors in liberal adult education. Their cultural standards derive from a narrow conception of culture and excellence. This precludes making accessible to all social groups the myriad features of the total culture and thereby enhancing the ideals of a community based on equality and diversity of ideas and feelings, values, lifestyles and artefacts. The current notions of excellence, judged from that view of culture, is seen as narrow, elitist and divisive.

9.   The concept of need is also challenged for reinforcing an ideology of individualism, which is desirable for some but inaccessible to many. The liberal ethos of need is seen to conceal the real interest in education in promoting competition and individual achievement. This works well for many middle class adults where education is a successful and reinforcing experience. Individualism has little appeal to working class adults whose experience of education has usually been in terms of rejection and failure. Expressed in rhetorical question form, who needs adult education if early experiences were off-putting and negative?

10. Finally, in underwriting a radical adult education service attention has to be paid to ensuring that the resource allocation is seen to be fair and equitable to all social groups and that in the educational process due emphasis is placed upon building self confidence, critical analysis and a commitment to praxis.

By way of summary, it should be appreciated that the purpose of this chapter has been to view adult education synoptically. This has meant that the finer details of the meaning of adult education as a term embracing definition, taxonomy and historical development have been sacrificed to the wider purpose of suggesting lines of thought about its nature and purpose in relation to society. From the generalised approach adult education has been presented as a number of ideological perspectives, expressing different ideas about the nature and purpose of adult education. This area of values and beliefs lies behind the thinking process of policymaking and practice. The connections may not be strong or articulate and may be relegated to the realm of the professional subconscious. The purpose of this chapter has been to bring these ideas to the surface in a speculative manner. By no means are these ideological perspectives to be seen as absolutes. Other interpretations may be just as viable or even better. The important point is to view adult education in an ideological way for it is on that basis that the ensuing social theory perspectives are more coherently related.

CHAPTER THREE
ADULT EDUCATION AND THREE MODELS OF SOCIAL WELFARE

It was noted in the preceding chapters that adult education has traditionally held a commitment to the welfare of the people through various kinds of provision ranging from, for example, basic literacy and life and social skills, to work with disadvantaged groups, work training, recreation learning, an appreciation of inner psychological life, and the cultural, economic and political issues affecting society. This approach has underlined a strong link with the ideas of welfare and well-being and have given adult education a strong theme of social purpose. This social purpose, at least in a general way, has been shared by the several different standpoints that exist in adult education although the commitment to welfare varies according to the ideas and beliefs helds in each school of thought.

This chapter explores the relationship between adult education and social welfare, mostly at the level of theory perspectives. This chapter is important in two ways. First it provides an opportunity to outline and discuss the broad concepts of social welfare and relate them to adult education involving provision with a social dimension. A second purpose relates to the question of funding adult education from the taxpayer and the public purse. This brings to the surface the assumption that is frequently made in adult education, to the effect that all kinds of provision, but especially that which is cast in terms of social welfare, is a legitimate claim on the resources of central and local government. In recent years it has been made very clear by a radical conservative government that traditional assumptions about the role of public expenditure and the obligations of the state to underwrite welfare services of all kinds is no longer taken for granted. Increasingly it has been argued that the citizen and the consumer of welfare services should assume greater responsibility for using some forms of provision, especially in the educational, health and cultural services, by paying a more realistic share of the costs. This view brings into question and focus different perspectives on the nature of social welfare and the role of the state in playing a leading part in forming ideologies and making provision.

The organisation of this chapter follows the lines of the preamble and begins with the concepts of social welfare. Attention then turns to discussing three models of social welfare and their different perspectives on the role of the state in public expenditure on what may be generally termed welfare needs.

With regard to the link between adult education and social welfare in a modern context the 1944 Education Act, which gave a recognised place to adult education, came into being during an era of major legislation which effectively estabished the welfare state. The idea was not new to Britain as forerunners of the welfare state had been in existence before, certainly since the reforming Liberal Government at the turn of the century. Some brief historical perspective is helpful [1].

The decisive event forming the legislative base for a national system of social security, health care, housing, education and other services was the experience of the Second World War. The sharing of risks and hardships and the pooling of effort and resources generated a broad psychological consensus. This collective state of mind prepared the way for a national scheme of social welfare dominated by the government with lesser parts played by the voluntary sector. Voluntaryism had flourished during earlier times where charity predominated. The establishment of a legal basis to welfare provision conferred a front line responsibility to the state.

Prior to the years of active thought and social planning which gave rise to the welfare state, generally between 1941 to 1948, the dominant ideology was expressed by the term laissez faire. This conferred only a minor role to the state, through central and local government, to provide for the welfare of the people. The belief was that free economic markets, unrestrained by government and working by an invisible process of mutual self interest and self-regulation would provide for all through the production of surplus wealth. Those unable to share in the production of wealth, through their own enterprise and labour, could at least benefit in part through the caring concerns of philanthropic charity. The term 'benefit' is open to question from a modern day perspective for the receipt of charity was often based on harsh rules of eligibility. Indeed the climate of public opinion was decidedly unfavourable towards the poor and they were held responsible for their own condition. The relief of poverty as determined by the 1834 Poor Law Act was based on the principle of 'less eligibility' which amounted to treating the poor as social deviants. Notions such as unrestricted economic markets, poverty as deviance and self-help were supported by the theories of classical economists who held that the 'iron law of wages', which was in effect subsistence pay for arduous toil, was necessary as a check against a population boom, the risk of famine and a drain on the productive capacity of the nation.

The roles of adult education in the context of these events and beliefs was of several varieties. On the one hand the pursuit of education for salvation through adult literacy suggests an altruism and practical form of compassionate welfare. At the same time education for vocation could be seen as playing into the hands of the interests of capitalists. Similarly the emphasis on self-help as an underpinning theme of adult education could be interpreted as a form of social control through its influence on thinking and behaviour amongst serious minded people seeking education for various purposes. In these ways adult education can be seen to be reflecting some of the currents of thought and action both in the context of the development of social welfare and political ideas.

Pressures for social reform and modification of the dominant political ideology and its hold over welfare came from several sources as the foundations of an industrial society took on a more definite structure. The development of a utilitarian outlook expressed in terms of 'the greatest happiness of the greatest number' fostered a more benign philanthropy concerned with human needs in a more compassionate way. It also to some extent influenced the early notions of collectivist minded socialist welfare, as a counter veiling force to the idea of the survival of the economically and socially fittest. The emerging middle classes with embryonic ideas of service to the community, rational administration through legislation and social planning, and protective self-interest influenced the development of public health services, the extension of the franchise and a national system of education. In the health field it was recognised that disease knew no social boundary and preventive measures were vital. Moreover education was seen as necessary to head off a fear of class revolution. Foreign economic competition created a need for a more literate workforce in an increasingly complex division of labour which was subject to the application of technological invention to the productive process. During this long period of industrial development the representation of labour, through the formation of trade unions and working class political parties, exerted some influence over welfare and educational matters as well as the traditional concerns of pay and work conditions. During these movements of ideas and the setting up of an emerging system of social welfare adult education was busy with the practical tasks of providing basic literacy, technical knowledge and cultural literacy, albeit for a small and elite sector of the adult population.

The view being expressed here is that adult education can be seen as part of a developing system of social welfare permeating the economic, political and cultural spheres of society throughout the last two centuries. Unlike other welfare services adult education was never incorporated into the activities of the state through legislation until the 1944 Education Act. Thus for much of its history adult education operated within the voluntary sector of welfare provision, acting as an unofficial and unacknowledged means of enhancing some sense of individual well being and a collective awareness of social needs whether primarily economic, political, cultural or welfare related.

This view begs the need for some definitions of welfare for it has been used in two main ways. The first idea is that of social well-being. In this approach adult education provides a service related to people's needs for intellectual stimulus, knowledge and skills in a wide variety of life situations, where some kind of organised learning is useful or necessary. Education in this sense contributes towards the quality of life by affording its users an opportunity to develop themselves as individuals. Knowledge and skills are only part of the product of adult education for learning also appears to enhance self-confidence, personal esteem and social belonging. Social well-being therefore is a personalised term for welfare arising, in this case, from the beneficial effects of adult education. Social well-being also derives from a number of people through adult education extending the cultural heritage as well as, through their needs, demanding the provision of cultural and recreational facilities. By such individual needs, collectively expressed, the well-being of society is extended, on the understanding that what is being demanded and provided meets with general social approval.

The notion of welfare, then, emphasises individual well-being. It is best understood as an individually perceived and experienced state of mind referring to some qualitative aspect of life arising through personal services such as adult education, or, just as appropriately, health care, leisure and recreation activities. Social well-being is based on the idea of meeting self determined needs. It also embraces the part played by experts in personal services, such as adult education, in making intelligent provision for needs which help to make people feel good about themselves, involved and stimulated by the world around them.

The second concept of the welfare state is more complex and far reaching. A short definition would be the many methods by which the state, through a host of different services, tries to raise the standard of living of the population and help people meet the various needs for security and personal development. There are a few points worth highlighting. First the stress on the role of the state through central and local government. Second the recognition of individual and collective needs as being a legitimate claim on the resources of society. Third, the conceptual vagueness and relativity of such terms as 'standard of living', and 'needs' and 'personal development', all of which have been considerably revised by government policies, fashions of thought and changing values.

A longer definition involves much more than the social or personal services, extending to the economic and social planning and control role of central government. This includes control of public expenditure and private consumption, through taxation and money supply; import and export policies; prices and incomes; industrial development; industrial relations and employment and re-training policies. To generalise, the role of the state in this context is to achieve a level of economic growth and stability compatible with the objective of enhancing the social conditions of the people by financing health, education, housing and social security services. The overall intention as originally conceived by William Beveridge, architect of the welfare state, was to combat want, ignorance, idleness, squalor and illness or the five grants on the road to post war reconstruction' [2].

The personal social services – health, education, social work and social security – are the main means of making direct provision to people in need. These services are mostly provided outside ordinary economic markets but some are provided by voluntary means and private enterprise as well as the traditional sources of personal support by family, friends and neighbours.

At the heart of the welfare state lie two principles – of individualism and collectivism. The first principle refers to civic rights to welfare, and collectivism refers to the right of the state to plan, control and ration the resources of the nation in the interests of all. The ideas of citizenship and state, in relation to each other, inevitably creates a tension between the demands for personal liberty, social equality and the balancing of different economic and political interests.

The original conception of state welfare envisaged an important role for the voluntary sector and individual choice to supplement and extend the essentially minimal provision by the state, acting as a kind of safety net during periods of prolonged or acute need. But the welfare state also sought to extend and further opportunities for people, as in the case of education, at any stage of life. The welfare state was also designed to provide optimum services, the best available services such as health care, irrespective of income and social background. The prevention of poverty was advocated through the creation of full employment in line with the influence of Keynesian economic theory. This was seen as one strand in dealing with the causes of poverty. Another was the insistence upon compulsory insurance in anticipation of future sickness, old age and other forms of dependence. The welfare state also contained egalitarian principles such as the redistribution of income, in the form of goods and services, from the able bodied to dependents, from rich to poor and from young to older people.

It was generally recognised that modern life generated all kinds of diswelfares, meaning unanticipated and structural hazards that beset people during their lives over which they have little or no control [3]. Examples of these include involuntary unemployment; obsolescence of work skills; industrial accidents and disease; road accidents; environmental pollution; cross infection in hospitals; adverse side effects of drugs; educational misallocation; religious, ethnic and class prejudice. State provided welfare is the only means of providing universal aid in such cases of diswelfare for private economic markets through insurance companies would not be prepared to provide cover for all kinds of diswelfare or spread the cost of risks across the entire population.

The description of state social welfare comprises several elements. It provides public cash benefits, such as pensions, which act as an aid to consumption as well as income supplements. Second, the welfare state provides benefits in kind, such as health and education, which act as a form of future investment as well as providing for immediate needs. Thirdly the idea of the welfare state includes a large element of public regulation through consumer affairs and industrial relations, social and environmental planning; health and safety measures; compulsory education of the young, etc. The taxation system combined with the provision of cash benefits and benefits in kind act as a redistributive device between social groups. Finally social welfare has a compensatory element arising from the many diswelfares caused by the complexities of social organisation in modern life [4].

The outcome of all these measures extend beyond a simple notion of benign paternalism, which conjures up an image of the state being motivated by a huge collective compassionate concern for the welfare of its citizens. In one sense this can be seen to be a truism but it does not go nearly far enough in describing the role of the state in the provision of welfare.

Social welfare as mediated through the enormous powers of the state performs two major functions – the reproduction of labour for the productive system and the control of the population. The first task is conducted directly through education and employment policies in the preparation of work skills, retraining, redeployment and the regulation of the size of the workforce through a wide range of economic measures. Indirectly the social care of the population, notably through health provision extending from the individual to the environment in the widest sense, attempts to keep the nation fit enough to work.

The second task extends through all aspects of life and sections of the population whether working or not by influencing thinking, attitudes and social behaviour. This is more clearly marked in the economic sphere of social welfare where the state exercises power over consumption through social benefit payments whether as contributions or in receipt of child allowances, unemployment pay, pensions, sick pay and so on. More strikingly, the fact that so much of social welfare is controlled by the state – education, health, social security, environmental matters – means that people are subject to its controlling powers mediated through regulations, officials and a broad consensus of opinion which has accumulated historically by the collective consent of the people. The latter represents a vague yet powerful force representing a central value that the welfare state is about our own good and has legitimate rights to regulate our lives.

These goals constitute the state organisation of social reproduction and should be seen as a third arm of the modern state. The other arms represent the production and accumulation of economic capital and social order. Social welfare operates in conjunction with the economic and social control functions of the modern state in a myriad of ways through social policies. Thus for example the training role of education can be seen as a form of economic investment as well as an allocative and selective mechanism for distributing relevant skills to the labour force. Education also acts as a means of socialisation into the prevailing norms and values of society. It also performs as a device for regulating ambitions. The former refers to the role of the state in achieving social control and the latter does that as well as manipulating ambitions in accordance with labour and economic requirements.

Three other themes emerge from this portrayal of the welfare state. The first, which has been alluded to briefly, equates the origins and development of the welfare state with individual citizenship in terms of civic, political and welfare rights. Civic and political rights were enshrined in welfare provisions, which conferred both obligations as well as entitlements on people for social security, health, education and so forth. In this way social welfare established a contract between the state and the people and legitimised the demands of the former over the latter in return for services and benefits [5].

Related to this theme is the idea of social welfare as a means of ensuring the integration of social structures – economic, political, cultural and community institutions, and social groupings, such as classes, races, genders, right down to families and individual members of society. The universal and compulsory principles of welfare, as well as those of redistribution, optimum services and equality of treatment, amongst other ideas, were seen as means of encouraging self respect at the individual level and one nation at the collective level. Social integration was expressed as a desirable value and as a strategy for overcoming the inherent divisions of a class based society with all its attendant diswelfares and inequalities and the natural greed and self-seeking behaviour of individuals.

These themes lead into a third which regards the welfare state as a positive fit between the state, the market economy and society as a whole by providing a set of institutions, performing recognisably useful services on behalf of society and its members, underpinned by shared social values. This view sees welfare as a means of social harmony both at the level of institutional relations and values. In these respects the welfare state plays a supportive role in the economy and labour market and helps to maintain social stability through its controlling and socialising functions. Taking the functional concept further the welfare state is a means of reproducing and maintaining social integration through the meeting of individual, group and societal needs. The welfare state in this context, therefore, emphasises the consensual nature of social relations and plays down the significance of social conflict and disorder in society. This perspective will be revisited in another chapter.

It is important, though, to dwell a little more on this functional and consensus perspective on the welfare state. This is best explained by noting that the welfare state has grown up as a result of political pressures from above and the working class from below. Together a social pact was drawn up over the central issues of social welfare rather than the more far reaching issues of social equality and power sharing between the social classes.

Keynesian economic theory, representing the interests of capital and the role of the state in fostering productivity, legitimised the intervention of government in the workings of the economy in order to create full employment and consumer demand. Political and economic opinion from above recognised the failings of the 'free markets'. The social and economic costs of mass unemployment, falling production and social unrest were regarded as too high and had to be dealt with by new economic and social policies. The welfare measures embodied by Beveridge and other reports, which later emerged in legislative form, formed the basis for a post war settlement between capital and labour interests. The latter were determined not to return to the pre-war conditions of mass unemployment and poverty. Arguably the greater political awareness of the working class, especially those in the armed forces, swept a reforming Labour government into power with a mandate to implement the welfare state. Thus economic and social policies enacted by a popular government in the immediate post war years formed the two main strands of a political censensus between the major parties that only gave way in the mid 1970s.

Moving into the modern age of social welfare it is clear that traditional practices, ideas and values have been considerably strained by recent economic and political changes. Thus it is possible to talk of a crisis in the welfare state which has in varying ways affected a wide range of services, including adult education.

Two major events have prompted criticism and change of the welfare state. The first is the escalating problems of the British economy which in turn prepared the way for the second event, the coming to power of right wing governments. The latter have launched a full scale attack on social welfare both of a quantitative and qualitative kind [6].

On the economic front Britain has experienced, along with other nations, inflation and recession, but for a number of reasons the problems have been more extreme and intractable than elsewhere. Britain has been in economic decline for a longer time, principally as a consequence of being the first nation to industrialise and the most resistant to subsequent updating and innovation in productive methods and capacity. One explanation is the failure to manage capital accumulation and investment because of a split between industrial and finance capital. Another reason lies in the persistence of class conflict manifested in defensive attitudes by capitalists and managers of the economy on the one hand and trade unions on the other. Working partnerships between capital and labour have been limited in number and success. A third explanation is that the existence of a comprehensive system of social welfare has been a drain on resources and a burden on taxpayers and capital investment programmes.

The election of a radical right wing government in 1979 hastened the process of attacking the foundations of social welfare which was set in motion by the Labour government arising from the oil and inflation crises in the mid 1970s. The most important attack was on the principle of full employment which was effectively abandoned and its place taken by mass unemployment. Second a programme of cuts in social spending has been applied to all personal welfare services, except for the growing costs of unemployment benefits and the various training schemes launched by the Manpower Services Commission (MSC). Cuts in public expenditure on social services, as a strategy for redirecting resources to the productive sector of the economy, is the quantitative means of changing the foundations of state welfare. The qualitative has been expressed as an ideological attack and has sought to re-privatize housing in the public sector; increase the real cost of services, such as cultural and recreational facilities and adult education to consumers; discriminate against strikers by withdrawing benefits; widen the gap between 'deserving and undeserving poor' by stigmatising the latter; and extolling the virtues of self-help enterprise and work seeking.

The ideology of the 'New Right', which characterises the radical conservatism of the Thatcher government, rejects the notion of the mixed economy shared by private and state capital and supported by social welfare. Instead it proclaims a belief in the doctrines of the free market economy and self-help individualism. This classical approach to political economy reduces the role of the state in the provision of social welfare to residual proportions, leaving room for private insurance and commercially run services.

This ideological shift introduces various models of social welfare which in their different ways highlights theories and approaches to the provision of benefits and services. One model reflects closely the perspectives of the 'New Right' with its residual conception of social welfare. Two other models in varying degrees uphold the conception of social welfare as a front line, universally provided range of benefits and services. These need to be outlined before pulling together the lines of thought in this chapter and relating them to adult education.

MODELS OF SOCIAL WELFARE AND ADULT EDUCATION [7]

THE CLASSICAL 'FREE MARKET'-ECONOMIC GROWTH MODEL

This model operates on the basis of allowing capitalist economies freedom to generate wealth. In enshrines the ideas of self-help individualism, survival of the socially and economically fittest and emphasises the importance of industrial achievement and performance as the main means of creating wealth and welfare. The model is based on the premise that there is no incompatibility between the competing interests of a free market economy for both competition and social inequality are natural features of life providing incentives to be successful. Social welfare is regarded as a last resort to be used selectively on hard core problems whose needs and means to help themselves have been rigorously tested by screening devices.

There are other related features of this RESIDUAL model, viz -

i.　Social welfare should only come into play when the normal means of meeting needs –the family, the informal network of friends and neighbours, voluntary bodies and the commercially organised welfare services break down or for other reasons cannot deliver the necessary services.

ii.　State welfare operating as a residual agency attending to emergency needs is designed to withdraw when other systems of welfare are able to work properly.

iii.　The resources of state welfare in this selective model can then be used more efficiently and sometimes generously on the most needy providing they are deserving and clearly unable to help themselves properly – i.e. the very old and infirm.

iv.　With the undeserving welfare cases where provision is still necessary, and cannot be dealt with by other agencies, state welfare is given on 'less eligible' terms, that is, on the basis of severe conditions of eligibility, stringently applied means tests, on minimal terms and involving social stigma for recipients.

v.　This last resort approach to social welfare reduces choice and participation in decisions about any aspect of state provision. On the other hand the existence of a developed system of private welfare markets, competing for the attention of consumers through the price mechanism, encourages choice and variety in the provision of services.

vi.　The consumer would pay the full economic costs of welfare services except for those provided on a voluntary or charitable and last resort basis by the state.

The model of welfare envisaged by the 'New Right' is founded upon a number of criticisms of the Keynesian-Beveridge principles of the liberal-democratic model.

i.　Political parties in ascribing so much importance to social welfare have made more promises than the means to satisfy them.

ii.　This openness of commitment to welfare has also arisen through the influence of pressure group politics.

iii.　Another inflationary pressure on the government budget has come from the sectional interests of the welfare services all pressing their own cases for more resources to tackle a widening range of commitments.

iv.   Welfare intervention is very imperfect and has produced too many expectations which were subsequently left unsatisfied through lack of knowledge, skills and resources etc.

v.   Welfare intervention by the state has weakened the traditional ways of dealing with problems (self-help, voluntaryism, etc.) which in turn has led to more dependence and thereby the need for more policies and bigger budgets.

vi.   The result of all these pressures is an overloading of government and a diversion of resources and policy making away from the wealth producing aspects of society.

With specific regard to adult education several types of provision could conceivably exist alongside each other. State provision could be based on two principles. First, adult education delivered through the existing organisation of agencies would provide services and programmes on a commercial basis recovering the full economic costs through student fees. As at present profits and losses across the programmes of each provider could be merged. The important point is that there would be no public subsidy through the state to offset uneconomic programmes. This enrollment economy survives or falls on the basis of the popularity of its adult education programmes and efficiency in delivery.

The second principle would enable adult education agencies, such as the LEAs to make provision for groups who were regarded as having special needs. Provision for such disadvantaged adults would be a political decision warranting an earmarked subsidy through public funds for educational programmes designed to meet approved needs. An example of these would be training programmes related to work skills and labour shortages or provision for designated socially disadvantaged groups such as the physically disabled, illiterates, people unable to understand the English language and so on.

In this second area of state assisted provision for adult education there would be some overlap with the commercial and voluntary sectors who would be just as capable of organising the appropriate programmes and services. The funding of such provision or other kinds in the liberal-humanities and recreation-leisure subject areas would be entirely commercial or subsidised by charitable giving and 'last resort' state assistance. For most intents and purposes, though, the role of public expenditure through the welfare state would be minimal and adult education would be characterised by free enterprise commercialism and a less eligible level of state assisted provision.

THE LIBERAL-DEMOCRATIC MODEL

The assumption of this model is that it is possible to co-exist with the free market economy and moderate socialism by emphasising the stabilising function of political pluralism and a comprehensive system of social welfare. This perspective on social welfare confers a key role for public expenditure through government intervention in the economic and social spheres. It also supports the complementary role of voluntary action at the level of institutional services and individual self-help.

The liberal-democratic model is essentially a pluralist approach to social and economic issues. Thus government in playing a leading part in social welfare provision bases its policies on democratic consultation with a variety of political, economic and social interests and works in partnership with other providing bodies. This approach emphasises consensus as a means of reconciling different political standpoints on social and economic issues. Therefore the reform of the excesses and failings of laissez faire economics in a capitalist society tends to be by gradual means. The collectivist principles of the welfare state are grafted onto capitalism leading to the mixed economy in the context of a democratic society. Social welfare is regarded as an important value upholding the idea of a common moral order in society. More specifically the values of the welfare state are expressed as universal security, equality, humanitarianism, social democracy and self-help in partnership with collective organisation.

The INSTITUTIONAL model of social welfare has other related features, viz -

i.   Welfare services are seen as normal and front line functions of the state.

ii. The complexity of modern life is recognised and the occasional inability of the individual to meet needs is considered a normal condition without implying failure or being stigmatised.

iii. The economic market is regarded as unable to render the equitable and fair distribution of opportunities and the meeting of a wide variety of social and personal needs. Only the state, representing the nation as a whole, can assume the powers necessary to meet collective and individual needs.

Adult education in the context of the liberal-democratic model is regarded as an integral part of the system of social welfare. It receives government backing and public resources in order to provide an educational service covering a wide variety of learning activities. Moreover it is expected to enhance the social well-being of adults and pay attention to disadvantaged adult groups whose needs for educational opportunities are relatively greater. In this way adult education forms working links with other branches of social welfare provision in order to provide a comprehensive means of meeting needs that extend beyond education for its own sake. Hence the extrinsic benefits of adult education are given the same recognition as intrinsic learning objectives. In its own right adult education is conceived as a means of work skill training, recreation through leisure, 'second chance' opportunities and, through liberal-conceptual studies, a means of developing useful knowledge. With respect to the latter point recognition is given to the value of fostering a pluralist democracy through raising the levels of public awareness over political, economic and social matters. This perspective has much in keeping with a gradual approach to social change.

THE SOCIALIST MODEL OF SOCIAL WELFARE

This model asserts that the competing economic interests in a capitalist society creates injustice, inequality and social conflict. The replacement of capitalism is the only way to create a more fair and humane society. It is the unequal ownership of capital and private property that lies behind the persistence of poverty, squalor, idleness and ignorance. Under those circumstances only radical political action and welfare policies can bring about substantial economic and social change. This entails the transfer of economic ownership, political power and control from the traditional ruling class, comprising only a small elite, to the majority working classes.

Like the liberal democratic model it is based on the same general features and operating principles with the main difference being in terms of emphasis on the role of social welfare as an agent of social change. The socialist model is more radical in its approach seeking urgent and far reaching changes, taking in political economy as well as social welfare matters.

Two schools of thought exist. The first advocates the front line role of welfare as a key means to changes in political economy. This approach advocates such means as positive discrimination in resource allocation and the equitable distribution of social and economic opportunities. The second school of thought argues that radical political action by class conflict is a necessary prelude to change in the distribution of power in society with welfare playing a supporting role in following through the effects of revolution.

The two schools of thought reflect a major intellectual conflict over the nature of the welfare state in post war Britain. Initially socialists saw the welfare state in beneficial terms. State power was regarded as a means of promoting socialism through the effects of its egalitarian principles of distribution of resources and creation of opportunities through education, employment and health. This view was held in common with other political persuasions that saw the welfare state in terms of a functional relationship with the market economy. It was seen as sufficient that the economy was being modified to incorporate some element of state control through nationalisation and fiscal measures. The opposite and more radical view held that the reformist traditions of the liberal democratic model only partly modified the classical economic growth model. The welfare state while extending the idea of citizenship rights did not impose any real threat to the balance of political power and thereby the means of controlling the production of economic goods and services and the control and distribution of wealth in society.

The radical position therefore challenges the assumptions of a pluralist democracy with the welfare state performing a key role as a means of ensuring integration and stability. Where these roles were being performed this was on the basis of existing inequalities in political and economic power in a class based society. In this view welfare was only a minor vehicle for social change and certainly had no major transforming effect on the distribution of power between the social classes.

Indeed the position of the moderate socialists upheld a particular view of social change where the welfare system was seen as a means of integration and restoring social stability following the disruptive effects of the war. From this perspective social change is an adaptive process dealing with problems of social adjustment through the building of new social institutions, practices and values. Social change therefore is about achieving stability and equilibrium in social relations rather than as an expression of conflict between social groups leading to more radical changes in political power.

Adult education in the context of radical social welfare takes off from the premise that it has the potential to initiate social change through the raising of social and political consciousness, leading to class solidarity and praxis. In that sense adult education is more than just a means of social welfare because of its commitment to political action through consciousness raising. Whereas social welfare implies being in receipt of services, like that of the consumer, radical adult education is about active participation in deciding the issues, controlling resources and learning by doing. The goal of radical adult education is far reaching. Social change in political economy generating through that momentum changes in the distribution of power and opportunities. Essentially it advocates a political approach to social problems harnessing the welfare system in a supportive role.

It should be clear that there is a strong link between adult education and social welfare in several ways. It has been argued that in one sense adult education is concerned with the social well-being of its participants, for learning has the inbuilt capacity to enhance personal growth intellectually, artistically, socially and so forth. In addition to fostering these several forms of self expression adult education develops specific kinds of instrumental knowledge and skills related to practical needs, employment and other economic activities. The assumption being promoted here is that individual and social well being are forms of welfare expressed in personal terms.

The second meaning of welfare incorporates the leading role played by the modern state and encapsulates the whole of society and its members. The point argued in this chapter is that adult education has reflected some of the earlier expressions and developments in social welfare thought and practice. This is particularly the case in its early concerns with illiteracy and work related knowledge, as well as in its practical expression of the virtues of the self-help ideology through the shining examples of self educated adults.

In a contemporary context adult education has been linked with the developments of the welfare state as part of a major piece of legislation through the 1944 Education Act, which formed one of the many strands comprising a comprehensive network of welfare provision. Just as significantly, the widening range of personal social services have formed working partnerships with mainstream adult education and have consciously adopted an educational dimension to their activities. This explains the widening concept of adult education and an interest in the practical and theory aspects by professional workers in the welfare services. This has also included several other workers, such as clergy, who see connections between the educational, welfare and more specific aspects of their roles.

Adult education, in its own right, has continued to seek ways of being socially relevant and of expressing the values of social betterment. This approach has embraced many aspects of the welfare state and the social problems it was designed to tackle. The various reports on adult education in recent years have taken pains to pursue these themes and concerns through a focus on the disadvantaged adult and commuity based services. This has led to the formation of inter-agency contacts and joint enterprises. This topic will be developed in the next chapter.

In outlining the different models of social welfare it should have been apparent that there are various attitudes towards the public funding of adult education. The residual model of social welfare, favoured by the 'New Right' would curtail many of the activities in the welfare related field as these are very dependent upon state finances. Indeed the subsidy of adult education would be removed and it would no longer operate as a public service. The marginality of adult education as a publicly financed service would be made worse. On the other hand the two other models of social welfare would confer a more significant role to adult education underwritten by adequate public expenditure to provide a social service. Needless to say, the emphasis on models confines this discussion to the ideal realm of thought. In practice adult education, even as an expression of the liberal democratic model of social welfare, has never been more than a marginal service within the budget of education let alone the welfare system as a whole.

A number of ideas have been explored in this chapter. The key idea is that there is a connection between adult education and ideas and models of social welfare, ranging from a primary focus on the well-being of the individual to radical concepts of collective organisation. Social welfare, then, is both a diverse concept and a mixture of ideological perspectives, just like adult education. This chapter has focussed on three models of social welfare that broadly correspond to the conventional, liberal-progressive and radical ideologies in adult education. This provides a certain depth to understanding the intellectual origins of these perspectives in adult education for at least in a broad sense the values and activities of the movement relate to ideas, ideals and practices in the wider field of social welfare. In more practical ways these connections help explain the resourcing of adult education from public expenditure. Each model of social welfare favours different approaches to public expenditure of community services, of which adult education is an element, and the changing nature of political belief and government policy is shifting the balance from front line responsibility by the state to an increasing emphasis on self financing. This has generated a major problem for adult education as a public service and has affected its commitment towards disadvantaged groups.

CHAPTER FOUR
ADULT EDUCATION AND SOCIAL WELFARE MODELS RELATED TO PROVISION FOR THE DISADVANTAGED

The chapter sets out the connections between adult education for the disadvantaged, models of social welfare and the different perspectives within adult education that offer varied interpretations on the nature of such work. In making these connections reference is made to several relevant concepts, particularly of poverty, for it forms the basis of related terms such as deprivation and disadvantage.

A useful starting point for bringing the elements of this chapter together is the significant impact of the Russell Report in 1973 and the research the committee commissioned which led to the important publication on the 'Disadvantaged Adult' [1]. Two lines of thought were behind the Russell Report recommendation that adult education should extend its range of activities to include the disadvantaged and thereby secure a partnership with social welfare services. The first reaffirmed the belief that adult education should have a commitment towards adults, who for various reasons, deriving from their physical, educational, economic and social circumstances, could not fully participate in the existing range of learning opportunities. This is the social relevance theme reaffirmed and updated.

The second line of thought and closely related to the first is that one explanation for the marginality of adult education is its limited appeal to a narrow section of the population. Adult education in this view simply reinforced the educational benefits already experienced by the middle classes. In performing this reinforcing function adult education had confined itself to the recreational and high minded cultural activities of an unrepresentative social group. This had rendered adult education peripheral to the needs of the wider community and had caused the service to lose its own way in relation to its longstanding concern for social relevance and betterment. The curriculum, teaching methods and its organisation in general had made adult education a marginal service in relation to a changing society whose social and economic problems were giving rise to renewed searches for solutions. Adult education for the disadvantaged and an emphasis on reaching out into the community were seen as relevant strategies for the future of the service.

The way to discuss adult education for the disadvantaged is to comprehend the major concept upon which its meaning is derived. Poverty as a concept is the obvious starting point. The concept has a long history but fell into under-use during the relatively affluent post war boom years in many western capitalist economies. Poverty was 'rediscovered' in the USA principally through the problems of a highly visible and vocal black population organised into a civil rights movement. In the UK poverty was identified in the 'never had it so good years' by academic research publicised by the Fabian Society and the Child Poverty Action Group and made into a political platform by the Labour Party [2].

Several explanations of poverty exist. Simply, people become poor because their wages are too low in relation to their everyday costs of living, or, unable to work and without enough capital assets to live off unearned income, depend upon inadequate state benefits. There is little point in providing statistical evidence to support this statement as the figures need to be constantly revised. However it is clear that the trend is always towards higher numbers in poverty, defined by those claiming supplementary benefits as normal state benefits are inadequate in relation to need. The main causes of poverty, then, for those beneath retirement age, are unemployment, one parent family incomes and others on low pay, and prolonged illness. It is interesting to interject this commentary with the note that the distribution of wealth is grossly unequal. According to figures produced by the Royal Commission on the Distribution of Income and Wealth, 20 percent of the population owned 84 percent and 80 percent owned 16 percent of the wealth in 1976. Similarly the distribution of income has remained rigidly unequal with the share of post-tax personal income of the poorest 20 percent of the population increasing in the period 1964-74 by only one percentage point [3].

The more important task is to conceptualise poverty in a broader sense for it is interpreted in political, cultural and behavioural terms as well as economic and material. Equally important is the need to understand two distinct ways of measuring poverty which form the basis of policy making, one in practice the other mainly in theory [4].

Poverty may be defined in absolute or relative terms. The absolute meaning measures the standard of living strictly in economic terms where income and expenditure fall below an agreed level of subsistence, just enough to survive on the bare necessities. Early attempts to construct a working definition of the poverty line relied on standardising nutritional requirements sufficient to keep alive and function with some acceptable level of physical efficiency. The poverty research of Booth, Rowntree and much later, albeit to a lesser extent, Beveridge, all attempted to define a minimum subsistence level without much success. Nonetheless governments of the day based their policies on the idea of an absolute poverty line set at a minimal standard before social security payments and other benefits became available. The important point is that there was no appreciation of psychological well being in this understanding of poverty.

The relative meaning of poverty uses both an economic and psychological perspective and derives its yardstick of poverty from the average expectations of people for adequate resources to cover a wide range of needs. The absolute meaning of poverty creates a poor class living on subsistence benefits. The relative meaning starts from the premise that people have common needs, both of an economic and cultural kind, so that they can participate in a standard of living shared by most people in society. This is more than the bare necessities of life and reaches out to an average sense of social well being relating to income, health, housing, personal security, access to leisure and cultural facilities, social esteem and self-worth. The idea operating here is that poverty and its relief derives from a comprehensive approach to human needs which goes beyond the parsimonious standards determined by authoritarian and paternalistic welfare policy. Instead use is made of the idea of comparative or relative need which relates poverty to average levels of living enjoyed by the majority. It is only too obvious that this concept of poverty has found little political support which brings into focus three quite different theoretical perspectives on poverty and social inequality. Each approach implies certain values and beliefs about the nature of social policy and the causes of poverty and inequality in society. These perspectives are relevant to any appreciation of the involvement of adult education with the disadvantaged.

The three approaches have been labelled as (i) conditional welfare for the few; (ii) minimal rights for the many; and (iii) distributional justice for all. Each relates to the models of social welfare introduced in the last chapter.

CONDITIONAL WELFARE

This approach to poverty held that the poor had only themselves to blame for their condition which was regarded as a symptom of moral deficiency. In spite of this harsh view it was acknowledged that some of the poor were unfortunate victims of circumstances beyond their control. But to be regarded as deserving poor they had to show willingness to help themselves. The way to do this was through work which prevents dependency and want. Keeping out of poverty through work was regarded as a moral virtue and a means of personal and social stability. Welfare in any form was linked to the willingness to work. The relief of poverty was on terms of 'less eligibility' – the meanest conditions. This theory of poverty is consistent with a laissez faire political economy and the classical 'New Right' model of social welfare. This view is enshrined in the 1834 Poor Law Amendment Act.

MINIMUM WELFARE

Poverty in any of its manifestations is regarded as an unavoidable 'diswelfare' of free market economies and other hazards of life and no blame can be attached. Two measures for preventing poverty and dealing with it are policies of full employment and compulsory social insurance as the basis of minimum benefits. This economic and social order is underpinned by the State by universal welfare policies, the 'safety net' principle and intervention in the labour market. This approach fits with the liberal democratic model of social welfare and moderate versions of the other two. The best expressions of this thinking in legislative form is the 1909 Poor Law Amendment Act and the Beveridge Report.

DISTRIBUTIONAL JUSTICE

This approach rests on the view that the majority of the people are denied their rightful share of the nation's wealth and access to political power, equality of opportunity for a wide variety of 'life chances' in employment, education and so on. Poverty begins whenever these rights are denied. This implies a far reaching approach to social equality in political economy and cultural values starting with the wider diffusion of power and economic

37

resources lubricated by active participation in decision making and an elaborate set of civil rights. This approach is only in embryonic form through the activities of consumer and welfare rights groups. This idea of poverty takes the concept of relativity to its extreme meaning and accords with the radical model of social welfare.

What emerges from this is that there is no single view of poverty and each interpretation contains quite different implications for social policy. It is not surprising, therefore, to learn that the meaning of disadvantage is neither singular or fixed. It is best understood as an umbrella concept with several meanings. As a concept it appears to overlap with the term deprivation which also represents a number of meanings. Both terms are overworked but that seems unavoidable as people strive for comprehension, which is the first rule of theory and practice. Disadvantage seems to have been favoured by community workers and adult educators as it better expresses the structural features of poverty; like the lack of economic and educational resources; poor environmental and housing conditions; restricted cultural worlds; various other political and social inequalities as well as the related psychological aspects of being dispossessed of the assets and opportunities enjoyed by the majority of people. The term undoubtedly includes an evaluative element to cover undesirable behaviour and marginal lifestyles deriving from rejection, hostility, discrimination, repression and exploitation. This view represents a consensual view shared by concerned opinion and middle class values. On the whole it does not heap moral blame on the victims of disadvantage but starts from the basis of understanding the prevailing conditions creating disadvantage, whether these are primarily psychological and cultural or political and economic.

There are many descriptions of the disadvantaged highlighting single or multiple kinds of conditions cited above and predisposed towards explanations that are either cast in individual behaviour terms or political and economic terms. These explanations reflect different political ideologies and related models of social welfare. Together these comprise the theoretical perspectives upon which policies and practices in adult education, community development and other kinds of welfare services directed towards the disadvantaged are based. This major theoretical framework will be developed later but meanwhile it is useful to dwell a little further on descriptive profiles of the disadvantaged.

Some descriptions deal in detail with the socio-economic characteristics of the disadvantaged [5]. This brief summary identifies the following characteristics which are most representative of social research findings -

i.   The very young and elderly are particularly over represented in poverty groups although age is not regarded as a causal factor but more of a contributory one.

ii.   Family and interpersonal relations are characterised by high rates of instability with a large number of families headed by women living on low wages or welfare payments.

iii.   The disadvantaged have the lowest pay and therefore have to consume a larger share of their income on basic necessities. They are less likely to obtain credit for house purchase, etc.

iv. They are more likely to experience prolonged unemployment and/or intermittent employment, principally because they are unskilled or have outdated skills or skills not currently in demand.

v. Welfare benefit is often the prime and only source of income which makes the disadvantaged very dependent upon political ideology and government economic and social policies.

vi. The disadvantaged often share the same poverty sub-culture, living in isolated areas or inner city areas with a transient population. They have less access to services and are less mobile.

With respect to educational characteristics the disadvantaged usually have low levels of attainment, particularly manifest in literacy, numeracy and basic social skills. This poor educational condition seems to be related to other factors such as lack of awareness of diet and nutrition; poor grasp of self care in health generally; limited abilities in verbal communication; conceptual and abstract thought; and a poor self concept with regard to learning new skills and attitudes. They have little interest in or knowledge of the larger society around them.

The psychological and cultural manifestations of disadvantage extend further into the area of personal values. They are reported to have a sense of helplessness and fatalism, reinforced by dogmatic and authoritarian views on personal, social and political matters. The desire for self-help and achievement is low. Instead the feelings of low status and esteem lead to withdrawal and dependency. This situation brings about marginality in society in relation to the majority of people.

In describing the disadvantaged there is considerable danger of treating the condition as if it was only a group phenomenon thus imparting to them a common identity and needs. Whereas the concept of disadvantage is used as a descriptive term for groups such as those living in communities with a high incidence of social problems; ethnic minorities at the receiving end of discrimination; the unemployed; various kinds of disabled groups and so forth, not everybody belonging to such groups is or regards themselves as disadvantaged. At the same time disadvantage can be experienced as an individual quite independently of any particular group affiliation. Moreover disadvantage is a relative term, with some lacking the skills resources and general wherewithal more than others or at different times and in different social circumstances. Taking this caveat one step further it is reasonable to question the appropriateness of using such blanket terms on whole social groups or even on individuals without considering the barely concealed propensities of the well educated and privileged middle classes to judge and label others in deficit terms.

Another relevant concept to understand is social equality which lies behind sometimes explicitly, more often implicitly, discussions about poverty and disadvantage in adult education. Social equality is both a policy outlook and an ideal which expresses the reformist and radical social change perspectives in adult education. By no means is there agreement over the use of social equality in education, welfare and politics generally. Different ideologies in these fields have varied approaches to its application, as will be discussed later. Nevertheless there is some general area of agreement about its meaning [6].

Social equality is mostly about the following -

i.   economic rewards from employment income and the acquisition of wealth by capital accumulation and inheritance;

ii.   recruitment to the labour market by ability rather than through social status determined my birth and personal connections;

iii.   opportunity to achieve through education and employment according to ability and effort;

iv.   citizenship rights in terms of free speech, entitlements to vote and access to welfare services and benefits, and freedom from negative discrimination on the basis of ethnic and racial origins, gender, age, religion and so on;

v.   rights to well-being such as the right to work, health, physical, property, environmental and consumer protection, access to cultural and recreational facilities.

The list is not exhaustive or static for ideas of equality change. They all point to various barriers to equality deriving from political, economic, social and cultural sources which have to be removed. In this sense poverty and the various manifestations of disadvantage are seen as barriers to obtaining equality as a member of society. Expressed in simple ideal terms, adult education for the disadvantaged starts from the belief, but does not end there, that the provision of learning opportunities is an initial step on the road to personal self-help at one end of a spectrum and social equality at the other. Hence the connections between these concepts.

Before examining the various theoretical perspectives relevant to adult education for the disadvantaged a summary account of the nature of the work is necessary. As the Russell Report defined disadvantage primarily in individual terms this gave an impetus to the adult literacy campaign which later developed into a basic education service. Target groups were identified, thereafter attention focussed on the educational requirements of individuals. Similarly, work with people having various kinds of physical or mental disability, although often conducted on a small group basis, was addressed towards individual needs. Adult education was cast in the role of providing useful tools to enable individuals to break out of their particular constraints or at least use newly acquired knowledge and skills as an aid to living, through the stimulus effect of learning. The 'useful tool' idea also applied to ethnic groups in need of language education and general coping skills. Adult basic education, meaning literacy, numeracy and 'life skills', was also seen as a remedy for the young unemployed with poor school attainments inhibiting job prospects. In other respects too the onus was on the provision of knowledge and skills that would enhance individual competence, self awareness and the basic motivation for self-help. Thus in the general curriculum area of 'coping' or 'life skills' basic knowledge, combined with literacy and numeracy skills, was seen to foster individual competence through such activities as domestic management, civic and community awareness, health and family relations, etc. Such programmes were available to a diverse range of adult education agencies and were genuinely interpreted as an expression of the social relevance theme. In such work adult education sought the help of fellow workers in community and institutionally based welfare services under the banner of inter-agency cooperation. Altogether in a short space of time adult education for the disadvantaged was no longer a piecemeal affair, that is, until the educational cutbacks started to bite deep in the late 1970s. Until then the hallmark of such work was innovative and enterprising and went a long way to dismantle the irrelevance of adult education.

No attempt has been made to discuss the idea of community development which is a particular aspect of adult education and the disadvantage. It requires extensive treatment in another chapter. In this chapter it is more important to relate adult education and the disadvantaged to models of social welfare. At the same time the different models of adult education will also be related to the work with the disadvantaged for they offer quite different perspectives which can then be carried over to the discussion on community development.

The four models of adult education, outlined in chapter two, all have different contributions and perspectives related to the work with the disadvantaged. Two models require only brief mention. The work training model, for instance, has been very active with basic education programmes related to various kinds of training schemes for young adults to improve their employment prospects. The role of the MSC, with its commitment to work skill training, has also played a very significant part in providing learning opportunities for a wide range of adult groups, many of whom would be described as disadvantaged – unemployed, disabled, ethnic minorities and some groups of women seeking work skill traning.

The recreation-leisure model too has been involved with the disadvantaged through a wide range of activities usually available to regular users of adult education services. The LEAs were, in the main, fairly responsive to such provision as it helped create new groups and provided a sound justification for adult education sometimes struggling with marginality problems. On the whole the response to this 'Russell category work', as it was sometimes called, was more inclined towards pragmatism and practical contingency than social idealism. The ideal realm was more the property of the other two models of adult education.

Both models share the general assumption that adult education could be a force for change and offer an alternative to the early education experiences of the disadvantaged which were seen as compounding rather than improving life chances. Thereafter real differences of interpretation emerge.

The liberal perspective adopted the position that disadvantage was personally experienced by individuals. The fact that they formed groups with others sharing the same circumstances was of secondary importance, although it provided a basis for intervention by adult education and social welfare services. The important matter was that adult education could enable disadvantaged individuals to break out of and contend with their condition. These conditions were interpreted primarily in terms meaningful to individual remedies, such as a lack of communication skills; poor self concept and lack of confidence; isolation; lack of basic knowledge and everyday life skills related to employment, health, domestic management and civic matters. Essentially its approach was humane, with a focus on helping individuals as people, not as role players, status holders or members of any cultural and socio-economic group. The line to be drawn between the individual and social membership through roles, status and larger group categories is a fine distinction and more a statement of philosophy than a sociological reality. Nevertheless as an ideal the concept of the individual has meaning, especially to those claiming that adult education through its work with the disadvantaged was improving society by providing opportunities to individuals.

This view accords with the liberal-democratic model of social welfare with its emphasis on organised provision and compensating people for diswelfares arising from a poor start in life and different kinds of poverty − cognitive, cultural and socio-economic. Work with the disadvantaged expresses the minimum concept of welfare, based on the diswelfare view of poverty, which blames nobody for the problem. It justifies state intervention to deal with hard core problems with the goal firmly fixed on helping individuals to help themselves through education and other services.

It should also be noted that the 'New Right' model of social welfare, with a more restrictive view of poverty giving rise to conditional social policies, has some favourable disposition towards work with the disadvantaged. Adult education work in this context, for example, has appeal as a means of fostering self-help individualism and character building through the acquisition of useful skills for the workplace and home. It is also quite cheap to provide for much of the funding for such work amounted to very little. Moreover it was often only a shift of resources from one area of public expenditure to another. Even the much acclaimed theme of positive discrimination entailed very little extra cost.

The radical perspective in adult education, in appraising the work with the disadvantaged, offers its own strong interpretation and makes several criticisms of the liberal approach. Starting with the criticisms these may be listed -

i.   The concept of disadvantage is too individually based and ignores the complex social, economic and political conditions that give rise to poverty and inequality.

ii.   Implicit in the work with disadvantaged groups is the idea of compensating people for their condition by providing educational and other services. This ignores the question of how can people be compensated for what they never had? The compensatory theme diverts attention away from the in-built deficiencies of education and welfare services onto individuals.

iii.   In focussing attention on individual needs there is some danger of regarding their disadvantage as caused by personal inadequacy which can be corrected by education.

iv.   The definition of disadvantage with its stress on individual pathology amounts to an uncritical cultural meaning which highlights deficits over differences and places those not labelled as disadvantaged as superior in personal capacities and social behaviour. What is being attacked here is the liberal philosophy which rests on the support of dominant groups in society, who have the power to define who shall be called disadvantaged and unequal. The disadvantaged have no say in the matter and have not been expected to define their own needs or kinds of provision.

v.   In ignoring the socio-economic and political context of disadvantage and inequality the liberal adult education perspective avoids a structural explanation of the causal factors, which lie in the way social relations are organised in a capitalist political economy. Poverty and disadvantage are end products of a competitive economy leading to a class based society which perpetuates social inequalities in economic, social and power relations. In taking a benign and optimistic view of disadvantage in society the liberal perspective at best is part of the problem and worse, helps sustain it. Thus the optimistic belief in social progress through individual achievement raises false expectations for there is insufficient political commitment to a major change in society towards greater equality.

These criticisms of the liberal perspective, applicable to the model of social welfare as well as adult education, do not deny the existence of the disadvantaged, for the most part. Rather the analysis and the policies and practical actions that follow from it do not go far or deep enough. The radical perspective starts with a structural explanation, meaning causes are identified which arise from social, economic and political inequalities that are built into a society organised into a hierarchy of social classes with very different life chances or opportunities. These 'life chances' comprise an extensive range of opportunities; in employment, education, economic activities (credit and capital accumulation, etc.), cultural freedoms (communication skills and access to leisure facilities, etc.), equality of social status and esteem and so on. Many studies have shown that the distribution of opportunities and the 'good things in life' which give a sense of personal and social well being are unequally distributed, principally according to social class background[7]. This does not rule out inequalities arising from gender, racial and other social group differences. It is just that social class is a major indicator of differences in various forms of opportunity and power in society – economic, social and political. The disadvantaged, measured individually and collectively by a wide range of quantitative and qualitative criteria, represent the extreme end of a spectrum of ascending privilege and power in society and their relative position is worse than others around them.

The radical perspective seeks to change the structure of society that is deemed to cause the diswelfares and disadvantages in society. The emphasis upon pathological features of individual and social behaviour by the disadvantaged mostly reflects symptoms not real causes. These arise from the ways in which poverty, in any of its guises, is inevitable given the inequalities built into the economic, social, cultural and political organisation or structure of society. The causative factor from the radical perspective, whether in politics, social welfare or adult education, is the capitalist system of economic organisation and the structure of political, social and cultural institutions that uphold it as a system of ideas and social relations [8].

Reference has already been made, albeit briefly to an illustration of the radical adult education perspective applied to social problems. It would be more appropriate to carry this over to another chapter where it is possible to deal in greater detail with the radical perspective. This is because in the link between adult education for the disadvantaged with the theories and practices of community development the ideas of the radicals can be more clearly described.

In summarising the theoretical perspectives on adult education for the disadvantaged it is necessary to employ the concepts of poverty and social equality. In the first case disadvantage is a wider meaning of poverty embracing deprivations of a qualitative kind in the psychological, cultural and social areas of life, as well as the economic and political areas. Second the relevance of social equality is that it expresses an end purpose for poverty policies and specific work with the disadvantaged. In this progressive view policies and practices start from the assumption that disadvantage is a relative form of poverty, rather than an absolute condition, and should be approached either through minimal welfare or distributional welfare perspectives. This accords with the liberal and radical perspectives in adult education respectively. Thereafter their views differ over the interpretation of the causes of disadvantage and the ways to remedy the inequalities that their condition reflects. These differences are more clearly visible in adult education for the disadvantaged in multiple deprived communities.

CHAPTER FIVE
SOCIAL THEORY PERSPECTIVES ON ADULT EDUCATION AND THE PROBLEM OF NON-PARTICIPATION

Closely related to the problem of providing adult education for disadvantaged groups, usually embracing ideas of community education and development, is the issue of non-participation. For many practitioners in adult education participation is the central question. Expressed another way, non-participation by large numbers of the population, especially disadvantaged sections, constitutes the major challenge to the idea of adult education being concerned about social purpose and relevance in a changing society.

There have been many research studies of participation and non-participation in adult education. These have ranged from local case studies of institutions and geographical areas to national surveys of sample populations. Behind these studies lies the issue of the appeal and relevance of education to the adult population. It is not intended to detail these studies, only to note their general findings. What is more important is to attempt to explain participation, and more particularly, non-participation. A simple way of putting this task is to answer the charge that adult education has an inherent bias towards the middle classes and is more relevant to those who have had more successful early educational experiences. But this would be to plunge into radical perspectives and critiques of adult education with undue haste. Moreover this might oversimplify the problem of explaining what is really a complex matter.

Central to an understanding of participation in adult education are the concepts of social class and sub-culture. Both have been used in participation studies, with social class as a key indicator in quantitative surveys and sub-culture used less often in more qualitative investigations. Furthermore the link between social class (or other social position indicators, such as gender, age, education, ethnicity, etc.) and participation has been used to discuss wider issues such as equality of opportunity. In this sense social class and participation in adult education is like a microscopic illustration of social problems applicable to systems theory perspectives in sociology. As there is a distinct connection between social class and sub-culture the relevance of participation studies to holistic theories of society and the particular issues of social inequality are strong.

Some outline of this chapter is appropriate. First it is necessary to clarify the meaning of social participation, both in general terms and as it applies to adult education. Second a brief review of research findings on participation and non-participation in adult education is useful. Attention can then focus on explaining non-participation. Implicitly this brings in the framework of ideas typical of holistic sociological perspectives for the reason stated earlier. Explicitly the key concepts of social class and sub-culture need to be explained as they are very important in participation research. These concepts also link with sociological explanations of the influence of social background and the educational system on the likelihood of adults returning to learning on a voluntary basis. In writing this chapter a selective approach has been adopted insofar as in other chapters ideas alluded to here are extended and discussed more fully. In effect this chapter serves the purpose of supplementing the other chapters and is as much about information giving as with theory building.

With regard to the idea of social participation there is first the need to clarify meaning and second to identify the values in adult education that make the issue so important.

Social participation is a broad concept and its specific meaning is somewhat dependent upon the particular context where it is used. Thus in adult education participation refers to various kinds of involvement in activities whose intention is to promote learning. In another context, such as party politics, it is more likely to refer to other kinds of actions. In the former participation includes a range of activities from attending formal education institutions and sustained study to the rather casual process of learning that may arise through clubs and informal groups. In the political context participation has similarly been described in terms of a range of activities from what is called spectator activities (i.e. voting, wearing a badge, listening to opinions) to transitional activities (such as attending meetings), to gladitorial activities (holding office, campaigning, etc.). For adult educators the issue of participation revolves around getting people to attend courses, join groups, visit an adult centre, make an enquiry or other steps towards learning. Thereafter participation can focus on interacting with educational institutions and tutors and taking account of the deeper psychological meanings people may attach to engaging in adult education. The point is that like so many other concepts in behavioural studies participation is an elastic, umbrella term with several levels of increasingly specific meanings.

Both sociology and psychology join together in examining participation in terms of engaging in adult education for an end purpose, such as personal goals or social change where learning appears to be a means to some end. This brings into account the question of motivations to participate, who they are, how they engage in learning activities and what transpires both in terms of individual outcomes and social effects on the broader canvas of society.

There are general ideas of social participation where a sociological perspective is applicable, without diminishing the relevance of psychological insights. For adult education participation is a group activity where numbers of people engage in learning pursuits through classes and courses. The interest is still primarily about group or social participation, even with the investigation of individual self-directed learning, for clearly it is also about numbers of people and their social characteristics who choose that form of learning. Thus there is a quantitative dimension to participation studies in adult education for policy making and practical reasons. Furthermore such quantitative data provides the basis for theorising about factors associated with participation and non-participation.

The values of adult education underpinning the social participation issue have already been described in an earlier chapter. It is only necessary to briefly allude to the rationales for participation in adult education. This embraces the idea that learning activities are a means of individuation and a liberal influence on the mind, to a means of occupational and social mobility; as a means of developing basic skills; to raising social and political consciousness, social action and adapting to a changing society. The point is that participation in adult education is essential to make operational sense of whatever values are being extolled.

The data on social participation is usually based on common social position indicators – social class, gender, age, occupational status and educational background – for they provide an easy guide to who participates in adult education and leisure time activities of other kinds. It is common practice to link these descriptive profiles with various means of eliciting motives for participation. Less work has been done on self-perceived satisfactions and benefits of participation. As stated earlier there are numerous small scale studies of adult education, voluntary association and leisure participation. Very few offer a distinct theoretical explanation of participation and non-participation but they are strong on descriptive data and as such are useful for general knowledge and policy making purposes [1].

There have been two major British studies, the most recent being by the now extinct Advisory Council for Adult and Continuing Education (ACACE) whose report in 1982 –Adults: Their Educational Experiences and Needs– is the most elaborate and up to date [2]. Twelve years previously the National Institute for Adult Education (now NIACE) published a comprehensive study called 'Provision for Adult Education' [3]. Both are too long and complex to detail here, although a few selected impressions are useful. These derive from other studies as well [4].

Taking a broad view of adult education, that is both formal and informal provision, it appears that about two million adults take part in a learning activity each year. This number is on the increase and grows at a faster rate than the increase of the adult population. It has been generously estimated that assuming just a one-off involvement in some kind of recognised adult education up to 40 percent of the adult population will engage in a learning activity. However it would not be wise to rely too much on such calculations and in any case it is difficult to comment upon their significance. What is abundantly clear is that formal adult education provision attracts only a minority of the population. It has been widely noted that the one consistent finding is a direct relationship between adult education participation and social class background.

Social class as a concept is difficult to pin down to a single meaning. Essentially social class is part of the wider concept of social stratification which refers to the division of the population into layers or levels of groups sharing certain common characteristics. The three elements of social strata most commonly used are economic position, status or prestige and political power. The point about stratification is that each layer in a hierarchy of social relationships experiences relative access to scarce goods. These range from material goods to the more elusive ideas associated with possessing socially valued objects, such as social esteem, power and authority, an exclusive lifestyle, even personal attributes prized by others. Mention will be made later of the different ways in which social stratification and particularly the inequalities of economic, social and political positions are interpreted by consensus and conflict theories of society. For the purpose of this chapter attention is more narrowly focussed on the economic dimension, usually known as class stratification.

Thus social class is usually defined in economic terms derived from the ownership of wealth and income, which is for most people earned from working for pay and reward. Class analysis springs from the ideas of Marx and Weber. The former saw social classes as real aggregates of groups with an inherent force to change society. Weber identified class in a more limited way to refer to people's market situation, which means for the most part their capacity to earn an income through work. Weber's ideas of class are closer to the way it is used as a tool for social participation research, insofar as it includes the notions of job skills, educational qualifications and other assets shaping a person's class and position in society in general as well as the economy in particular.

The practical approach to social class as a concept and variable in social research hinges around occupation. Implicity in this is the idea that a person's social class is largely shaped by occupational status and rewards and this influences life chances. The traditional assumption is that a broad distinction in life chances exists between non-manual and manual occupations commonly known as middle and working classes. Further refinements can be made between higher and lower levels within these broad classes corresponding to the increasing refinements of rewards, status, power and other manifestations of the complex division of labour in the occupational and economic structures of society. Life chances, meaning the variable opportunities people have to gain a share of the economic and cultural goods of society, is seen to derive from membership of a social class.

Practically these ideas of social class are translated into distinct occupational, socio-economic categories that rely on the judgement of sociologists and demographic experts through such bodies as the Office of Population Censuses and Surveys. These standard instruments are widely adopted by others doing market and academic research. The ACACE survey, for instance, discusses the use of social class categories in the appendices to its report. Nonetheless the element of interpretation that goes into these standardised instruments is often open to debate for the boundaries between social classes is sometimes quite blurred. In adult education participation studies a frequent issue is where to place housewives as a social class category. Indeed such problems of definition and labelling are the common experience of participation research as there are no definitive rules of guidance. This sometimes confuses comparative analysis, making it a somewhat speculative activity.

The most salient finding in participation research is the influence of social class background and behaviour on whether or not adults use education. The middle classes are the dominant users of adult education, especially of formal provision, with the professional occupational groups being over-represented. The key idea that emerges from this is that early educational experience at the compulsory school stage establishes a taste or distaste for more education on a voluntary basis in adult life. This depends greatly, although never absolutely, on the level of successful attainment and the everyday experience of school education. The position seems to be that adult education participation reinforces the mainly positive experience of school and this operates mainly in the opposite way with the working classes. The connection between social class and educational background is very strong and this carries through to adult life. Thus social class and educational background could be used interchangeably in participation research with the same general findings emerging. But it should be noted that this is only a general observation for one of the attractions of adult education is its capacity to provide second chance opportunities for those whose early education was not successful.

In general the various studies of participation both in adult education and leisure activities come to the same conclusion that there is a strong connection between social class and previous education. This is not the only connection though, for the same studies have also shown that the participants in adult education are likely to be involved in a variety of other social and cultural activities, many of them formally organised, in the community. It is helpful to summarise some other main connections between participation and the social characteristics of adults.

Most participation studies confirm a higher level of involvement by the 30 to 50 age range, peaking in the mid 40s for many adult students. Motivation varies with age with younger adults being more inclined towards vocational studies linked to earning a living. Older people in the main seek adult education for a wider variety of purposes. With regard to gender women outnumber men in most kinds of adult education with the possible exception of narrowly based work training. Some studies have examined in detail the relationship between adult education participation and a range of other social indicators, such as urban/rural residence, race/ethnicity, religion, civil status, family size and so forth, but apart from their case study significance these findings are not really generalisable. Expressed another way, their importance is overshadowed by the principal finding that adult education by attracting the middle classes and better educated is a reinforcing activity rather than a remedial one. This is in contrast to the social relevance theme and the concern to make adult education accessible and meaningful to the disadvantaged and the majority who are not attracted to continuing learning.

In examining the profiles of adults there appears to be a continuum of attitudes towards their own education. Those who regularly join adult education courses are knowledge seekers willing to take the trouble to study and learn in a formal way. These are usually drawn from the ranks of the better educated middle classes who are familiar with participating in such organised activities through voluntary associations and relatively organised leisure pursuits. To all intents and purposes these represent a minority of the population. The next level are those who are interested in learning but unwilling to make the effort to join courses and the like. The rest, estimated to be about half the population have descending levels of interest ending in indifference to antipathy. This impression of a hierarchy of positive to negative attitudes has been implicitly juxtaposed with the pyramid shaped hierarchies of the class structure and educational attainment levels of the adult population. At least two leading studies, a nation wide investigation in the USA and the other a smaller scale British one, came to the same general summary [5].

Whatever the accuracy of such a generalisation the impression has a plausible ring of truth. Attention now needs to be paid to the idea that non-participation is characterised by indifference or hostility towards adult education. This is especially relevant where adult education has attempted to be innovative in the nature of provision, especially for disadvantaged groups in their own communities. This involves looking further into the meaning of social class, not as a research indicator or measure of occupational and educational standing but in terms of cultural values and behaviour. This introduces the idea of class sub-cultures.

Before doing that a very brief profile of non-participants is required, based on the ACACE study. The ACACE study identified 15 percent of its sample as a negative non-participant population grouping, that is, with no experience of post school education and no desire to become involved. According to the study these non-participants tend to be older (over 55 years) and mainly from the lower social class groups −semi to unskilled occupations. This group with the least potential for participation not only lack educational motivation but express very little interest in active leisure interests. Instead there is a premium on passively passing time. Their lack of interest is compounded with a lack of knowledge about educational opportunities, chiefly because they are seen as irrelevant. It should be recognised, as suggested earlier, that this is an extreme group. Other participants are by no means as negative. This led the ACACE report to argue that there was evidence of latent, unexpressed demand, given the appropriate kinds of provision. Indeed adult education certainly experimented with innovative forms of provision long before the findings and recommendations of the ACACE report was published.

The concept of class culture lies behind many studies of working class life and these are of general use in considering the issue of non-participation in adult education. The concept simply refers to a set of more or less distinctive values, attitudes, beliefs and lifestyles of a social group. A sub-culture is relatively different from but at the same time inter-linked to the dominant culture of society. Hence the distinctiveness of the sub-culture of a group while implying special properties does not mean isolation from society.

Within the context of adult education the working class, as the major disadvantaged group (although the feminists might dispute this point), are seen as a sub-culture and a deviation from the culture of the dominant classes in society. Some adult educators are disposed towards treating working class sub-culture as a problem manifesting pathological behaviour. This fits with those views of poverty and disadvantage that favour psychological and cultural explanations and end up blaming the victims for their own condition. On the other hand working class sub-culture is seen by others, usually of radical political persuasion, as a healthy statement of an alternative set of values and lifestyles, not dependent upon the ideas of the dominant, ruling classes.

These varying views uncover some key questions about the meaning of sub-culture which cannot be ignored or conclusively answered. The problem is to resolve two different ideas − the first of the distinctiveness of class cultures and the other of a common culture cutting across class groups. It appears as if an extreme view of either position is not applicable for it has been shown that both exist together with cultural diversity and a common culture. At the same time the lower social classes have managed to cultivate certain differences of culture, expressed through behaviour and styles of living, that are sufficiently different to merit further description. These are summarised in the following paragraphs.

What emerges from the many studies of working class culture, both British and American, is a host of descriptions of various dimensions of the idea of sub-culture [6]. On balance there is more description than theory, principally because many studies were concerned with political issues and social policies. These descriptions emerge as fairly consistent themes of working class life, revolving around the expressions of values, through attitudes towards various topics, such as education and leisure, politics and authority, work and wages, family life and members of other classes. Before outlining these attitudes and common themes two preliminary points need to be made. The first concerns the assumed homogenity of the working class, which is clearly not the case. And the second point also implicitly adopts another typology to outline a schema of class related values.

As explained earlier, social change, particularly the continuing diversification of a complex division of labour, has considerably transformed the Marxist idea of two social classes. Although there is broad agreement with the idea of a middle and working class it is now accepted that there are several strata within each class. This has been the case in studies of class cultures and values. As the example shown later illustrates, values are aligned behind three broad classes. Other studies point to more specific variations within the working classes. Thus studies identify variations within the aggregate of the population comprising the working class. For instance, distinctions have been made between what working class people themselves describe as 'respectable', 'ordinary' and 'rough', suggesting a hierarchy of status and esteem, with the 'respectables' more closely situated and emulative of the higher placed middle class and their values and lifestyles [7]. It might be supposed that from the ranks of the respectable working class there is a greater disposition towards education, emphasising the importance of doing well at school and of being willing to learn in adult life. By contrast 'ordinary' working class lack educational aspiration and the 'roughs' are antipathetic. There is such a large element of speculation in these suppositions that they have to be treated as ideas, rather than as facts.

Another distinction is between 'traditional' and 'modern' working class, closely related to staple and newer industies and geographical regions where these economic activities are located [8]. In this typology the traditional working class demonstrates established customs and behaviour, often conservative and conforming in manner and attitude. The traditionals represent the images of deference towards authority and higher classes and the idea of the proletarian in Marxist thought. They have also been described as 'status assenters', that is, with habits of thought and action belonging to inherited socialisation and cultural mores. By contrast the 'status dissenters' are the new working class who having made the break with their traditional pasts seek new lifestyles. The latter are believed to be more materially minded and concerned that their children do well enough at school to compete for the better paid jobs. The problem for the status dissenter is of not having a sense of belonging, unlike the more traditional, status assenting working class. Status dissenters are the more 'privatised' working class regarding work as an instrumental means to material ends and eschewing the traditional values and solidarity of status assenters.

The important point is that working class is not a single, homogenous grouping but a relatively diverse set of sub-cultures reflecting different relations to production and economy, location and community, values and tradition, and so on. Moreover the working classes are changing, albeit in uneven ways, from established patterns of living in the family and marriage, community, work and economic activity to a more loose knit set of relationships providing a greater scope for individual choice. These changes have been depicted as a merging of certain sections of the working class into middle class lifestyles and values. So in education, for instance, there is more recognition of the importance of education and a stress on personal achievement. This has enabled some working class children to climb up the ladder of individual achievement and escape from their class backgrounds, not always without some personal anguish.

Yet another image of the working class, though, is of the 'earnest minority' who never got away from their class backgrounds, either through choice or lack of opportunity [9]. These have been described as the joiners and volunteers in politics, trade unionism and serious minded cultural and learning activities through working class associations and classes run by the Workers' Educational Association. From the ranks of these serious and earnest working class men and women labour politics built its early foundations, dissenting religions thrived and the toil and perseverance of the self educated carved out some remarkable scholars. The earnest minority seemed to have co-existed with their less serious minded contemporaries, some by becoming community leaders, without much rancour. Part of the explanation is the sheer doggedness of the self educated. Another explanation is that working class culture is quite rich with self-directed, independent organisations and activities, providing an ambience more supportive of intellectual activity than might be supposed from a superficial examination. A different view altogether is that the 'blue collar joiner' is a rather marginal figure in two respects. First the blue collar joiner is not well knitted into the informal relationships of the locality because of recent mobility. Second, this drives the person to seek friendships through membership of associations, organised leisure and educational activities. But note that the British earnest minority and American blue collar workers experience very different worlds, with the latter having more opportunity and acceptance of moving home and job.

One of the ways of putting these themes and differences of working class sub-culture into perspective is to construct a typology of values. The hypothesis behind this typology is that social class influences behaviour (such as disposition towards adult education participation) and pesonality, by providing different kinds of socialisation, learning experiences and cultural milieus. The way of expressing this idea is to combine all these behaviours and present them as stemming from social class values. A simplified model presents three main classes –middle, working and lower class –related to value dimensions, as shown below[10]:

	Middle Class	Working Class	Lower Working Class	
ACTIVITY	Mastery and manipulation, open world view	Security minded, belief in luck and fate	Powerlessness in achievement areas	PASSIVITY
RATIONALISM	Faith in rationality, preference for order	Pragmatism, oral tradition	Anti-intellectual, prejudiced	TRADITION
UNIVERSALISM	Stress on equality of opportunity for those prepared to strive	Person centred, home and neighbourhood centred,	Simplification, narrow views	PERSONALISED
INDIVIDUALITY	Emphasis on individuality and personality	Them v. us feelings	Deprivation, misanthropy	GROUP ORIENTATION
FORWARD LOOKING	Orientation towards change	Immediacy	Toughness, insecurity	PRESENT/PAST LOOKING

It would be impractical to detail social behaviour characteristic of each value dimension but it would be useful to provide selective examples. These are mainly focussed on working and lower class values and lifestyles often expressed in the American literature as behavioural themes.

An example is the work of Hoggart who identified what he regarded as typical British working class values, such as an oral and local tradition, home centredness and neighbourhood centredness, both concerned with personal and immediate issues [11]. The personal and the concrete is preferred to the vagaries of abstract thought. There is also a strong 'them and us' attitude derived from a lack of power and authority, which leads to the need for in-group solidarity to fend off the intrusions of 'them'. There is less faith in the idea of a ladder of success for those who achieve and work hard. Instead more reliance is placed upon luck and putting up with things when it runs out.

American literature, stemming from the 'War on Poverty' projects of the 1960s, focussed attention on the values and lifestyles of what they termed the lower class sub-culture. The behaviour of the disadvantaged sections of American society is largely shaped by the values of simplifying the world around them and through the experience of deprivation base life on feelings of powerlessness and insecurity. The struggle to survive at the bottom of the social pile gives rise to the tough minded outlook, intolerance and anti-intellectualism[12].

On the other hand the traditional working class American with better job opportunities is more concerned with achieving a good standard of living, but without necessarily trying to emulate middle class values. An awareness of class differences does not seem to foster antagonistic class consciousness, although illiberalism over matters of race and gender equality is reportedly common. With regard to education limited experience and a sense of failure rules out much enthusiasm for adult involvement. This attitude is compounded the lower the class sub-culture where education is very far removed from the everyday necessity to survive economically and psychologically.

This negative attitude towards education has been labelled cognitive poverty which expresses an unwillingness to learn and develop. Thus there is a contempt for talk which involves general principles, abstraction or imaginative ideas going beyond the concrete and familiar. In brief, 'book learning' and theory are seen as irrelevant and cynically dismissed as being more suited to 'them'. At the same time it has been noted that working and lower class adults value the education of their children more then they do of themselves. Therefore self improvement, with the exception of an earnest minority who have found their way into adult education histories, has very little appeal. Attention is paid to the present not to the future.

These generalisations have been subject to a great deal of criticism on a number of grounds [13]. There is little point in labouring these criticism for the generalised nature of the observations of working class sub-culture is sufficient to suggest their weaknesses. Allowing for these criticisms it is useful to outline a select number of sociological studies that put forward theories of class and sub-culture. These are useful in a general way as insights into working class values and indirectly to the question of non-participation in adult education.

There are four theories of particular note with some overlap between them. All the theories deal with the moderation of the British working classes, in contrast to their predicted radicalism. More specifically they provide clues to help explain non-participation.

The first theory puts forward the idea that there are three class related value systems [14]. Behind this theory lies the notion that there are divergent values reflecting class groups and differences in society rather than a set of values held in common. This latter point represents a different theory to be outlined shortly. The problem with a divergent class structure and related values is of achieving a satisfactory level of order and control, given the prospect of class values clashing through industrial, economic and political conflict. For some values to override others, say in the interest of national unity, it is necessary for these values to be institutionalised and disseminated across the social groupings of society.

The essence of this theory is that the ruling and middle classes have taken possession of the main institutions of society and from that power base have secured their own values and placed them in a dominant position. Thus the values of the middle classes noted earlier are the dominant values of society. These values uphold individual achievement, competition and the legitimate nature of various kinds of social inequality.

The sub-ordinate values of the working classes generates both an imitative form of aspiration and deferential behaviour. Both are accommodative responses, the former through opportunities for achievement and upward social mobility and the latter by encouraging an acceptance of lower status as a consequence of lower levels of achievement. This acceptance of subordination is reinforced by 'us' and 'them' attitudes with 'them' being seen as the strivers for whom educational and other kinds of opportunities have really been designed. Even the bargaining strength and solidarity of trade unionism does not fundamentally alter the commanding position of the owning and managerial classes —the

54

dominant class culture.

For those members of the working classes with aspirations (status dissenters) educational achievement has represented a limited ladder of opportunity for mobility. This opportunity really arose through the expansion of non-manual jobs, particularly in the welfare sector, where educational achievement was a ticket of entry into the lower ranks of the middle classes. Social mobility in this respect has acted as a kind of safety valve, defusing potential class antagonism by providing chances for some to 'get on' in the world.

For the rest subordination means acceptance of the status quo. In this respect adult education has very little relevance as a means of opportunity, for the world is not perceived in those terms and in any case such activities are seen as the province of 'them'. It is 'them' who find education meaningful whereas for 'us' it is about failure, pretension, unrealistic ambition and other things beyond the reach and ambit of the immediate social milieu.

The only alternative to status assent or attempting to become like them, that is an aspiring member of the dominant value system by status dissent, is to become radical. This involves a conscious awareness of political and other forms of inequality based on class differences and how the dominant value system of society manipulates and controls people. The traditional routes to this form of awareness, leading to a radical alternative value system, is through membership of the trade union movement and labour politics, both using adult education as a means of consciousness raising. Depending upon the political perspective adopted this form of adult education may be seen as merely initiating working class people into the prevailing value system, disguised under doctrines like 'democratic citizenship', 'liberal studies', and other themes related to the institutionalisation of industrial relations and social conflict. Such activities may be seen as a muted form of radicalism rather than the alternative political values of educational activists such as Freire and others with a strong conflict perspective.

It is reasonable to claim that the great disappointment for the radical seeking an alternative to subordinate values, with the expressions of deference and acceptance of inequality, is the accommodative nature of working class culture. On the one hand the objective class position of clerical and manual workers, as determined by economic rewards and working conditions, is unequivocal. By the objective measures available these occupational and class groups comprise the proletarian working classes and through the raising of their consciousness could become a 'class for itself' and gain real power. Yet on the other hand there is so much acceptance of subordination.

This position can be explained by the use of reference group theory [15]. This theory holds that people form their attitudes and values from the actions of others whom they emulate and model their behaviour upon. The material presented on class values and sub-culture would suggest two kinds of responses by working class adults. The reference group for many is their own class members and they simply model their own attitudes, values, behaviour and lifestyles on the example set by those with whom they share a common and often inherited and traditional cultural background. This is usually formed by a common economic class position. Several studies of working class culture implicitly make use of the idea of a membership reference group, illustrated by the behaviour of the status assenter and the values of the subordinate class.

Another kind of reference group is of a higher placed social class whose culture and lifestyle sets the standards and aspirations of the status dissenter. It is not clear whether the earnest minority within the working class derive stimulus, motivation and personal goals from the examples set by higher placed social groups and their cultural values. It would appear, though, that some feeling of relative deprivation, that is, an unfavourable comparison with self-perceived circumstances with those of higher placed social groups, may be an incentive to regard adult education as a means of personal change and upward social mobility. Whatever the empirical truth of these observations it is generally believed that the reference groups used by working class adults and the sense of perceived relative deprivation or contentment helps explain a disposition towards or away from participation in education. In general working class culture is not largely disposed towards the voluntary commitment of time and effort to pursuits seen as the hallmark of middle class culture.

Nonetheless even for those working class adults who show some leaning towards middle class values and lifestyles it is important to recognise that having an aspirational reference group may not be sufficient to maintain the level of personal ambition required to succeed at typical middle class goals. Adult education taken seriously demands a great deal of effort and application, perhaps more than learning power. While endurance and tenacity may be traditional virtues of the working classes this may not carry over to the demands of sustained learning. The truth of this is questionable, of course, for so many self educated working class people testify otherwise. Yet in people's minds education represents a daunting prospect of taxing effort and fear of failure. This might be sufficient cause not to take the risks involved. The traditional compensation for individual success is the security of a familiar class culture.

This whole area of working class cultural values has been examined from another angle. The underlying question is the extent to which the working classes, particularly the more mobile and affluent workers in the newer industries, have merged into the middle classes. More specifically the questions are whether the new working class (the status dissenters) share the same broad economic position, normative outlook (similar values, attitudes and behavioural standards and goals) and relate to their middle class counterparts (paticularly clerical and service groups representative of the lower middle class) on a freer and accepting basis. This has been called the embourgeoisement or class convergence theory[16].

This theory is really about the decline of working class radicalism as a consequence of rising affluence and the securities of the social wages of the welfare state. In a narrow sense it is also a vision of working class life being absorbed by status and acquisitive concerns typical of the middle classes. The major research project that tested these propositions produced mixed findings. There was evidence of some class convergence, more often led by the clerical non-manual workers turning to white collar trade unionism as a means of maintaining their relatively declining economic position. At the same time working class unionism was less a means of social solidarity but more an instrumental means of securing better pay and working conditions. There was also evidence of normative convergence over the importance of children's education and a more home and family centred lifestyle and leisure time use. The latter similarity has been described as a privatised lifestyle reducing community related activities to the fringe of the new working classes' cultural values. This compounds the traditional marginality of working class participation in adult education and other consciously 'improving' cultural activities in the community. The significance of home based learning through the influence of television and recently the home computer is still unchartered. What is reasonably clear is the decline of community participation and the ascendancy of a private, home and family centred culture. On the larger political canvas the embourgeoisement thesis has not been proven beyond reasonable doubt. Inequality persists and rising levels of unemployment, work insecurity and inflation have substantially weakened the idea of a new affluent working class.

In spite of these findings the idea of a pervasive and classless value system persists and cannot be ignored. Much of the material presented here has started from the basis of distinctive social classes and lifestyles derived from different cultural values. The value stretch theory challenges those assumptions[17].

The starting point of this American theory is that there is an underlying common value system. This corresponds to the assumptions of structural-functional theory in sociology, another predominantly American inspired perspective. The argument is that the lower working class, even though they may lack the wherewithal for middle class success, still subscribe to their values and strive for a similar lifestyle. The solution to the problem of the gap between expectations and realistic prospects for the attainment of middle class goals is to stretch the values, without abandoning them or seeking alternatives. Thus the lower class value stretch is a means of coming to terms with lower levels of success and more modest attainments. This strategy enables people to be deprived in dignity and also satisfies the middle class value of striving for respectability. Adult education concerned with basic skills and work training may well provide the vehicle for enabling the disadvantaged to imitate middle class values while settling for lesser levels of attainment and reward.

As with several theories and field based observations there is a need for caution in jumping to general conclusions in this area of sociology. The implications for adult education have to be tentative. It would be foolish to regard these findings as facts. Instead their value is in pointing to lines of thought and research possibilities. With regard to the former there is much to be gained from an awareness of social class as a cultural phenomenon and it is fairly clear that the non-participating working classes have other priorities, needs and interests than joining adult education classes.

Undaunted, adult educators have continued to seek ways of relating to the working class. From this has sprung innovative and enterprising forms of provision closely attuned to working class culture, especially modes of communication and learning. This is the story of adult education for the disadvantaged through basic education programmes, work related training and in partnership with ideas and practices of community development in conspicuously deprived inner city areas. These efforts have been rewarded, albeit on a small scale, and it suggests that the barriers to cultural communication can be lowered providing the appropriate approaches to provision and modes of communication and learning are observed. Above all the question of relevance has to be based on felt needs rather than on an outsider's assessment or grand slogan.

CHAPTER SIX

THE SOCIAL RELEVANCE THEME: THE NON-PARTICIPATION PROBLEM, PROVISION FOR THE DISADVANTAGED AND THE IDEAS OF COMMUNITY ADULT EDUCATION

Along with the disadvantaged adult education enthused just as much with the ideas of community education and development and in many ways the terms were used synonymously in pursuit of the social relevance theme. In discussing the disadvantaged in the context of community education and development reference needs to be made, by way of preface, to the meaning of community. Once more, there are several meanings and theoretical perspectives to comprehend, as indeed there are in the ideas about community education and community development.

In understanding the concept of community two kinds of meaning are in use. The first is the association of community with various kinds of idealism. This approach may be called the romantic view of community where it performs the imaginary function of solving a wide range of problems. Hence community as a panacea. The second is a sociological meaning of community involving classical and modern attempts at definition. This approach reduces the element of romantic idealism but never totally for sociologists are just as given to using concepts to suit their vision of the world as anyone else. That is why reference is made to the view that the idea of community is a myth, for it helps to correct such tendencies.

First the romantic idea of community in which it is generally held to be a 'good thing'. This moral dimension may explain why some adult educators and other workers concerned about the well-being and social welfare of others have latched onto the concept so avidly. It is as if the existence of the concept of community is justification in itself. Moreover the appeal of the concept has acted as a kind of connecting thread, bringing together adult educators with social workers, youth leaders, librarians, clergy, health workers, counsellors and the like in the common cause of creating and preserving a sense of belonging through the provision of services held together by the unifying idea of community. This alliance around a concept has stimulated mutual developments in these services on the general understanding that as their work has a community dimension it must be a good thing to support. Behind the practical and sometimes costly ventures in community based services lies the idea that people need a 'world of our own', to coin a phrase, where everybody is known and respected and where care and services and concern mixes with interest and mutual support amongst neighbours, friends and even strangers. Community expresses that idea of social relations extending, as it does, beyond the immediate support and mutual obligations of the family and kin into a wider group.

In the sense that community is being used here there is a whole person ideal being expressed [1]. The whole person theme means that people relate in the totality of themselves through all their social roles. This is in contrast to the fragmented way typical of modern industrial society with a complex division of labour and status groups hierarchically arranged. Industrial society prevents the inclusiveness of social relations which the romantic ideal of community, by contrast, naturally fosters through the customs and practices of everyday social interactions developed through long historical ties. In tandem with this idea community represents a means of enabling people to rise above their selfish interests and by so doing broaden their social experience. This perspective encourages the belief that through such an experience of community the foundations of conviviality and cooperation are established. These in turn act as stabilising forces in society and are seen as especially welcome during turbulent social changes.

Earlier commentators on society, as it transformed into an industrial and mass social organisation, saw the consequences as a loss of human simplicity, naturalness and cooperation, which placed man in conflict with himself. Thus the spirit of industrial capitalism with its competitiveness and acquisitiveness led man away from his true nature into a society of divisions of wealth, labour, status and influence. The lesson to learn from this perspective on community is that it is used to convey personal visions and ideal values concerning the predicaments of man in society. Some critics of the community idea have argued that by clinging to these romantic notions it cannot be adequately understood as a concept applicable to the real world. This may be the case but nonetheless it is best to recognise the force of ideal outlooks irrespective of their empirical merits.

The history of the community idea stems from the intellectual interest in the social consequences of industrialisation, as indeed does sociology as an intellectual discipline. The founding figure was F. Toennies who published a book entitled 'Gemeinschaft und Gesellschaft' in 1887 which is usually translated into 'Community and Society' [2]. His work has provided a fund of ideas on the concept of community which starts from the basis of depicting the development of society from traditional to modern form. It also has an implicit lament for the supposed 'break-up' of the ideas of community as envisaged by the romantic idealists.

Like many ideal type models in sociology use is made of dichotomous, polar differences in social relations. The apt example is Toennies' gemeinschaft and gesellschaft model, as shown below -

GEMEINSCHAFT
(Community)
1. Blood and kinship ties are predominant.
2. Locality and ties to the land are emphasised in
rational thought and change.
3. Tradition and stability are seen as virtues.

GESELLSCHAFT
(Association)
1. Impersonal and contractual social relations predominate.
2. Emphasis is placed upon social relationships.

In this 'ideal type' model gesellschaft represents the polar opposite of gemeinschaft, everything that community is not. Thus modern society is more like a mass, impersonal association of people relating to each other through contractual obligations underpinning social roles. Rational – legal authority governs social relations rather than the traditional and customary authority typical of gemeinschaft – community. The specific features of community as outlined in Toennies' ideal type model can be listed -

a. Human social relationships are intimate, that is, based on long standing and a high degree of face to face interaction.

b. People know where they stand in relation to each other because status is largely determined at birth and is therefore ascribed rather than achieved.

c. Social roles are clearly prescribed and 'fit' easily into personal life and relations with others.

d. There is little mobility from their locality or up a social hierarchy.

e. The culture of the community is shared by all because there is little movement into or out of the group and customs are socialised uniformly from birth.

f. The custodians of the culture are strong and pervasive in the transmission of moral values and everyday rules of social interaction.

g. The moral code emphasises a fierce loyalty to the community, often expressed as a strong sentimental attachment to the land or environs and a personalised way of interpreting social issues affecting the life of the community.

It is useful at this point to provide a note on the concept of ideal-type models, such as that exposed by Toennies. It is relevant because there will be other examples in the book. Ideal type refers to a hypothetical or imaginary model which is based upon observed social behaviour or features of a social institution. The observations are then translated into a general, pure and abstract model which forms the basis for further empirical research and reality testing. Thus in the case of the gemeinschaft contrasting with gesellschaft, what is being described are the pure features of both models, abstracted from the complexities of the real world and highlighted for illustrative purposes in an ideal form. In the first instance the ideal types do not have to be proven right or wrong but simply understood as ideas and concepts purporting to explain some aspect of sociological thought. Thereafter the models may be critically examined. Hence the description of gemeinschaft, which is used to explain the existence of social solidarity (and its demise in gesellschaft), allows for intelligent discussion about the meaning of community and the effects of social change arising from industrialisation and urbanisation on social relations.

This ideal type model serves two purposes. First, it reminds social commentators that gemeinschaft represents a particular type of society which may be for the most part lost but still surviving or potentially revivable. This is the romantic ideal for some kinds of community developer, which will be explained more fully later. Second, the gemeinschaft community in whatever form it exists can be observed and analysed. This is the stuff of several studies of working class commuities. These studies are of relevance in gaining insight into the issue of non-participation by the working classes in conventional forms of adult education provision. This topic will be dealt with at length in another chapter. Both the romantic and empirical aspects of Toennies' ideal type model are of relevance in discussing adult education and community development for the disadvantaged.

For all the explanatory power of Toennies' dichotomous model the search has continued for a more rigorous empirical description which tests a theory of community against firm evidence drawn from observation and experience. One notable attempt to do this using the dichotomous, ideal-type model approach is through the work of R. Frankenberg who constructed a rural-urban continuum[3]. His model incorporates the ideas of some of the founding figures in sociology as well as modern surveys of a more closely observed kind. In the model there is a movement along the continuum from gemeinschaft at the rural end, to gesellschaft at the urban end, as shown belown in reduced form -

RURAL
Gemeinschaft-Community

1. People are related in diverse ways and interact frequently and have many common interests.
2. A small number of people comprise the social arena of individuals.
3. People have multiple roles which they play to the same people over and over again.

4. The economy is simple with little division of labour.
5. Social solidarity is of a mechanical kind – collective consensus and beliefs hold the group together.
6. For the individual family life fixes social position. Social status derives from given social positions rather than achieved ones.

URBAN
Gesellschaft-Association

1/2/3 The social arena is much larger but role relationships are specific rather than overlapping. Whereas people may share common needs they do not have many common interests. Roles are played to different people and there is comparative infrequency of interaction.
4. Economy and division of labour is complex and differentiated.
5. Social solidarity is of the organic kind – interdependence of economic and social ties organised by contractual obligations.
6. Family ties are still important but emphasis is placed upon achieved status through education, occupation and social mobility.

The point about the model and others like it is its simplicity. This means that at one level it is quite plausible as an explanation. At another it is too generalised and sometimes erroneous. The best example of this is the idea of the urban village where some of the features of the rural community are incorporated, in a small sized local enclave, into the structure of a large metropolis. This idea is of importance in considering the commuity life of traditional working class culture resident in the inner zones of a large urban setting. It is also a reminder about relying too much on ideal type models to approximate social reality.

In addition to constructing models of types of community much attention has been paid to defining its meaning. One classic study identified over ninety definitions and since then the onus has been on reducing and sorting out the semantic nuances into key ideas and elements comprising the generally agreed meanings within a sociological framework[4].

Two major areas of meaning emerge. The first has been termed the horizontal meaning of community and the second the vertical meaning[5]. The horizontal meaning refers to the ideas of community being associated with geographic area and territory, combined with a sufficient time span allowing for settled patterns of living within defined boundaries. Together the elements of space and time encapsulate a distinguishable way of life which has common economic, social and cultural elements providing identity, shared experiences, a sense of belonging and common meanings to its members. The size of the community is not fixed nor do the members have to share exactly the same sense of belonging and so forth. On the one hand the horizontal meaning implies an all embracing, comprehensive view of community. On the other hand the really important point is that the horizontal meaning of community is relative rather than absolute which nonetheless provides a starting point for comprehending a very elusive concept.

Similarly the second meaning of community is also relative and elastic by necessity. In the vertical meaning community has a narrower conception, arising from the pursuit of specific interests such as those in clubs and other kinds of voluntary association. This meaning leaves aside any need to include common lifestyles and wider forms of inter-dependence of an economic or social kind related to a locality. Another vertical meaning recognises that community may exist only as a temporary experience, often in response to external threat (like wars and disaster) or internal conflict (like racial tension). These experiences induce a temporary sense of community-in-the-mind involving a limited kind of social participation around a common concern (like Silver Jubilee celebrations). Finally, a vertical meaning of community may be of a limited liability form, such as residents in commuter villages or weekend cottage dwellers, spending most of their time elsewhere who nonetheless have some sense of belonging to a place where they have attachments and interests[6].

The vertical meaning of community considerably extends, some might say stretches too far, its value as an operational concept. Yet it reflects the effects of social change, such as rapid urbanisation, geographic and social mobility, the emergence of the nuclear family structure and other changes to social relations in society. A complementary concept is social networks. It may be usefully compared to a fishing net. The close mesh net represents the traditional community described by Toennies as gemeinschaft and Frankenberg as rural in their dichotomous/continuum models, and depicts close knit social ties. A loose knit social network, seen as a large mesh fish net, depicts the wider distances between points of social interaction. This is typical of more mobile people in modern day society, where a residential pattern of community life is of lesser personal significance and meaning than, say, the social interactions of the occupational community. The close knit social network is more akin to the horizontal meaning of community and the loose knit of the vertical community. Above all the idea of social networks is not geographically bound but represents a more fluid pattern of social interaction.

A final item in discussing community as a concept is to question its validity as a workable idea[7]. Criticism is directed at several aspects of the concept. The first argues that the persistent use of the concept to express idealism in any of its forms is an outmoded romanticism and too subjective to be of much use in real life. The second criticism is that the idea of community is unrealistically bound by the geographical and territorial meaning. Social relations, especially in modern society which are more open to flux and change, are less confined to specific localities. Hence the social network and vertical notions of community rather than the all-inclusive, traditional ideas. People have networks of social relationships that extend well beyond immediate contacts and place, many of which are also out of their control. City life, for instance, is characterised by secondary rather than first hand, personal social relations, simply because the need for social order and control gives rise to remoter forms of management of everyday life (i.e. traffic control and other kinds of environmental management).

Two other criticisms are apt. The first is that community is often regarded as a means of socialisation through the transmission of cultural norms and values. This is an over-simplified idea. Whereas it is clear that people living in communities influence each other, through the family, local friendships and informal networks, it is also true that other institutions, such as schools, with cultural values determined from outside the locality, also act as socialisation agents. In this view, therefore, it is false to simply equate community, by itself, with socialisation outside the family for other, more formal social institutions are involved who are located within but not of the community and whose values and practices are often determined by some government bureaucracy or the like from outside society.

The other point is that in stressing the idea of community as a sense of belonging and well-being there is an implicit emphasis on value consensus and social order. Whereas this may be true it is at the expense of ignoring the social divisions in any community, reflecting the class, status and power differences in society, and a source of tension and conflict arising from the effects of social inequality. This view challenges the idea that community is a kind of benign haven removed from the tensions and conflicts of society. On the contrary, community reflects social reality in every way.

These criticisms do not demolish the idea of community for it holds too much sway over the imagination for that. But it does question its validity as a concept, where clear meaning is essential. Community is a vague term once it is examined closely. Nonetheless for all its flaws it has power as a vision of a desirable microcosm of society. It provides a generally understandable idea of small scale society within a geographical boundary and within which social life in all its manifestations may be observed. It also introduces the idea of communities of interest which are not geographically bound but centred around needs, activities and other specific interests as expressed in the idea of social networks. Finally, and in a more practical way, community is a useful prefix for a range of services concerned with social issues and problems within a territorial context or focussed on specific groups that has more administrative utility than sociological meaning. This leads to the major section of this chapter.

Two main concepts relate to adult education for the disadvantaged – community education and community development. Both have a short history much of it recently connected to the disadvantaged and these need to be outlined briefly and then clarified as concepts.

The early post-war history of adult education was about expansion and diversification of the curriculum. This reinforced the hold the middle classes and better educated had in adult education, leaving it with a conscience about the needs of the working classes and, later, the wide range of groups under the umbrella term 'disadvantaged'. One important development was adult education located in or serving the interests of the industrial community, particularly trade unionists, through industrial relations courses[8].

This important development was still quite small and specialised and left out the wider problem of reaching the working classes as a whole. The response was to argue for the dissolution of conventional ideas and practices in adult education. The rallying calls were community education and community development, or some variant of the latter term[9].

Community education has been used as a symbol for innovation in provision and this has required an elastic approach to the term for policy and practice under this banner has been varied. In this sense community education is what practitioners want it to mean. Once more the term embraces a diversity of ideas and practices. In one sense it has meant that educational agencies adopted a 'community outlook' by finding ways of reaching outwards to attract adult students and casual users of the educational and recreational facilities available in establishments. Sometimes this approach led to specific appointments to comunity education posts either based in an establishment or with an 'outreach' commission. At this end point of the spectrum of meanings in community education the emphasis was on working on the inside of various groups or gatherings of people located in the community.

The theme of this form of community education for adults (which is an offshoot of the innovations in the mainstream of school and colleges under the community education banner) was expressed as 'educational priority'. This theme has sought to reorganise adult education around the local issues, problems and needs of the people, leading to a new curriculum and learning addressed to practical problem solving and learning-by-doing. Some of this community based adult education was intended to promote social action, which amounted to the combination of learning, organisation and political pressure group acitivities arising from direct involvement in local issues.

Neither of the terms community education and community development were new. The former had its origins with the pioneer work of Henry Morris and the Cambridgeshire Village Colleges and the latter can be generally linked, for example, to the early years of the educational settlements in the deprived inner areas of some British cities at the turn of the century. But they both received a boost from a climate of opinion forming in the mid-1960s and often prompted by several official government reports. These should be mentioned in passing as they provide a useful historical background to this section of the chapter[10].

The ideas of Henry Morris have been linked to the Hadow Report on secondary schooling in the 1920s. Similarly the reference in the 1944 Education Act to County Colleges for part time learning influenced the development of Community Colleges in some rural areas, many acknowledging a debt to Morris and his village colleges. In the early 1960s two reports on youth work encouraged a wider view of education by recognising the needs of youth, particularly the value of informal educative activities extending beyond the school years. A few years later the Department of Education and Science (DES) was encouraging schools to share their facilities with adult users. More significantly, both the Russell and Alexander Reports on adult education supported the ideas of community based learning and outreach work. Of equal importance were the recommendations of the Plowden Report on primary schools. The Plowden Report promoted the idea of the community school which in its limited form simply opened schools to wider use[11]. But in its more radical interpretation the report regarded the school as a base for community development and introduced the concepts of educational priority areas and positive discrimination. These were focussed on the problems of children living in areas of multiple deprivation where educational underachievement was associated with the adverse effects of wider social and economic problems.

These developments in community education were paralleled by reports in the wider field of social welfare provision. The Seebohm Report on the social services urged more integrated organisation, concerted approaches and a wider awareness of the community dimension to social problems experienced by individuals and families. The Skeffington Report on planning raised the principle of public participation in decisions affecting the local environments of people[12]. Probably the most significant policy of central government was the setting up in 1969 of several Community Development Projects focussed on the problems of deprived, inner-city areas.

The recent history of community development, therefore, stems from the setting up of the Home Office projects, called CDPs for short. The background to the projects, alluded to previously, was the persistence of poverty and disadvantage in an intractable, concentrated form in the inner city areas where the traditional economic base had eroded away leaving behind an array of social problems. The deprived neighbourhoods or zones of transition, as they were sometimes called, were characterised by a multitude of social problems. Amongst these was a high rate of unemployment, low income and debt problems associated with evictions, property possession orders and emergency housing needs. To this list could be added overcrowded housing, poor health, including infant mortality rates higher than the average, crime and a variety of educational problems of children. Such areas marked by these and other kinds of social malaise are very unstable and can give rise to ethnic and class conflicts sometimes pursued by violent means, as the riots of 1981 in London and Liverpool testify[13].

A political response was demanded in the interests of social justice and order. CDPs were part of a range of educational health, youth and welfare projects, all of them different in organisation and methods from traditional practices, especially casework, across-the-counter services and in the case of adult education, formal teaching. Above all the view was that these services could not rely on clients coming to them, often as confused and deferential supplicants, but instead they had to reach out into the community. This was to discover how people in general and clients in particular experienced and felt about their problems and needs.

As a model of community development (which will be shown later) will demonstrate, there is no single perspective in terms of basic aims and principles. Nonetheless some common characteristics exist and these can be listed below -

1.   Community development expresses the idea of a process by which people, in partnership with professional workers employed by government and other official agencies, combine to improve the social and economic conditions of communities. The term community mostly refers to the geographical (horizontal) meaning and to groups living within having some clearly defined problems which makes them relatively disadvantaged.

2.   The process of community development emphasises three related elements – active participation by the people themselves to tackle problems; the enabling support of skilled help and extra resources; and the importance of self-help as a basis for taking initiatives and engaging in social action.

3.   The emphasis on dialogue between government and people highlights the trend away from paternalistic bureaucracy, typical of political and state welfare institutions, towards a more client or people centred approach to policy making and provision where they have some say in determining priorities, objectives and practices.

4.   The role of community workers is that of a catalyst and enabler in promoting social action.

5.   The specific objectives of community development are diverse, ranging from the concrete activities of urban renewal projects, welfare rights and other information giving services; to acting upon issues of discrimination and the quality of welfare services; to such intangibles as improving community relations, encouraging a sense of belonging and raising consciousness. The central strand running through this diversity of policies and practices is the idea that community development is aimed at altering the distribution and

allocation of resources and opportunities in favour of those who experience inequality and disadvantage and providing access to power to those who lack it.

6.   Implicit in these processes are ideas about social welfare, particularly the concept of distributional justice of which positive discrimination is an expression. Community development relates to both liberal and socialist models of social welfare and has attracted the radical perspective in adult education.

7.   Community development is usually regarded as a means of social change because it is involved in economic and social relationships and fosters participation in political decision making, self-help and social action rather than just debate.

The idea that community development acted as a lubricant bringing about social change is a main area of agreement amongst workers. But the nature and extent of social change differs according to the perspective or model of community development favoured. These should be outlined first[14].

MODELS OF COMMUNITY DEVELOPMENT

The Universal Model

This perspective derives its inspiration from Toennies' gemeinschaft-community model and focusses attention on the social problems of modern day gesellschaft-associational society, particularly the breakdown of personal contacts and communication. These emerge as loneliness and isolation; lack of mutual support and cooperation; uncertainty about moral values and understanding of the norms or rules of personal and social conduct; alienation caused by a loss of personal autonomy.

The approach of workers emphasises the ideas of bringing people together to share activities and work cooperatively through collective decision making. Value is placed on self-help as a product of social action, whether concerned with recreation or problem solving over local issues.

The role of education is to act as a catalyst, bringing people together to share activities and interests. This involves reaching out into the community and using educational resources as a means of promoting a sense of community and self-help.

As a political means this perspective on community development leans towards a benign liberal democracy which in any case is secondary to a concern for inter-personal social relations and well-being. This perspective is attractive to the recreation-leisure and liberal progressive models of adult education for it is not so much concerned with social change through political action but rather with people as rounded human beings who then have the self-confidence and skills to act upon their needs and change their circumstances.

The Mainstream Model

This perspective is concerned with problems of poverty, disadvantage and social inequality. Hence the focus on disadvantaged or deprived neighbourhoods and communities where groups with multiple social problems are usually concentrated. But it does not involve a radical political perspective and relies instead on the tidying-up and 'safety net' approach to social welfare characteristic of the liberal-democratic and reformist socialist models.

In this view the social problems dealt with by community development have arisen through a combination of factors – cultural and social deprivation, ineffectiveness in the delivery of educational and other welfare services and inequality in the distribution of economic resources and social opportunities. What is avoided, for the most part, is a political and economic explanation of social problems arising through the effects of the inequalities of a class based society, typical of a predominantly capitalist political-economy.

There is an emphasis on social change by concentrating on the presenting problems of the disadvantaged and by equipping them with relevant knowledge and practical skills to cope with their problems for themselves. Self-help through compensatory education and welfare provision, therefore, is seen as personal and group forms of innovation leading to relatively minor changes in the socio-economic, cultural and environmental conditions within communities. Essentially the model takes a localised view of social problems and seeks remedies through personal change.

The Radical Model

The model starts from the premise that social inequalities in any form are the result of gross power differences whereby a ruling class of closely connected political, economic and cultural interests dominate society in order to consolidate their own position relative to other groups in society. In this view poverty and disadvantage is structured into the organisation of economic life through the unequal distribution of income and wealth and opportunities in the employment market to find jobs with good pay and conditions. The poorest communities are those that experience the worse effects of these structured inequalities, highlighting the oppression of capitalism and the class system which derives from it. This form of political economy, from the radical perspective, has to be challenged by grass roots political action. The basis of such political action is the raising of class consciousness so that the disadvantaged become more aware of their common plight and develop the potential to change their circumstances through class solidarity.

The role of education is to provide the means of raising consciousness and supporting political action. But the consciousness raising is pitched at the community level through active groups rather than at individuals. In that respect the radical model is not primarily concerned with individual achievement which is seen as a traditional, middle class value concerned with personal mobility and success. Reference has already been made to the ideas and practices of P. Freire, who is the best known exponent of this radical perspective.

Shortly other examples drawn from British adult education experiences will be illustrated which in their varied ways have attempted to effect Freire's idea of education as 'the practice of freedom'.

These models of community development, allowing for all the defects of the generalised ideas behind such thinking and the varieties of actual practices, relate to different explanations of social problems. These social problems represented by such terms as the 'deprived neighbourhood' and 'disadvantaged' can also be aligned to poverty policies and the models of social welfare referred to earlier.

In the light of experience gained by community development projects workers found that they were dealing with five different explanations of urban social problems[15]. These explanations spanned the range of political beliefs and together with different perspectives on social welfare and poverty provided workers with a wide theoretical framework on which to base their policies and practices. This framework can also be related to the models of adult education.

DIFFERENT EXPLANATIONS OF SOCIAL PROBLEMS

The Culture of Poverty explanation argues that the problems of poverty, disadvantage and other manifestations of social malaise, outlined earlier, arise from the way the disadvantaged relate to each other and to other groups. Their internal group relationships are such as to reinforce their particular problems simply because they share a common experience and circumstances. This promotes a group dependency and a distinctive way of life centred around their problems. Because they are disadvantaged they regard themselves, and are regarded by others, as a marginal and minority group separated from other groups in society. Viewed from the outside such groups appear to hold a set of beliefs and share a behaviour pattern or way of living which sustains a distinct culture of poverty or disadvantage. This leads to the opinion that the disadvantaged have themselves to blame for their position and are deviant.

The core of this explanation is that the individual and the group develop a social-psychology, based on the experience of being disadvantaged, which gives rise to an outlook on life described as a culture of poverty.

The role of the community development and adult education worker, in this explanation, is to work with groups to help them break out of their negative view of themselves and, often, hostile view of others. This requires group work and counselling skills as well as knowledge of practical self help matters concerned with their position in the wider community. The emphasis is upon social adjustment to the mainstream values and norms of society through practical knowledge and skills. This perspective encourages the view that as the disadvantaged cause their own problems social policies should be of a minimal kind or even conditional, so as to prevent regression and dependency. This view has ideas in common with the classical model of social welfare. Because the explanation focusses so much on the individual this has appeal to these models of adult education that are concerned predominantly with personal needs and social adjustment.

The Cycle of Deprivation explanation takes the view that disadvantage is culturally transmitted from one generation to the next through family and group socialisation. The focal point in this explanation is that disadvantage is a psychological inadequacy acquired or learnt from others sharing the same problems and conditions. The purpose of community development is to break into the cycle and enable people to lift themselves out of the pattern of social behaviour and psychological attitudes which perpetuates their disadvantage. The emphasis, therefore, is on acquiring new skills and changing attitudes.

Like the culture of poverty explanation it shares the assumption that poverty and disadvantage are a result of personally acquired deficiencies. In that respect the social policies and models of social welfare, as well as the person orientated adult education models are similar for the cycle of deprivation explanation.

The Institutional Malfunctioning explanation moves away from the individual-cultural pathology perspectives of the two previous explanations and focusses attention on the ways in which welfare services are organised. This view has attracted the attention of adult educators who regard the irrelevance of the service to working class adults as arising from rigid recruitment procedures, inappropriate publicity, too much emphasis on formal, classroom based learning and other organisational matters.

In the social services a similar view is held that too much emphasis is placed on complex rules of eligibility for benefits. Worse still, the bureaucratic organisation of welfare has spawned too many overlapping and duplicating agencies which confuse and alienate clients. What is required is a simpler form of organisation with fewer points of contact with clients through generic and community based workers. Moreover the role of community and adult education workers is to act as brokers, helping to explain the rules of entitlement of a bewildering array of benefits or assist members of the community express their views on social planning and organisation to officials and politicians.

This perspective on social problems is in keeping with the ideals of distributional justice policy and both the liberal and socialist models of welfare. In adult education the institutional malfunctioning problem is generally understood and would find support from all four models, partly because its perspective is mainly politically neutral. Furthermore the persistent marginality of adult education has also made its workers conscious of institutional failures and the need to deliver a relevant service efficiently to keep in business or earn recognition and support.

The Maldistribution of Resources and Opportunities explanation of social problems moves closer to a radical perspective and away from psychological to structural causes of disadvantage. Structural causes of disadvantage derive from the way in which aspects of society are organised so as to create inequality. In this particular explanation the resources of society are inequitably distributed through the wage structure, occupational pensions, welfare benefits and capital wealth. These economic differences reflect social class and gender based inequalities. These inequalities are compounded by inequalities in educational and employment opportunities which also correspond to social class and gender differences deeply seated in the structure of social relations in society.

The policy responses to this accord with the distributional justice perspective and the socialist model of welfare. Social policy works towards the re-allocation of resources through the distributional mechanism of cash benefits or the social wage. In a wider economic context this approach favours a minimum wage, equal pay and higher levels of welfare benefits. It is particularly associated with the concept of positive discrimination. This means the conferment of additional benefits, whether economic, educational, legal, social and cultural to those groups in society who are deemed to have experienced a long history of negative discrimination rendering them unequal. By providing positive forms of discrimination it is hoped to overcome and make up for historically determined disadvantages. This concept has been applied in a limited form in educational priority areas (EPAs) following the recommendations of the Plowden Report on Primary Schols. It has been enthusiastically adopted by the women's movement as a policy principle and applied to occupational recruitment and the workplace.

Positive discrimination has had appeal to a broad spectrum of adult education opinion and particularly the radicals. The development of provision for the disadvantaged has often been interpreted as priority work for which special funding and efforts were required over and above the traditional forms of provision.

The Structural Class Conflict explanation widens the positive discrimination perspective by advocating political action arising from consciousness raising and the organisation of the disadvantaged into coherent pressure groups. Its basic premise is that social problems, particularly those in conspicuously deprived communties where CDPs are located, arise from the social inequalities which are an inevitable feature of an economy based on private profit and the unequal ownership of capital resources for production. It is only through the redistribution of power and control in the political, economic and cultural spheres of society that the working classes and the other relatively disadvantaged groups can obtain equality.

As this perspective is the most controversial it is better elaborated through the examples of various community development projects which involved adult education policies and practices in new forms of provision.

At this juncture it is necessary to revisit the earlier piece of contemporary history in adult education where it became associated with community development. In the late 1960s and through the early 1970s adult education involved itself with a number of experimental projects in community action aimed at reaching the working classes whose participation had always been limited. Five projects have been extensively recorded and discussed[16]. The first was instigated by Keele University which set out to make direct provision for working class adults in their neighbourhoods, chiding the local Workers Education Association (WEA) in the wake of this innovative form of provision for having failed in their traditional role. The second project, another coming from the university adult education department at Southampton University, focussed attention on the perceived educational needs of adults living on a large public housing estate. Probably the best known examples were based in Liverpool with the WEA closely involved in an innovative educational priority area project (EPA) in one part of the inner city and the university extension department involved with a CDP in an inner city dockside area. The latter represented the more radical adult education and community development perspective, closely modelled on the structural class conflict explanation of urban deprivation which was the subject matter of all the projects. The last example, this time from the Inner London Education Authority (ILEA), approached the issues of disadvantage and participation through the idea of 'outreach' adult education. It is useful to note that the high water mark of innovation in provision was not confined to these much publicised projects. Many LEAs set about new practices in the timing and location of adult education classes, recruitment and publicity, curriculum content and learning methods and cooperation with social service agencies in an effort to secure more participation and appear socially relevant. But it is the experimental projects that best highlight the connections between theoretical perspectives and practice.

There is little point in detailing the projects for they have been extensively documented but some summary is necessary.

The Keele project started off with a social survey of two predominantly working class communities in order to profile their social and cultural conditions and lifestyles. Particular attention was paid to adult attitudes for it was important to consider how adult education could relate to people in the communities. The survey finding was that the local culture had little room for adult education, regarding it as remote and irrelevant. The lesson derived from this knowledge was that adult education had to start from working class needs and interests. This prompted a sounding out policy leading to more locally based programmes.

To make any judgement about the theoretical perspectives behind the thinking of the university adult educators involved in the Keele project, or any of the others, is difficult and must be very generalised. The only really useful measure, albeit a rough and ready one, is the actions that transpired from the project. Another, equally general measure, is the rhetoric of advocates of particular lines of action and theoretical perspectives. On balance some projects were better at rhetoric.

The Keele project appears to have been based on the horizontal concept of community which focusses on culture and lifestyle, in this case of the traditional working class. The assumption was that working class culture was relatively impoverished because educational matters had little influence on adult attitudes to life. By changing the style of adult education and making it more accessible and related to needs and experiences, working class culture might be penetrated. This could be the starting point whereby these adults who responded to education could begin to raise the level of their intellectual awareness and increased activity. Two pathways opened up. The first was to step on the ladder of educational achievement as an individual. The second was to become involved in local action programmes to deal with local problems. There seemed to have been more response to the first pathway.

Although poverty and disadvantage was not central to the thinking of the Keele project nonetheless working class culture was viewed in terms of cultural impoverishment and the cycle of deprivation. The welfare perspective was closer to the universal models on the understanding that it was quite appropriate for adult education to provide for the cultural needs of adults on a positive discrimination basis. Moreover it adopted the view that adult education provision had become irrelevant and was therefore malfunctioning with respect to its ideals of social relevance and service to the relatively disadvantaged working class.

The Southampton project started from the premise that adult education had to be remodelled if it was to hold any appeal to the working class living on a post-war 'overspill' housing estate. It also acted on the belief that adult education should serve the whole community, not just those who traditionally used the service. This meant having a commitment to identify working class needs, many of which were concerned with social and economic problems. This led to the formation of interest groups that involved learning through interaction and discussion. By this process of non-formal education people communicated with local politicians and professional workers about a range of issues. Similarly the process of working with groups of local people and various agencies led to the idea of forming networks of local groups under a flexible federal type structure to collectively represent needs. The venture in a cooperative on social issues found through further study that there was evidence of inbalanced resources and opportunities for local residents. This reinforced the process of communication to welfare agencies the needs and wishes of local people.

Before outlining the theoretical perspectives related to this project a note on the concept of non-formal education is useful. It has five features which distinguishes it from traditional formal education characteristic of institutionally based education. Non-formal education is usually about specific matters of a short term nature, such as local social issues. People engage in learning on a part-time, sometimes casual basis as and when time and inclination permits. The content of their learning is mostly concerned with doing things related to the local community. This flexible approach starts with the interests of the learners and is under their control. It is not about academic awards, timetables, selection procedures and all the other paraphernalia of the educational establishment. The emphasis on autonomy, which is the central theme of non-formal education, is the basis for extending provision for through such a direct experience adults may enhance their own confidence and see the relevance of education for themselves. This is the groundwork for the development of local networks and social action.

Unlike the Keele project the concept of community, whilst operating within the context of a homogenous working class area, nonetheless recognised the operational value of small group learning based around the neighbourhood or street. This acknowledges the vertical concept of communities of interest. The advocacy of consciousness raising mediated through the enabling role of the adult educator, leading to self-help group activity and inter-agency cooperation suggests a changed institutional role. A redistributive approach to social change is implied in the problem and issue focus, with its implications for positive welfare policies consistent with universal models of social welfare. In leading towards social action through political pressure group activity this contrasts with cultural and psychological explanations of disadvantage. The emphasis on learning as the basis for action leans towards the liberal adult education perspective. A radical view would have made more about the necessity of a class conflict approach to social problems.

The ILEA outreach project grew out of a survey of the population profile of the areas served by adult education centres. Noting the unrepresentative social backgrounds of the adult students a working party recommended the appointment of field based education workers to investigate the needs of the community as a whole and work towards the setting up of groups and inter-agency networks to facilitate provision. The roles of the twenty or so outreach workers varied according to the specific characters of the communities they worked within. Most worked from the community towards the adult education centres which operated in the capacity of resource providers and some became prime movers for inter-agency liaison.

The concern with the needs of non-users of adult education implies a cultural explanation of relative disadvantage, remedied by changes in the delivery of the service. This was achieved through approaching the community, initially on a geographical area basis and then, secondly, through interest and activity groups – horizontal and vertical meanings of community respectively. The models of social welfare implicated are of the universal kinds, especially as outreach work urged more comprehensive and integrated community based services. On the whole the outreach programme emphasised non-formal learning and the welfare needs of the community rather than radical forms of political action. In that way it accorded more with the liberal adult education model.

The two Liverpool based projects illustrate varying degrees of radicalism. In many respects, though, their methods of working and activities are similar to the other projects. What differs is the interpretation.

The WEA project operated in conjunction with an EPA action research investigation. Both started from the premise of reassessing the role of education for children and adults living in a deprived inner-city area set against a background of under-achievement and non-participation. The policy perspectives were, first, to recognise that education was only one of the means of comprehensively dealing with the problems of social and economic inequality and manifestiations of disadvantage. The second policy perspective was the advocacy of positive discrimination, through the local schools and through the distribution of additional resources to the community. A third perspective was to emphatically raise the level of social class consciousness, through the school curriculum as a means of replacing competitive middle class values with traditionally cooperative and supportive working class ones. The emphasis on children's class background, as experienced through their personalities, culture and local environment was seen as a means of developing social awareness, learning motivation and the abilities to tackle the problems of working class communities. The idea of the community school reflecting and promoting a positive rather than deficit working class culture was central to these perspectives.

Adult education was incorporated into these perspectives with a specific role to offer relevant learning opportunities based on the immediate needs and interest of local people, rooted in their community and outside the usual conventions of provision. To reflect these aims the term community adult education was coined, rather than the more specific labels of recreational, liberal or vocational education. As the inner city area where the project was based was alive with community development undertakings working partnerships were common. This encouraged the network approach to adult education provision in contrast with the 'centre-periphery' model, as the usual institutional framework was called. The learning network approach was a practical outcome of having a detached or outreach adult educator linking with other community based workers and agencies, all with relatively free ranging roles.

The learning network concept was the more significant radical departure in adult education thinking and practice. It enabled the adult educator to perform at least three related tasks – bringing people and agencies together in a cooperative learning network; acting as a resource for such groups and agencies in the learning process; being a guide through the educational services and teaching. Some of the conceptual inspiration was drawn from the ideas of Illich, especially of learning webs and exchanges, but most of it grew out of direct practical experience.

Working with adult groups involved informal discussion in the manner of liberal education but located in the community and addressed to local issues democratically decided by the group members. It was re-discovered that working class adults were quite able to use abstract concepts in their thinking about problems within their own language forms. This led to the idea of using the dramatic and personalised communication style of live radio programmes linked to discussion groups taking up the issues afterwards. The simple and effective idea was that local issues, presented in a straightforward manner, by commanding easy understanding laid the foundations for the discussion of wider issues about causes, accountability and possible solutions. This was the educational route through to political awareness and action. It moved beyond the immediate problems towards their complex origins in regional and national, social, economic and political policies. In so doing there was a noticeable departure from psychological and cultural explanations of disadvantage, representative of minimal poverty policies and models of social welfare. Moreover the idea of community development and social action being bounded by territorial limits and a deficit class culture was seen as unduly restrictive in conceptual and practical terms.

The WEA project initiated a great deal of thinking about social problems and adult education which has since continued. The relationship between community action and adult education has come under scrutiny, for it is clear that practical experience has given birth to several interpretations. These range from community action for personal development, through to improving relations between local people and social welfare institutions, to the more radical ideas of building alternative institutions and launching ideological attacks on the perceived forces of economic and political oppression. Similarly, adult education reflects the individualism theme in the form of liberal, recreational and work skill activities to the more collectivist minded ideas of forming social and political action groups arising from the analysis of social problems. The latter radical perspective really emerged strongly in the dockside project in Liverpool which was led by a team of university adult educators.

Once again there is no useful purpose in describing the project for it has already been done in several articles. What is important is to reach the heart of their theory of social action for adult education in a working class inner-city area of noted deprivation. Their work instigated a number of criticisms which exist in tandem with theory. These should be itemised -

1.   Their approach criticised community development project perspectives on poverty and the working class. In their view some CDPs, in adopting the defining feature of their work as dealing with a sub-culture of conspicuously deprived working class, assumed two things. The first was that poverty was a residual problem of a clearly defined minority and not a relative problem of the entire working class. Second, this view confined community development to a tidying up role (the mainstream model) and in emphasising self help implied a cultural rather than socio-economic explanation of poverty. This view ignores the way in which economic resources are distributed throughout society and the relative inequality of the working classes, who are dependent on the lower rewards of manual labour. Moreover the cultural explanation avoids the question of how much control the working classes have in determining economic rewards and social opportunities in education, employment recruitment and other key areas which affect life chances.

2.   The EPA project emphasis on curriculum relevance and working class culture is also questioned. Such a re-shaping may inadvertently encourage a parochial, locality and class-bound outlook which is both stifling and patronising. The only exception to this would be if such an approach fostered constructive discontent as the basis for political action. But that has not been the theme so far.

A related criticism of the curriculum relevance theme is that its pretensions are mere rhetoric. The stimulation of social awareness of the grim realities of inequality and disadvantage is a long way from having control over the forces that create such conditions. Nonetheless it is acknowledged that awareness may lead to action and ultimately to power and control.

The ethos of the educational system as it relates to the working class is also criticised. Essentially, by placing importance on individual achievement middle class values are reinforced and made predominant. These values conflict with traditional working class life styles, with their greater stress on direct experience and group solidarity. For those working class children who climb the middle class ladder of success they do so alone and in leaving their class origins relatively weaken those left behind.

A real dilemma exists, therefore, between the limitations of the relevant school of thought and the pre-existing middle class cultural bias of the educational system. Neither of these value positions and their attendant educational policies and practices do much for working class people with regard to various kinds of social equality. The radical position is that the working class require an education that faces inequalities in society and stimulates an informed and far reaching discontent. Community education that ducks these issues and approaches is limiting the horizons of working class people to help themselves in a thorough-going way. In this view community education is intimately involved in the political life of working class people of all ages.

The role of the adult educator in the specific context of working class community is not to be confined to simply providing services on a consumer basis or to assume that existing services are relevant. What is required is a new concept of adult education which is characterised by organisational flexibility and consultative dialogue with the people relating to the worker as a resource agent and enabler of socially constructive learning. In this perspective adult education is about the mobilisation of resources and the kinds of knowledge, skills and conceptual awareness relevant to the analysis of social problems as perceived by adults experiencing inequality and disadvantage. Moreover this perspective urges adult educators to commit themselves both personally and professionally to the outcomes of such learning by showing solidarity or supporting the actions of the groups representing the interests of the working class. The consequences of such action of traditional concepts of the professional educator role are inevitably conflicting.

In this explicit commitment to class conflict, from its embryonic beginnings, radical adult education in the context of community development criticises the failures of the Labour party and the trade union movement for ineffectively representing the working class. The Labour party are accused of siding with the interests of capital rather than labour. The trade unions are criticised, in turn, for being overly concerned with wages and working conditions rather than wider community issues and social inequality. These criticisms promote the alternative idea of building a democratic and politicised working class through community based 'grass roots' participation, with both the self-confidence and power to represent their interests.

An important ideological prop in this perspective is the relative concept of poverty, working towards redistributional justice, underpinned by a strong version of equality within the framework of the institutional models of social welfare. In using the concept of community reference is made to the adverse social effects of the gesellschaft model, which fits the description of some aspects of inner city life with extreme forms of social deprivation. At the same time gemeinschaft provides a relevant conceptual base for identifying the common cultural bonds of the working class as a basis for stimulating social action. This perspective on community goes further than the simple idealism of the universal model or the cultural and residual poverty notions implicit in the mainstream model. By advocating the idea of advancing the whole community through a conflict approach to social problems, by an unequal yet potentially powerful working class, the radical perspective prescribes a very different role for adult education as a facilitator of community development.

Whatever the adult education perspectives favoured the importance of community development as an instrument for bringing about social change can be questioned. Four main points may be made, several of which have already been noted in passing by the radicals. They are worth repeating, though, as a safeguard against too much naive optimism.

a.   The role of making services available to the community has been criticised on the grounds that too much is assumed about the relevance of conventional forms of provision in relation to the specific needs of people living in disadvantaged circumstances. The criticism implicates the idea that sub-cultural differences in society often renders ordinary ways of delivering services and communicating ideas useless.

b.   The idea of enabling some people to leave their disadvantaged communities by providing a ladder of educational opportunity is criticised for draining off potential leadership and creating personal marginality for those who leave.

c.   An emphasis on sub-culture and the attendant ideas of special forms of provision has been criticised for promoting ghettoism, reinforcing rather than changing the values and attitudes of the disadvantaged. Moreover there is a tendency to ignore the wider inequalities in the political economy which give rise to sub-cultures of the poor and disadvantaged in society.

d.   Community development as a process has been criticised for its marginality[17]. This means that community development is seen as operating on the fringes of the political process and has very little say in decision making beyond those institutions such as welfare and education which are distributive agencies. Community development is rarely concerned with the major institutions of production and control in society which radicals see as the major determinants of social, economic and political inequalities.

The preceding chapters, including this one, have presented in a condensed form a variety of theoretical perspectives on the nature of adult education, and on community development projects. Similarly a range of social concepts such as poverty and disadvantage, equality, social class sub-cultures and community have been illustrated. Together they provide the practitioner with a wide range of conceptual frameworks and tools for approaching the practice of adult education, particularly in the social problem areas covered by community and disadvantaged work.

Running through the commentary reference has been made to the idea of social change, as an end purpose and core value in adult education theory and practice. This concept provides a rationale for a wide range of policy and practice especially in activities that have a political dimension and involve the consideration of social, cultural, economic and power factors in society, to which adult education invariably relates.

The concept of social change as it relates to adult education in society has to be approached through an introduction to sociological theory. More precisely, the general pitch of the discussion of adult education and social change leads to the introduction of two major sociological theories. These provide quite different interpretations of social problems, as represented by adult education's involvement with poverty and disadvantages in specific communities, and the perspectives of the service in relation to the wider concepts and models of equality, social welfare and so on. These 'social systems' theories of society not only introduce a branch of sociological theory they also provide a means of linking all the concepts, models and perspectives into one general scheme of ideas. This is the task of the next chapters.

CHAPTER SEVEN
AN INTRODUCTION TO TWO SOCIOLOGICAL MODELS OF SOCIETY APPLIED TO IDEOLOGY IN ADULT EDUCATION

Introductory textbooks on sociology are legion[1]. It is inevitable, therefore, that this chapter will overlap with what others have written about sociology. A major difference, though, is that these introductions have to be brief as the focus is concerned with more advanced theoretical perspectives which are intended to provide a conceptual framework for the material of the preceding chapters.

The mistake in introducing sociology is to define it tightly and convey the impression that it has only one meaning. Sociology is made up of several perspectives and this chapter deals with 'social systems' theory. Another chapter will deal with other perspectives which are not concerned with explaining the nature of society and social relations as wholes. This is exactly what this chapter does and this generalised and abstract approach has to be appreciated for its strength to discuss some of the major issues raised about adult education and social problems.

Sociology may be seen as the study of society, or more precisely, of social interactions and relationships between people as members of various groups and institutions. The range of groups and institutions through which people relate to each other is enormous and pervasive throughout our lives. The most common groups we belong to are those determined by gender, age, occupation and social class, most of these having a clearly defined character and structure in society. Group membership and the interactions and relationships with others that arise is also shaped by family, economic, political and many other social institutions which also have a clearly defined outline. Our lives as individuals are very much influenced by the experiences of social relations, through these groups and institutions, for they are the means by which ideas and rules of social behaviour are devised and enacted. In emphasising the idea of studying social relations, as they increase in size and complexity from group membership to social institutions, social structures and whole societies, an attempt is being made to be systematic, disciplined and scientific, in the observation and analysis of social behaviour. Hence a concern with methods of research.

But sociology is also in search of general statements about social behaviour which are based on sound observation and evidence. This search for a wider understanding of social relations in society leads to several different theoretical perspectives, each purporting to explain social behaviour. Some theory perspectives focus on everyday interactions and social relations in a microscopic way. Other perspectives focus on society in general and within this approach there are distinct and contending interpretations on the nature of social relations, as will be shown later. The study of human behaviour, whether viewed as history, anthropology, economics, psychology, demography or politics, as well as the arts and natural sciences, are all philosophies of thought which are based on some general images or ideas which determine methods as well as frames of reference or perspectives. No single view of human behaviour can comprehend the infinite variety and complexity. But they can offer ways of seeing and speculating in the best manner of considered thought. Sociology is very much involved in perspective making in this philosophical and disciplined tradition.

Further understanding of sociology can be derived from its origins and development as an intelligent discipline. Its emergence as a branch of knowledge can be traced back to the closing years of the eighteenth century. It developed throughout the turbulent decades of industrial and political revolution and the formation of a mass organised, urban based society. These quite dramatic changes concentrated the minds of several social philosophers who sought to explain the nature of social transformation, from an agrarian to a capitalist economy. These changes to the economic base of society transformed in its wake social relations between groups. These changes in the nature of social relations could be observed in capital and labour relations, as the capitalist political economy established roots, and in other aspects of life such as community relations, authority relations, traditions and beliefs.

These philosophical observations were not metaphysical. On the contrary, the influence of the scientific method of observation, which tested theories and hypotheses by empirical means, owed a great deal to the methods of the natural sciences, particularly the investigations of Darwin and his contemporaries. But sociology was also strongly guided by moral and political concerns especially directed at the problems of working class poverty. Both the scientific-empirical and the moral-political or visionary dimensions of sociological thought coexist albeit in an uneasy partnership at times.

Much of the early sociology was concerned with grand theories of society which would explain social relations as a whole. This holistic approach, as it is called, is the basis for social systems perspectives. These holistic perspectives start from the notion that social behaviour is largely shaped and determined by forces outside the control of individuals. These are common features to these perspectives which are listed below -

1.   There is stress on large scale units of analysis of social relations in society, such as social systems (the economic, political and cultural spheres), social structures or institutions (educational, religious, political parties, media and other organised bodies), social groups (classes, races, gender, etc.) and social roles (workers, owners, managers, teachers, etc.). What is analysed is the inter-relations between these various elements. It is assumed that social system refers to organised patterns and processes of social behaviour. These have a clear outline or shape sufficient for analysis because they are reasonably predictable expressions of the way social relations and society as a whole works.

2. This approach comprises a global view of social relations and society (which is the final level of analysis). Such a global view, by necessity, involves a high level of abstract generalisation based on positivist theory, which is the scientific method of empirical investigation using rules of evidence for the testing of theory.

3. This holistic, global view of society is concerned with the question or problem of how social order is achieved and maintained. This concern with social order gives rise to different interpretations of how it is achieved, ranging from the idea of a collective consensus based on common values to the ideas that repression, fear, manipulation and the exercise of power by some over others is the basis of social order.

4. The hallmark of the social systems approach is the determination of the social behaviour of individuals by external influences. The outcome of this view is that society exists independently of its individual members. It also suggests the puppet like nature of the individual in relation to the external influences on behaviour coming from society. However, this absolute view is not really subscribed to in the exact manner of its presentation. One modified view is that society is a construct of man's organising abilities and a means of meeting universally shared needs. A more radical view, yet still broadly within the determinist framework, is that man's ideas and actions can change social relations, and ultimately the nature of society, through the redistribution of power. Social behaviour would still be subject to external forces but on the basis of a new political and economic dispensation.

After this brief introduction it is now appropriate to proceed with an outline of two distinct systems perspectives called consensus and conflict theories of society. Both provide explanations of social relations relevant to the kinds of social problems encountered by adult education[2]. They also offer different interpretations of social change and provide a useful framework for bringing together all the concepts that have been used so far, as well as extending them. Together this material should provide adult educators with a wide view of their work and a useful underpinning to the contemporary expressions of the social relevance theme in adult education.

In approaching systems perspectives the heartland of classical sociological theory is entered. It has already been suggested that this holistic approach leads to the conception of society as an embracing term for social relations and interactions, which is the core material for sociological thought. A few more points in this idea are necessary. It is also the case that classical sociology provides a means of introducing many major theorists. Their thoughts underpin both the consensus and conflict perspectives and after the central features of these have been presented their individual contributions will be noted.

As indicated earlier, society is a concept which is founded upon the activities of individual human beings but which cannot be reduced to its parts. Thereafter views differ as to its further meaning for there is a major divergence between those who regard society as an expression of mind and consciousness and those who deem it to be a construct of physical and material properties. The former comprise the idealist and the other the materialist conceptions of society. The idealist perspective on society argues that the products of the human mind, that is, thoughts and feelings, lay the foundations for social norms (prescribed guidelines of behaviour) and values (important beliefs). Norms and values are regarded as central features of society and explain its existence and order. The materialist conception, on the other hand, argue that society is essentially built upon physical factors such as economic goods, physical power and elemental forces of the natural environment. The idealist perspective rests on reciprocity of social behaviour whereas the materialist perspective emphasises the importance of economic and political power. The former takes a benign view and the latter a power view of social relations as the basis of society. Upon further examination it is clear that this dualism of perspectives is really a continuum, like so many conceptual frameworks in sociology. But for illustrative purposes it is relevant to consider them as poles apart.

The two models of society emphasise different ideas about the nature of social relations. The consensus model starts from the idea that social order is brought about by people's commitments to norms and values of behaviour. These prescribed forms of social relations determine social cohesion and stability, making society a naturally integrating system. By necessity man is constantly seeking ways of ensuring predictability and continuity in his social relations. Norms and values are the key elements providing the means of social cooperation and consensus over most areas of life. The divisions that arise between people and groups are countered by a fundamental unity of purpose. Social purpose is the basis of legitimate authority and power, exercised by some on behalf of all society's members through a wide range of institutions. As an example, the educational system performs important tasks in communicating and transmitting social norms and values and represents a collectively agreed means of legitimate authority, backed by legal force and the prescribed duties of the teacher's role to uphold social values.

The conflict model places emphasis on the power of certain economic, political and cultural groups to determine the norms and values of society in their own interests. This implies that social relations, at the workplace and in many other areas of interaction between interest groups, are based on inducement and coercion. Thus social relations are often characterised by divisiveness, leading to opposition and conflict under certain conditions (such as anger at discrimination and awareness of exploitation). This perspective implies that social life, particularly in the political and economic spheres, generates all kinds of sectional interests and groups with differing amounts of power. This explains the existence of social stratification whereby social groups form into differing levels of economic, social and political power. This hierarchial arrangement is often the basis of conflict between groups in society for interests are neither identical or equally shared. Those holding power and having privileged positions to maintain use the means at their disposal to resist other interest groups. This provokes a pressure to change and in this perspective of society stability is uncertain and fluctuating.

Comparing the two perspectives, conflict theory rejects the view that society rests on a fundamental consensus of values and contractual commitments towards common goals, which are believed to exist as a natural product of social relations. Therefore consensus is regarded as a myth designed to help the holders of power. In the conflict perspective social order is achieved through domination and force. The consensus perspective, on the other hand, argues that the unequal distribution of power reflects natural differences in abilities and efforts. Elite rule not only provides a means of advancing the development of society it also ensures its stability. This is achieved through the influence of good examples of cultural standards, economic success and leadership qualities, which in turn act as incentives for others to emulate elite groups in society.

The concepts of social stratification (meaning hierarchically ranked social differences in income, wealth, status and power), inequality and power are clearly central to both perspectives. The consensus view of stratification (which includes the idea of social class) is that the social differences that are expressed by the concept, such as unequal economic and political power, are inevitable outcomes of a well developed division of labour, typical of advanced, industrial societies. Thus social stratification, in any of its forms, is seen as a system of incentives and rewards for those individuals and groups prepared to work hard and use their brains. This incentive system is an unconsciously evolved means of making society operate effectively. This means that the various parts of society, within the economic system, and between the economy, political and cultural systems of social relations, are inter-locked into a functional whole. This system serves the needs of individuals and society.

From this perspective social inequalities are tolerated because the majority of people share a consensus view about the core values of society. These values legitimate social differences in economic, status and power positions. Rather than social inequalities being seen as 'system disturbing' they are regarded as natural elements of social integration and stability. This view has important consequences for the disadvantaged groups in society, as will be discussed later.

Power and social inequality are closely related. Power refers to the means of determining outcomes in social relationships and making things happen through the use of knowledge, economic resources, physical force and psychological persuasion. In consensus theory power is derived from the norms and values shared by the majority in society. Power is regarded as a resource for the coordination of social relations in economic, political and cultural activities. Whereas it is possible that some people misuse their power, nonetheless the overall purpose of power is a functional one in society.

By contrast, the conflict view of power argues that its possession is derived from the productive system, with those having greater access to economic resources gaining control of many other commanding heights of society; in politics, education, religion, military, the media and so forth. Power is the currency for determining social norms and values which are then broadcast by elite groups to the rest through the institutions of society (education, religion, media, etc.). Power defends the interests of privileged groups and is therefore the base root of social inequality.

More closely related to the concerns of adult education, both social perspectives provide different interpretations on social problems. This means that a particular perspective on society affects the explanation of social problems and the measures thought necessary to overcome them. It was shown earlier that there are at least five different explanations of urban social problems, as perceived by community development project workers. Each explanation relates to different kinds of poverty policies and the three models of social welfare, also outlined earlier. Although these are invariably simplified connections being made with these ideas it does suggest that the explanation of social problems, and the policies and practices that follow, are to some extent the products of a broader view on the nature of society and the definitions of social problems that follow from these views.

In the consensus perspective the underlying assumption is that society has in-built, natural tendencies towards integration of the parts into a functional whole. This arises from the inherent stability of commonly agreed core values of society which are transmitted and maintained through socialisation and social control. Where malfunctions emerge in society the theory holds that self-correcting mechanisms come into play to re-integrate and stabilise social relations. In this view social values are re-emphasised to correct any behavioural deviations. Social values lie at the heart of social policy.

From this highly abstract view of society the various social problems encapsulated by the terms poverty and disadvantage are seen predominantly as the result of deviance and social disorganisation. More specifically the consensus perspective believes that social problems are caused by breakdowns in the communication of core values and norms (such as achievement and ambition, tenacity, thrift, hard work, self-help and other long term goals of life). The problem of communicating values lies in the socialisation process which is ineffectively transmitted in the family, neighbourhood, schools and so forth. These explanations are embodied in the culture of poverty and cycle of deprivation perspectives on social problems. These place emphasis upon various forms of psychological deviance, evidenced by the social behaviour of the disadvantaged.

Another causal explanation from the consensus perspective is that faults exist in the delivery of social welfare services —the institutional malfunctioning view. This perspective and the two related social-psychological and cultural explanations lean towards social policies that seek social rather than political-economic solutions. This implies minor rather than major social changes, or, expressed in a similar way, small adjustments to existing ideas of social welfare. These ideas are more in keeping with conditional and minimal approaches to social policy; with their thinly concealed emphasis upon the moral failure of the disadvantaged; their personal and social inadequacies, and the use of stigma and less eligibility as forms of social control.

The conflict perspective provides an alternative view of social relations and fits with the distributional justice notion of social policy and socialist models of welfare. Whereas the consensus perspective regards conflict as a deviation from central values the conflict view treats it as a fact of life. Conflicts of interest centre around vested economic and class positions held by powerful elites in society and the various forms of opposition that arise

86

periodically from discontented groups. Thus there is no natural tendency towards social integration and stability for unequal and disadvantaged groups. It is only by ensuring greater equality and social justice that the social problems that divide society can wither away, to be replaced by integration and stability between equal members of society.

The conflict view of social problems places greater weight on inequality in the economic and political spheres of society, where resources are allocated and life chances determined, as the main causes of social problems. Hence the emphasis upon the re-distribution of economic resources, social opportunities and policies of positive discrimination as the basis of welfare provision. These also serve as lubricants of social change. As outlined earlier, there are two versions of conflict theory as it relates to dealing with social problems. The pluralist approach seeks a gradual transformation of social problems through progressive welfare measures, such as positive discrimination programmes. Pluralism in this context means political power. This provides the basis for egalitarian welfare policies aimed at bringing about far reaching social change. Essentially the pluralist approach starts from the idea of solving social problems and resolving conflicts within the framework of a parliamentary democracy. Such a democracy could include room for the expression of the wants and needs of all kinds of community groups. This is a participative democracy and a more developed forum for consulting the people than the existing representative system. These ideas are particularly attractive to radically inclined adult education and community development workers.

So too is the more extreme conflict perspective whereby social problems are regarded as only resolved by operating outside the existing social order. This is seen as too vested with entrenched interest groups to desire much social equality and change. Ultimately this conflict perspective regards violent revolution aimed at fundamentally changing the prevailing system of economic and political relations in society as the only realistic solution. This is implicit in the radical version of social welfare presented earlier.

It is important to note an obvious point about both social perspectives. They embody ideal visions of society, irrespective of their grasp on observable truth. The conflict perspective puts forward the idea that the elimination of inequality, in the possession of resources, status, wider life chances and political power, leads to social stability. Thus equality is a utopian vision of society where social conflict has been drastically reduced through man's collective humanity and sense of justice. The consensus perspective views inequality as natural and inevitable, even a means of social betterment. What is important is the pervasive power of elite groups to uphold and transmit those values that are associated with the successful functioning of society.

Running through these social perspectives are different ideas about social change. It has been argued that social inequality and the problems related to poverty and disadvantage are central concerns of social welfare. More specifically, it has been noted that adult education and community development workers have a developed social conscience and devote a great deal of thought and action towards solving social problems. They therefore have a general commitment to social change, more so with the radicals. This means that they consider the question of what constituted the central needs and interests of society and what should be done for the disadvantaged.

For those with a preference for the consensus perspective they approach such concerns from the standpoint of what is desirable for society as a whole. Note the implicit statement of social values contained in the idea of desired goals. Given the previous line of thought, it should be clear that what is desired is compatibility between the needs of the individual and society as a whole, for they are seen as necessarily integral. This encourages the belief that the central values of society, having been evolved and tested by custom and practice, are the mainstays of integration and stability. The task of adult educators and others is to socialise people into an awareness and response to these values. This places the communicators of knowledge and skills, such as adult educators, in the position of representing the mainstream values and goals of established and leading groups in society. The existing social system, that is, its institutional structure and values, is regarded as the basis of order and stability. This framework is not regarded as challengable in any major respect. Change occurs, therefore, from the centre of the value structure of society, usually as an adaptive process in response to revised ideas derived from new insights and knowledge. Adult education may facilitate such change through the dissemination of knowledge by a two way communication of ideas. Usually, though, adult education communicates outwards and downwards from the core culture of society. This means that maintenance and conservation of society takes precedence over more urgent ideas of social change. With regard to social problems the task of social welfare, of which adult education and community development are constituent elements, is to strive towards the social integration of the disadvantaged into the mainstream values and behavioural norms of the majority of members of society. This supports cultural and psychological deficit explanations of social problems and residual welfare policies. These have already been outlined.

The conflict perspective starts from the premise of advancing the causes and interests of unequal and disadvantaged groups in society in the idealistic belief that comprehensive social equality is the only guarantee of stability. Far reaching social change is the end result of attacking the root causes of inequality and disadvantage in society, by changing the distribution of economic rewards and political power. In short, the class society has to be dismantled for social justice and stability to prevail social relations.

The implicit idea of social change used by radicals and reformers in adult education is that social systems are dynamic and prone to flux and transformation, not inherently stable as seen by the consensus perspective. Adult Education and community development have the means at their disposal to organise, inform and initiate political action arising through the generation of an analytical awareness of the causes and remedies of social problems. This constitutes an important instrument of change which can challenge existing social values, ideas and practices in the political economy and welfare services. Many of the slogans of political action, such as liberty, democracy and equality, have acted as cutting edges in society. Often after prolonged conflicts of interest between groups such ideas have brought about change both in the currency of ideas and social values and institutional and economic arrangements. The development of the welfare state may be seen as an illustration of the power of ideas to change society.

The element of ideology, meaning in this case social and political beliefs, is entwined with these major social systems perspectives on social change. Different social and political ideologies line up behind these perspectives and they warrant some description. They also relate to the various models of social welfare, adult education and ideas of equality that have been outlined earlier.

Closely related to the consensus perspective are three ideologies – Eugenic, biblical fundamentalism and classical capitalism. Each needs to be briefly outlined along with their interpretations of social issues.

The Eugenic ideology rests on the belief that genetic endowment determines behaviour and the life chances of individuals. The social strata that exist (economic, status and power strata) are simply the outcomes of different endowed abilities. Some are born to become clever, rich, powerful and the leaders of society. Others are not so fit and do not survive or thrive in the naturally competitive struggle to live. The prime movers of social change are the naturally endowed elite whose abilities and efforts generate momenta in society, particularly in the economic-material and cultural-ideas realms. Taking this ideology into the social welfare realm, the emphasis upon the survival of the fittest means that the view of the disadvantaged is to regard them as a burden on the rest. In this extreme view social welfare is seen as a gradual means of weakening the powerful social value of self-help. Social inequality has a natural root in genetic biology not in political systems. Intervening is ineffective and a weight on the capacities of the most capable individuals to create wealth for society. Eugenic ideology upholds the ideas of individualism laissez faire and residual welfare.

Biblical fundamentalism operates as an ideology from the basis that God is sovereign in social affairs and determines who is rich and poor; strong and weak; leaders and followers. A related view is that Man, because of his greed and exploitive character, has fallen from grace. Inequality, poverty and disadvantage reflects the outcomes of Man's nature and God's disfavour. Social welfare is a limited form of redemption which should be in the form of charity and voluntary altruism. This form of welfare emphasises personal rather than state directed services. It also upholds self-help as a virtue of individual behaviour. Only after life will God redeem the inequalities that existed on earth.

Elements of Classical Capitalism as an ideology have been mentioned before. For instance, inequality is seen as inherent and natural for man is neither born equal nor lives in such a social environment. By nature man is competitive and acquisitive and only by leaving men free to pursue their economic interests can social progress be made. Restraints on self help individualism causes stagnation and prevents the generation of wealth for all to share. Profits provide resources for consumption, providing employment and income for others. Unemployment provides competition for jobs and ensures that labour is directed to where it is most needed and efficient. Similarly, wages reflect real market circumstances of demand and supply for goods and services in society. In this view life is a challenge and opportunity for those who have the skills and make the effort to succeed.

There are obvious common ingredients to these ideologies consistent with the consensus perspective. For example the values of self-help individualism are applauded. Inequality is regarded as natural. These views reinforce the idea that society operates from a central bank of agreed values and norms of social behaviour. These values confer meaning and stability to social life. A competitive economy and a hierarchical political order have evolved through the necessity to survive and as a reflection of different endowments of social man. Social change occurs through the adaptive process of new ideas and techniques applied to economic production through science and technology. Essentially change happens from inside the established social order in accordance with the values held in common by the majority. Society in this vision is like a giant organism with the capacity to evolve gradually into a higher form, while leadership, brainpower and hard work function as the lubricants of the system. Several of the early sociologists have lent analytical weight to these ideas about man in society and they still provide a coherent perspective.

The conflict perspective is expressed through the writings of Marx and permeates in modified form much of the rhetoric of socialism and other 'left wing' ideologies. They all attack the ideas of consensus ideologies, particularly residual ideas of social welfare, natural equality and ascription (qualities of individuals, whether natural abilities or social positions, conferred by birth rather than by achievement). These are seen to conspire to justify disadvantage and other perceived injustices of a class based society. As the sociological ideas of conflict theorists will be described later only a summary note is needed here.

Expressed simply, there are two poles in political ideologies within the conflict perspective. One pole and the nearest to the centrepoint of an imaginary spectrum of political beliefs, from right to left wing, may be termed the 'soft version'. The other is the 'hard' left wing. They have different views on social welfare as explained earlier. The 'soft left' favours the liberal view of equality and a partnership of state and voluntary effort in the provision of welfare. This encourages self-help individualism through educational achievement, for instance. This leads to the idea of a meritocracy which allows for inequality on the basis of achieved differences of social position arising from ability and effort. Social welfare is seen as a vehicle of social change through the sponsorship of equality of opportunity for individuals to fairly compete for higher rewards and status. Conflict in this sense is channelled through the democratic process and rational arguments designed to change attitudes and values to bring about greater social equality.

The 'hard left' conflict perspective argues that capitalism with its concern for profits and supporting political-cultural ethos, which hardens the domination of powerful groups, is the source of inequality. The wage or reward system in the economy highlights the exploitation of the owners of productive capital over those with only their labour to sell. Wages and profits are the basis of class differences and inequality. Yet the wage worker produces for the owners of capital surplus value or profits. This position is viewed as indefensible and socially unjust. Only by recognising the source of their oppression can wage workers, that is, the working classes (and other disadvantaged groups) change their circumstances and create an equal society. Social class, therefore, is a means of change by the process of raising the level of consciousness – from a class by itself to a class for itself –and acting upon the injustices through a class based political solidarity.

In addition to the ultimate action of political revolution this 'hard left' ideology stresses the centrality of universal needs of members of society, and following from this, policies of positive discrimination and equality of results. This last point expresses the main differences over the idea of equality. From the liberal and social democratic or centralist political ideologies, equality is seen as having freedoms of choice and opportunities to develop abilities. This leads to the position of justifying some forms of social inequality. The rewards should be on the basis of need and not competition, achievement or inherited advantages. Needs can only be fairly provided through collective action represented by an institutionalised and positive system of welfare and egalitarian policies in the economic sphere. This means gaining control of the productive system to serve the needs of all, not for the advantages of the few. Equality of results means the use of government controls to minimise economic, status and power differences. This idea of equality is more concerned with outcomes than with means. Thus equality is about the distribution of power according to group membership – equal representation for women; greater proportional representation for the majority of the working class and the same for ethnic minorities in proportion to their numbers in society. This form of proportional representation extends to other areas of life where life chances are determined.

Having surveyed the various meanings and interpretations of the consensus and conflict theories of society, relating them to the equality theme, models of social welfare and political ideologies, it is useful to complete the description by briefly outlining the ideas of the social thinkers that gave rise to them. This is where classical grand theory sociology is introduced as a background to the more immediate concerns of adult education with the problems of disadvantage and community development.

The main elements of consensus perspective warrant some reiteration. Like the conflict perspective, human or social behaviour is seen as being to a very large extent structured by the social environment. This view even allows for the Eugenic ideology. Similarly, the biblical fundamentalists share the same idea that social behaviour is determined by forces outside individuals. For those seeking a social explanation of behaviour, rather than a genetic or spiritual one, the consensus perspective argues that it is the existence of collectively evolved and determined values that forms the core of society as an interlocking system of inter-dependent relationships. The imagery is of a seamless web of inter-connecting threads, social relations, held together by roles, institutions, social structures and values, together forming a complete social system. This explains the persistence of social stability and order.

The early beginnings of this perspective evolved from the ideas of three sociologists –Comte, Spencer and Durkheim. Comte (1789-1859) is credited with introducing sociology as a separate discipline and inventing the term. He divided sociology into two areas of study – statics and dynamics. Statics focussed on interrelationships of parts of society and dynamics on the ways society changed. He adopted an evolutionary view of social dynamics and saw society as having developed from two earlier stages, the theological and metaphysical, to the positive. The positive meant that man had learned to understand his relationship to nature through scientific knowledge. This gave him mastery over nature and the means to reshape and control society. It was noted earlier that 'positivism', another invention of Comte, is the scientific method which he regarded as a 'religion of humanity' providing the means for man to shape his own destiny. Scientific thought, then, represented a core value around which investigations of universal human laws could be made and the nature of society determined. In this sense knowledge is the basis of social order and control.

Comte's positivism was also blended with a vision of the moral perfectability of mankind. It is through the desire to know and develop mental powers that mankind may improve society. Positivism as a new science of man also functioned as a religion, freeing man from dubious doctrines and clearing the way for a common moral commitment to social progress. Sociologists with their capacity to foresee social progress with their knowledge would be the consultants and advisers to political leaders; a new priesthood of the wise.

Comte's analysis of social relations was also based on a conception of the importance of practical activities. Society, therefore, was built upon man's need to survive. This material base arising through economic production, the accumulation of capital and division of labour into greater specialisation, gave purpose and structure to social relations. But for Comte the guiding element was man's capacity through language, communication, knowledge and progressive mental development to control and determine society. Thus social change arose from material progress and the power of man to make himself through his intellectual prowess and moral ideas. The thinking and feeling realms, though, were of supreme importance in the making of a new society. This perspective laid the foundations for further developments of the consensus view of society.

Herbert Spencer (1820-1903) has the distinction of having developed an embracing theory of social evolution, similar to Darwin's theory of the origin of species. Like Comte, the social thought of Spencer advocated an optimistic view of the ascent of mankind to higher forms of social cooperation, analogous to the evolution of higher animals from lower forms. The social evolution was regarded as being a material development, through the establishment of economic cooperation and institutions, and higher forms of ethical and moral values. This concept of society was broadly compared to an organism with each part of the structure interrelating to form a functional whole. Society, like a natural organism, was characterised by the struggle for survival. Hence his reliance on an evolutionary theory of society where a pattern of development from simple to complex (or compound stages) was proposed, together with a typology of either military or industrial systems. Whatever the stage or type Spencer argued that all societies performed universal functions –regulation, distribution and sustenance or government, economic production and socialisation into culture (attitudes, norms, beliefs, ideas and values determining social behaviour). Evolutionary development arose from economic activity and the division of labour, leading to structural changes in the rest of society, and changes in the way social relations were controlled; from the despotic force of military based to the cooperative nature of more democratically inclined industrial type societies. Successful societies were those that had adapted to their environments through the process of structural differentiation and change. This idea was made famous as the 'survival of the fittest', which really meant an evolution from simple to more complex and highly organised societies.

The elements of Spencer's evolutionary theory of society that have been much criticised are those that support the economic and social doctrine of laissez faire, status ranking according to levels of authority and skill and the demise of centralised bureaucratic organisation. Within this theory these elements were quite consistent for Spencer regarded the centralised control of military type societies as ill-adaptive to the changes brought about through free market economies. Free enterprise was for Spencer a symptom of man's capacity to master the environment and the emergence of social strata reflected natural inequalities of ability, effort and initiative. Individualism in his view was a key ingredient in social evolution for man, unrestrained by the dogma of government controls, would naturally evolve forms of social cooperation based on universal needs to survive. These forms of cooperation would constitute the core values of society. This form of natural consensus would be further reinforced by the developed forms of inter-dependence and inter-connections between the economic, political and social structures of society. These structures function as enduring and institutionalised ways of organising the complex activities of individuals in society.

Probably the best known of the classical social theorists in the consensus perspective is Emile Durkheim (1858-1917). He elaborated the thinking of Comte and Spencer into a theory which has become widely known as structural-functionalism and was later developed by the best known modern social systems theorist, Talcott Parsons. Durkheim, following in the wake of Comte and Spencer, also compared society with a living organism, with the separate elements or organs linked together and dependent upon each other in order to function property for the benefit of the whole.

Durkheim's approach insisted that society existed in its own right, being more than the sum of its individual members. Society as an organism had a discernible structure – institutions like the law, religion, education and welfare – whose function was to provide the common rules and laws or norms and values for the control and organisation of social behaviour. This is the basis of the structural-functionalist or consensus perspective within social systems theory. For Durkheim the unifying element in his structural-functionalist analysis of society was the existence of a broadly shared collective consciousness. This state of mind, as it were, provided the ground rules of social relations, in effect the norms and values upon which a common moral order rested. Thus the myriad political, economic and cultural institutions (Spencer's regulatory, distributive and sustenance functions of society) base their principles of social interaction and relationships from the norms and values derived through the complex processes and ideas expressed by the collective consciousness of social man. This moral force provides meaning and purpose to social life as well as operating as a means of social sanction and control. Durkheim's theory differs from Hobbes' notion of social contract which he interpreted as based on self interest, rather than moral obligations. Social contracts for Hobbes required a more overt political control whereas Durkheim stressed the voluntary basis of moral and social values.

An illustration of Durkheim's theory of social order and stability is the educational system, a federated body of institutions concerned with learning, training, selection, allocation and other social functions. For Durkheim education has a structure and functions designed quite purposefully to maintain the core values of society. The curriculum of educational institutions is determined by the values of the common moral order, as represented by leading members of society ideas about what constitutes useful knowledge, appropriate teaching and learning, criteria for successful achievement and so forth. These ideas are designed to facilitate the smooth working of society through the interaction between education and the other institutions of the social structure in the economy, politics and culture. The transmission of knowledge, skills and appropriate social behaviour is an important task for education, expressly for the benefit of society as a whole.

Durkheim, in keeping with the theoretical obsessions of his intellectual peers, was seeking to explain the nature of social solidarity, that is, the persistence of society as a structural and functional whole while individuals acted out their lives on the social canvas. His explanation is of relevance to some of Toennies' ideas about community and society and may be regarded as broadly akin to the latter's gemeinschaft and gesellschaft dichotomous model described earlier. Social solidarity varies according to the type of society which Durkheim divided into two main types – pre-industrial and industrial. Social solidarity in the former Durkheim termed mechanical and in the latter organic. Mechanical solidarity arises where society is simple and undifferentiated with little division of labour and customary roles and traditions typical of a subsistence economy.

Spencer's description of simple societies fits Durkheim's idea of mechanical solidarity and his treble compound society largely reflects the industrial, based on organic solidarity. The latter is characterised by a high degree of individuality and variety in the nature of economic and social roles, making society very unalike. Social relations instead of being bound by custom and tradition are held together by inter-dependent roles based on contracts. These social contracts are honoured by a broad consensus of norms and values underpinned by positive rewards and negative sanctions. As society evolves from mechanical to organic solidarity, through the effects of economic activity and the division of labour, collective consciousness permeates the widening network of social relations.

To give more emotional meaning to the importance of social contracts, religious, educational and other institutions find ways of symbolising their place in society giving them sacred qualities. Some important social values that have formed the bonds of modern social relations are loyalty, trustworthiness, teamwork, ambition, hardwork, fairness, service, patriotism and achievement. Much effort has been made to symbolise those values related to work, for instance. Not only are they manifestly concerned with productive efficiency they also serve to integrate individuals into the group by providing the credentials for social belonging and self-respect. The absence of these values was for Durkheim the cause of anomie, meaning the breakdown of the norms governing social interaction. For those concerned with community relations anomie described the condition of social isolation and the transient, rootless lifestyles of many people forced to live in the anonymous urban environment where traditional values had collapsed. Anomie highlighted the problem of individual adaptation to social change but Durkheim was also aware that modern day society placed great stress on the viability of collective consciousness as a means of stability.

In the modern era of grand social theory Talcott Parsons (1902-1979) stands as the last giant in the systems approach. His theoretical work encapsulates much of the earlier work of Comte, Spencer and Durkheim. The essence of structural-functionalism is embodied in their collective works. Some repetition of these ideas is warranted and can be blended into Parsons' theory of society.

For society to exist as an entity certain basic functions have to occur. These functional prerequisites of social survival are fourfold -

1. Adaptation to the environment – organised means for the production and distribution of goods and services – Economy.

2. Goal attainment – organised means to identify, select and define the collective aims of the members of the society – Polity.

3. Pattern maintenance and tension management – organised means of motivating people and committing them to the norms, values and sanctions of society – Kinship.

4. Integration – organised means of communication and coordination of the diverse activities of the members and institutions of society – Community and Cultural Organisations.

Society in this perspective is a system of interlocking structures comprising, in ascending levels of complex organisation; roles (regulated by specific norms giving concrete guidelines to social interaction; social institutions (economic, political, religious, educational, organisations, etc.); and major sub-systems (economy, polity, kinship, cultural and community organisations), governed by the four imperative functions listed above. Moreover each sub-system has its own AGIL structure, meaning; adaptation, goal attainment, integration and latency or pattern maintenance. Thus the economic sub-system of society, in addition to being concerned with production (adaptation), also interacts with the other sub-systems and their primary functions to create an interlocking structural and functional system of social relations. To complete this model of society the four main functions may be grouped into instrumental (adaptation and goal attainment) and expressive (pattern maintenance and integration), corresponding to the economic and political systems and the kinship and cultural/community systems respectively.

Underpinning this holistic model of society are fundamental social values which have evolved through time and custom to assume an agreed importance in the workings of the system – the consensus perspective. Society, then, is the combination of those structures which work in such a way as to meet the needs of its members.

Central to the structural-functional perspective are the norms and values of social behaviour. Parsons has developed Durkheim's ideas on social values as the basis of consensus and stability in society by making use of the concept of social equilibrium. Equilibrium in this perspective means the absence of conflict arising from people having a clear idea of the expectations of social behaviour. These expectations are channelled through social roles and institutions, pervading all the sub-systems of society. The processes of socialisation and control are the means of learning role expectations and the metaphor which best conveys this idea is the carrot and the stick (or rewards and punishments). Society has established two key socialisation processes – institutionalisation (where social expectations are communicated in a deliberate, regular and standard manner, as in educational institutions) and internalisation (where expectations are understood and learned). Role learning as an aspect of socialisation enables people to incorporate the common culture (attitudes, beliefs and values), find their places in society and discover ways of meeting personal needs and coping with change. The process is relatively straightforward because people seek social approval and are willing to conform to what is expected of them. Therein lies the determinist view of social behaviour which compares people with empty vessels waiting to be filled with social knowledge. This view leads to the idea that there is a basic compatibility between the individual and society.

Parsons developed a classificatory schema for identifying possible sources of conflict and dis-equilibrium, where the norms and values are out of step with society as it changes through the effects of industrialisation and concentrations of populations in urban environments. His concept of 'pattern variables', as the schema was called, could be generally compared with Durkheim's mechanical and organic solidarity and Toennies' dual model of social relations. Both these early theorists were concerned to pinpoint sources of breakdown in the values of society as a consequence of major social change. The schema serves the purpose of prescribing the appropriateness of some values according to the type of society. These prescribed values may be seen as statements about what ought to be seen as desirable expectations and behaviour in society. These beliefs have percolated through to the background assumptions of social policies in relation to education and welfare. Some of those have already been noted, especially in relation to the treatment of social problems.

The 'pattern variables' schema is available in most sociology textbooks and is not reproduced here [3]. It can be understood in two ways. First it identifies the kinds of values consistent with a type of society. Then an advanced industrial society maintains equilibrium by emphasising such values as achievement, self-discipline and individualism. These largely instrumental values accord more with the economic and political systems. The instrumental realms of modern society fashions the predominant norms and values. In the other realm of the social system, the expressive, the more diffuse emotional needs of peole are met. This provides a counterbalance to over specialisation and allows people to become more rounded as personalities. Secondly the values of both realms (in the expressive realm the values of ascribed status, broad relationships, communal pursuits and immediate gratifications to satisfy emotional needs) complement each other. People are socialised into moving between the instrumental and expressive realms smoothly and learn the role playing and norms/values appropriate to each situation. In this process of role specialisation and normative behaviour social equilibrium is achieved. Social change in this model is an adaptive process whereby new norms and values emerge to support the increasing complexity of role specialisation. Like the earlier models importance is attached to the effects of economic development and the division of labour fuelled by scientific knowledge and technological innovation – a deterministic view of social change.

Not surprisingly the large scale abstract generalisations of structural-functionalism have met with much criticism, from within and outside this school of thought. As the leading theorists of the conflict perspective will shortly be outlined their criticisms are only to be temporarily assumed. Instead attention is paid, by way of summary, to modifications to classical consensus theory from the inside, as it were.

Refinements to Talcott Parsons' work comes from his former student Robert King Merton whose criticism rested on the view that the elaborate nature of the structural-functional perspective made it impossible to survive the rigours of empirical analysis. Merton set out to refine Parsons' theory, chiefly by critically examining the semantic meaning of key concepts. Thus the term 'function' came under scrutiny and Merton's analysis introduced the ideas of dysfunction, manifest and latent functions, all of which modified the sweeping nature of Parsons' work, making it more amenable to research. Essentially Merton reversed Parsons' approach to social theory by moving from the analysis of particular social issues to wider generalisations. Merton's work marked the demise of grand theory and introduced the more modest 'middle range theories'. These were seen to combine conceptual analysis with scientific methods of investigation to produce testable knowledge within a theoretical framework.

An example of middle range theory is the re-examination of the concept of anomie – a specific social condition where the usual norms of behaviour have broken down or are in abeyance. Merton worked within the general assumptions of consensus theory by implicitly recognising the importance of social goals and values as the basis of social order, such as economic and social success through hard work and achievement. But this pattern of interaction between individuals and the values of society is neither universal or uniform. Merton hypothesised that the social structure created different opportunities. For many, simple conformity to expected social behaviour was a normal and compatible response. But for others to obtain their personal needs and goals some forms of deviation from the general or conventionally accepted norms is necessary. Some have to become innovative, which might include learning sharp practices in order to 'work the system' to personal advantage. This means that while they accept the goals of society the means they use would not always be approved. Yet others engage in a kind of ritualised relationship with the goals and values of society where a slavish conformity acts as a compensation for limited success in life. Two other responses are more typically deviant insofar as neither the goals and values of society or the means of conforming to them are accepted. Thus the retreatist become marginal members of society, whereas the rebels attempt to create new goals and means.

This kind of theory has brought the generalisations of the consensus perspective within closer range of the diversity of social behaviour and the complex processes of maintaining stability. Above all it moves away from simple determinism. Nonetheless it has to be acknowledged that the consensus perspective, founded upon the anthropological and natural organism leanings of structural-functionalism, has probably been the model informing so much thinking in social welfare generally. The explanation for this is simple, as the starting point for social welfare workers is that social problems arise from malfunctions in a system of social relations that appears to work for the majority. The behaviour of clients appears as deviations from the normative values of society and need correcting. The onus falls on fitting people back into a large jigsaw of inter-connecting pieces, that is, society as a whole. Compassion, altruism and practical help are seen as civilised responses to the needs of people who have fallen out of the system, either through their own fault or because, somehow, the correct 'fit' between the individual and society has not been found. Whatever the explanation, the common assumption is that society works for most people. Change starts with the individual who has to be resocialised and has to re-learn the prevailing norms and values of social behaviour so as to conform and function effectively in society. If the incentives or carrots of society fail to modify behaviour there is always recourse to the punishing stick.

The ideas of the various social theorists in the consensus perspective have contributed a powerful conceptual framework which has provided plausible explanations of social behaviour from the individual to the societal level. As explained this perspective has held a prominent place in social welfare generally and the approaches to social problems by community development and adult education specifically. The opposite perspective of social conflict theory has already been shown to provide quite different explanations. The conflict perspective too has been pieced together through the ideas of a number of social thinkers. The giant of these is Karl Marx but there are other modern day theorists who warrant attention as well. But first the ideas of Marx and Marxism.

The difficulty of describing the essence of Karl Marx (1818-1883) is of not doing justice to the enormous range of his intellectual achievements. As with all the theorists mentioned in this book it is only practical to scratch the surface of their works and convey their main ideas in support of a particular perspective. Thereafter the diligent reader has to delve further, hopefully aided with these brief sketches, and relate them to the theory and practice of adult education.

Marx offers the most comprehensive alternative to the evolutionist and latter day structural-functionalist perspective by focussing attention on the economic forces determining social relations. Before plunging into this interpretation of social relations some background description is necessary.

The conflict perspective relies a great deal on political ideology as an explanation of the historical process and change in society. There are two themes running through the conflict perspective which overlap with each other. The first is that there is an inherent streak in man's nature, such as competitiveness and power seeking, which brings about conflicts of interest between individuals, groups and nations. Utopian thought is the pursuit of a formula which will control such behaviour, either through the imposition of a superior force or through some mutually agreed re-arrangement of the social order.

The second theme argues that man's nature is a product of a particular social order whose contradictions in organisation brings about conflict. Only radical social change can render such conflict obsolete. Marx based his thinking more on the latter theme. As a utopian using revolutionary means to bring about social change and a new social order his ideas have held wide emotional appeal throughout the world.

Although Marx provided a different conception of social relations nonetheless he held some ideas in common with the theorists in the consensus school of throught. Above all Marx was a disciplined observer seeking testable theories of society by the use of orthodox research methods. He also located his observations within an evolutionary framework which rested upon a process of change whereby society evolved from different stages of economic production and their attendant social relations. Thus Marx employed an inter-disciplinary approach to social theory embracing economic history, economic theory, social survey data from government reports on the condition of the working classes and industries, political and comparative analysis on an international scale. Marx, like the other social theorists referred to earlier, believed that the psychology of man was essentially social, that is, created by historical changes in society and the forces acting upon his nature (economic, political and cultural) contemporarily. Where he differed was in advocating a political revolution to transform society according to the will of man, or from his ideas and social consciousness. His own particular contribution to the science of society, as well as to revolutionary ideas, stems from his emphasis on the importance of the material base of society as a means of understanding its structure and function and the sequence of social change. Through such analysis Marx provided an array of sociological concepts that are still very much in use.

Marxian theory starts from man's struggle to survive through the production of necessities. This process of producing from nature is the basis of social relationships. Throughout the different types of productive systems (tribal subsistence, slave or serf based or modern industrial, which is wage-labour based) man engages in distinct types of social relations. Expressed another way, there are forces of production (comprising the raw materials, technology and knowledge of production methods) and social relations of production (ranging from the simple division of labour in a hunting party or subsistence farming economy to the complex divisions of specialisation, authority and ownership characteristic of modern industrial production). Together these constitute the material base of society – the productive economic system or infrastructure of society. The infrastructure, through the production of goods and services and the particular form of social relations that arise, largely determines the nature, or structure and function, of the superstructure of society. These are the social institutions of the family, law, military, education, media, political parties and the complex organisations of the State. Simply, the infrastructure causes changes to occur in the political and cultural spheres of society – the superstructure.

In this view of society Marx argued that social life was characterised by flux and change rather than by natural forces of stability such as the values and norms evolved by members of society. The key to social change is man's economic relationships. In each type of economy (subsistence, slavery or serfdom or industrial) there are basic contradictions which prevent them from remaining in their present state and which will eventually cause changes throughout society. A major contradiction is the exploitation of one group by another. This creates a conflict of interest as one group gains wealth, prestige and power at the expense of the other, whose labour has contributed towards the supremacy of the dominant group. The root of the contradictions lie in the forces and relations of production.

The nature of capitalist economic organisation represents an ideal type illustration of such contradictions. For Marx, labour produces wealth which is mostly appropriated by the owners of capital (who have possession of the forces of production – land, property and technical knowledge, etc.) as profits, leaving the workers with very low wages. The source of the contradiction, therefore, is between the labour force of production (which produces goods and services and wealth) and the relations of production which involves the control of that wealth by a small capital owning class. Similarly, whereas production is a collective endeavour of labour, ownership is a private matter.

The result of these contradictions is the exploitation and oppression of those who have no capital, only their labour to sell in a market situation where low wages are the norm. The origin of various forms of social inequality stems from this imbalance of economic power. Exploitation has several features. It arises from impersonal market forces governing the relations of production, whereby the owners of capital in order to maximise their profits in volatile markets force down wages to retain their competitiveness. The capability of the capitalist to maintain an 'iron law of wages' is upheld and protected by the exercise of political power, including the use of physical and legal force and domination of the creation and dissemination of social values and knowledge.

The contradictions of the economic system, therefore, fostered conflicts between owners of capital and sellers of labour. Moreover, according to Marx, such contradictions wrought other changes in the economic system generally, such as polarisation between the two groups as traditional and often independent occupations withered away in the wake of the concentration of capital into industrial forms of production. These displaced workers having no capital had to join the ranks of the labouring classes. Furthermore this sharp division into two classes made many poor and a few very rich. Finally even the competitive nature of free enterprise capitalism gave way to monopoly capitalism as powerful groups gained more control over production.

Marx saw these factors as alienating man from his natural world insofar as life was controlled by impersonal forces, intensified in the capitalist organisation of an industrial type economy. Neither capitalists or workers can escape the dominance of this particular form of social relations until they reach a new stage of consciousness, producing new ideas as the basis of revolutionary action. This is the utopian vision of Marx. On the one hand the owners of capital had every reason to profit from an economic system of production which alienated the rest. Their purpose was to retain control whereas the workers had nothing to lose through change and everything to gain. But this awareness had to be stimulated so that the labouring classes could form themselves into a coherent political force. This is what is meant by becoming a 'class for itself', with the necessary solidarity of purpose and organisation to take action. This revolutionary action functioned as a prime mover of social change, bringing about major transformations in the relations of production with the transfer of ownership from individual to collective hands. Economic change in this case forms the basis of social equality and major changes in the institutions and values of society. Change therefore starts from the infrastructure and permeates to the superstructure with revolutionary ideas of equality and justice providing the ignition to spark off direct political action by the working classes.

Running through Marx's analysis are a number of important concepts. First, Marx introduced the concept of historical materialism which brings together the philosophical views of idealism (emphasising the centrality of thought as the basis of social change) and materialism (whereby the physical world shapes man's thoughts). He argued that the real makers of history were the workers, who through their labours in the productive system created history. Once these workers develop a consciousness of their place in history, and realise the source of their exploitation and oppression, they have the power to change society. Thus labour and ideas (the material and ideal) combine to produce a force for change. Earlier stages of economic development transformed through an interaction between ideas (new technology), replacing traditional modes of economic and social organisation. Thus in the earlier feudal system industrial production as a new force rendered the traditional obligations of lord and vassal inflexible and introduced the practice of wage labour, a new development in the relations of production. The essential point is that historical materialism is a philosophy which interprets social change as determined by the forces and relations of production, arising in the infrastructure of society.

The best known concept used by Marx is social class which he employed to explain social change. Class has two meanings. First it refers to particular relationships to the means of production, where people and groups can be ranked according to the different levels of property value, capital and income they possess and acquire. Marx observed two main social classes by this objective criteria – the class of capital owners and wage workers. The history of the social class structure since the writings of Marx has been one of increasing complexity as the division of labour in the economy gave rise to more and varied class groups between the polarised classes he depicted.

The second meaning of class is the one Marx used to explain social change. This is the idea of a class forming into a self conscious group – subjective class – where an awareness of common identity and plight leads to the development of class solidarity and political action. This notion of subjective class consciousness is implicit in the formation of trade unions, political parties and grass roots pressure groups based on working class communities. 'By itself' objective class has no power. 'For itself' subjective class has the will and the means to change society. Class 'for itself' arises when their position in the productive system is so exploited that workers react against the alienating conditions of inequality and lack of autonomy to change society. Marx envisaged a society of equals with common ownership and control of the economy and social institutions, replacing the inherent contradictions of class based capitalist society.

Marxian analysis of capitalism led to the study of state power which was seen as providing a supportive structure of legal edicts and administration on behalf of capitalist interests. This analysis has since provided working class political movements with a way of looking at society, sufficient to rouse consciousness beyond the specific concerns with wages and working conditions into the operation of the capitalist economic and political system. Marx also provided an analysis of knowledge and culture which he regarded as being determined by the ideas and values of leading socio-economic groups to reflect their own interest. This view has been a source of ideas for subsequent studies of the relationship between the social classes and ideas of knowledge and culture mediated through the educational and religious institutions of society.

Not surprisingly Marxist thought has come under considerable criticism and revision. His economic theory has been regarded as outmoded, so too his predictions of a revolutionary class struggle in capitalist societies. The social classes have not polarised in the manner of his predictions. Nor have his utopian visions fulfilled their original splendour in the living examples of modern day socialist nations with communist aspirations. Yet the emotional appeal of his ideas live on. So too does the immensity and range of his intellectual attainments, even though some of his ideas failed.

Some of the specific limitations of Marxist thought have challenged the minds of others within the conflict perspective. For instance, the rise of the managerial and technical occupations have been seen to mitigate class conflict, along with a broadening base of private ownership of capital resources. Another view is that the institutionalisation of industrial conflict has removed the source of class conflict from the political sphere. This has been accompanied by a weakened link between capitalist interests and state government. Then there is the moderating influence of state organised social welfare, a widened franchise and relatively more attainable middle class lifestyles for the aspiring working clases. Finally there is the appeal to nationalist, ethnic and religious emotions which are seen to tanscend class interests and loyalties. All these questions and more have thrown doubts on the salience of some of the original ideas of Marx. What follows is a summary of revisions and reiterations from other writers.

Max Weber (1864-1920) was the first noted sociologist within the broad ambit of the conflict perspective to question the economic determinism of Marx. Whereas Weber agreed that power was a key factor in social relations he parted from Marx in arguing that dominance over others stemmed from several sources. Weber put forward the idea that social stratification was multi-dimensional, not simply economic. This view incorporated the ideas that social status and the organisation of group interests into parties were independent elements, operating alongside the market situation of social groups in the economic sphere of society.

Weber also debated with Marx the significance of ideas in producing change in society. As evidence he put forward the historical connection between religion and the development of capitalism. He drew attention to the connection between Calvinism and the free enterprise ideas of capitalism. The predestination beliefs of Calvinism encouraged the idea that Gods elect would show signs of their blessing by being prosperous and successful entrepreneurs. Being a tool of God justified the quest for productivity and profits.

The other significant contribution of Weber was in drawing a connection between the possession of power and the exercise of authority in society. Two types of authority, traditional and rational-legal, reflect pre-industrial and modern day societies, and legitimates the actions and values of powerful groups. Both types of authority consolidated the interests of the powerful. A third type of authority, charismatic leadership (as typified by revolutionaries), is system disturbing and brings about change in the balance of power between social groups. In all these ways ideas have greater currency than Marx allowed and in those respects Weber refined the crude economic determinism of the conflict perspective.

Ralf Dahrendorf writing in the 1950s re-assessed the nature of conflict theory in the post capitalist era, after the impact of two world wars and the ascendancy of socialism and the mixed economy had exerted changes on society. Dahrendorf noted key changes in the relations of production, principally the weakened link between ownership and control of industry with the demise of the old style capitalist and the institutionalisation of labour relations. Similarly labour had become more specialised and divergent in their relations to the means of production. Moreover the class structure was no longer divided into distinct groups with uniform interests. This reflected the creation of an opportunity structure through social welfare, education and social mobility, enabling some people to move away from traditional class attitudes and lifestyles.

Like Weber before him Dahrendorf also questioned the economic determinism of Marx and specifically criticised the way power was linked to economic production. Like Weber he observed that social class is more than the sum of economic relationships. Furthermore social policies are not entirely governed by economic considerations nor do all social conflicts arise from property struggles. Social class in Dahrendorf's view is only one source of conflict in society. Authority relations constitute another arena for conflicts of intersts. These are much more diverse than conflicts about economic issues and are not specifically tied to social classes but to many kinds of interest groups and role relationships in society. These non-economic power struggles stemming from complex authority relations sets off diverse forms of resistance to such coercion. These become the sources of social change, albeit more subtle than the outright class conflicts that Marx predicted would lead to the new society.

Dahrendorf's interpretations have been challenged by more traditional Marxists on the grounds that beneath the apparent benevolence of state welfare and greater control over industrial conflict the old class divisions remained. This has led some theorists to examine the values of the working class in pursuit of the question of their supposed absorption of middle class ideas. One major study found that the working classes, especially those near to the boundary between non-manual and skilled manual labour, had not become more bourgeoise, even though their political beliefs had grown apart from traditional class solidarity[4]. Instead they had become more private in their personal lives and regarded work solely in terms of rewards.

For a modern Marxist the question is, why the disadvantaged do not revolt? Modern society is on the whole more stable than torn apart by conflict. Only exceptionally does the State resort to the use of naked force to retain control, although to the common observer the use of police and armed forces in riot gear seems on the increase. One explanation is that control is exercised through safety valves or social mechanisms, such as job mobility, pay incentives, gambling, educational opportunities and religion. These provide the appearance of opportunity, justice and the 'fair go'. In reality few really benefit and deeply entrenched inequalities remain largely undisturbed.

Another explanation, which Marx himself employed, is the ability of dominant social groups to devise and transmit the leading ideas, mores and values of society, usually in their own interests. The ideas reinforce existing inequalities and forms of dominance by upholding arguments in support of the need for authority, the logic of industrial and capitalist organisation and appeals to the national interest. The ideas of the ruling class as the leading ideas of the age, as Marx expressed it, became enshrined in the major institutions of society permeating the economy, polity and the cultural spheres.

There are several responses to this dominant value system. One is to accept the values in a resigned way, living in accordance with what 'they' expect. This subordinate value system operates in response to the dominant value system. It fosters adaptation manifested by fatalism, low expectations, 'us and them' thinking and powerless working class communities. Some might adapt by imitating and aspiring to the values of the dominant classes in society. Others make a virtue out of being ordinary. The least likely response is to become radical and oppose the dominant ideology by asserting another view. This would involve underlining the exploitive and self-seeking nature of dominant groups, as well as promoting a working class consciousness affirming the dignity of labour and the justice of equality as a political ideology. These values have failed to make much impact on working class consciousness, except sporadically and without much success.

This chapter has outlined the main ideas of leading contributors to the systems theory approach in sociology. For the purposes of illustration two extreme models of society have been presented as they interpret social relations in a distinctly different way. These models, the consensus and conflict perspectives, align to different political and social ideologies, models of social welfare and explanations of social problems. The purpose of all this theory and model building is to provide adult educators, in search of wide perspectives giving context to their work, with a framework of ideas that helps to explain the often implicit thinking that lies behind policy and practice. To complete this part of the book, which has concentrated on a widening and embracing range of social theory perspectives, the next chapter attends to systems type theory in the sociology of education. This will lead to a summary of the main ideas presented in the foregoing chapters.

CHAPTER EIGHT
ADULT EDUCATION AND SYSTEMS THEORY PERSPECTIVES FROM THE SOCIOLOGY OF EDUCATION

A major departure point for this book is the idea that adult education is in search of a socially relevant role. This explains the involvement of adult education with social welfare agencies and community development projects in makng provision for disadvantaged groups in society. This work with a social dimension is an important thrust in adult education. Invariably such work brings into the framework of adult education policies and practices a host of social ideas and concepts. Many of these have been outlined.

Before pulling together all these ideas and concepts and relating them to the different models of adult education, also outlined previously, some reference must be made to systems theory applications to the sociology of education[1].

Education occupies a central role in modern society and consumes resources on a scale comparable to a gigantic industry. The educational system relates to all the systems and institutions of society – economic, political and cultural – through its role in transmitting culture, socialisation, training, selection and allocation to the occupational structure. Education also performs important social control functions. It is relevant to make these points for so much conventional wisdom stresses the notion that education is only concerned with the development of individuals, not more far reaching and yet just as obvious social functions. This is the starting point for examining the nature of the relationship between education and society.

Theory perspectives on education divide into the structural-functional and conflict approaches and sub-divide again into what is called technological and evolutionary functionalism and the conflict perspectives of Weber and Marx. These perspectives can be briefly outlined and, wherever possible, links made with adult education. It is also relevant to relate education to theories of social change for it is a connection that is central to both consensus and conflict perspectives on the role of education in society. Change in this context refers to modifications to the institutional structures and main values of society of a significant and enduring kind.

The technological functionalism approach appeals to advocates of continuing education, or any of the variants, that extends the skill training and upgrading role throughout the working lifespan. The argument is very simple. Modern society is dependent for its economic growth and wealth on the efficient working of the productive system, especially in more competitive world markets. Economic efficiency is based on two key factors – the application of scientific knowledge and technological innovation to production and the supply of skilled workpower. The two factors are integral to each other. The role of education is two-fold. First, to develop knowledge applicable to production in any of its forms, and, second, to train and supply a skilled and adaptable workforce. The anticipated consequence is that increasing numbers of people have to spend longer periods on their initial and subsequent training on a recurrent basis to prepare themselves and remain effective workers. Their own success in life and the wealth of the nation are seen to be the same.

This 'fit' between the individual and society and education with the economic system is an apt illustration of the functionalist perspective. The key element holding everything together is technical knowledge and skills related to the occupational structure of an industrial economy. The fundamental problem and task for society is to find ways of matching skilled people to labour intensive job skill requirements. Educational policy and practice is concerned with the identification, training and continued selection and allocation of people to labour intensive job skill requirements with the minimum of obstruction to its flow into the occupational structure and the economy in general. This perspective on education has appeal to those lobbying for equality of opportunity, for those with ability and willingness to work hard, irrespective of social background. Moreover this view of equality argues the case for a meritocracy with education playing a key role in selecting talent and promoting social mobility.

The technological-functionalism perspective takes issue with social and political ideologies that assume the concentration of ability amongst elite groups in society. The rate of social and economic change is such that the need for high level skills far exceeds the supply of available abilities from elite groups. Furthermore these fixed ideas about the availability and distribution of ability do not match experience. Studies have shown the wider distribution of ability than sometime conventional wisdom held. Hence such ideas act as a constraint on the capacity of education and society to find equilibrium. To use an image, the trawling net used by the educational system to find and select talent is of the wrong mesh and located in the wrong place. Viewed from a more radical ideological standpoint, the search for talent theme grossly simplifies the immense difficulty of creating educational opportunities in an unequal society. Educational opportunity by itself is not sufficient to provide equal chances because of deeper seated social, economic and political inequalities in society.

The relevance of the technological functionalism perspective has already been noted in the advocacy of continuing education. It has specific bearing on the work training model of adult education and reflects the thinking of governments concerned about employment training schemes. This equation of education with the fostering of human resources as a form of capital investment has commonsense appeal. It leaves unchallenged, though, the supposed consensus of values about the primacy of economic growth as a social ideal. It also certainly ignores the consequences of economic growth in terms of environmental pollution, the exhaustion of natural resources and the human effects of competitiveness stimulated by achievement and social mobility values in education.

The determinist nature of structural-functional theory is very evident in the technological view of the role of education in society. The same applies to evolutionary functionalism. This perspective focusses attention on the socialisation and cultural tansmission functions of education. These are seen to reinforce the training function by educating people into the appropriate attitudes and values consistent with the technological nature of modern society. It is assumed that the family and other social institutions lack the wherewithal to adequately initiate the younger generation into these values. To refer back to Parsons' pattern variables model, the educational system is charged with the task of inculcating the values of achievement, independence, delayed gratification and so forth. This complex task requires specialised skills. Implicit in this perspective is the assumption that as technology advances the functionally related social ideas and values are advanced too through the socialisation and social control elements of the school curriculum. This is seen as a natural process stemming from the leading ideas of elite groups in society.

It should be fairly clear that this perspective, by emphasising the communication of cultural values, has direct relevance to the liberal adult education model. The connection might be weakest in suggesting that the purpose of liberal adult education is to serve the needs of industry and the economy. Clearly it is not, but in a general sense the communication of ideas, many of which touch on social concerns including basic values in society, is very much the province of the liberal model. The high minded, academic culture of traditional liberal adult education is frequently cast as an elitist activity. Worse still it is seen as a ploy by the ruling class to spread their values. This perspective on education comes from radical political and educational ideologies drawing their inspiration from conflict theories of society.

Implicit in the structural-functional perspective on education is a version of social change theory, extending from classical sociological thought to modern technological determinism. The modern champion of the idea of a post-industrial society is Daniel Bell whose book depends greatly on a structural-functionalist perspective and incorporates the framework of thought of technological determinism as the prime mover of social change[2]. Bell's work reflects a long line of thought reaching back to the early work of Comte and Spencer. The former regarded modern society as the product of a prolonged gestation, evolving from earlier stages by a linear and ascending path to the positivist stage where scientific thought determined the nature of society. Spencer also posited the idea of an evolutionary pattern of increasing complexity and differentiation of the institutions of society arising from role specialisation in the emerging industrial economy. Durkheim too regarded the main impetus to change in society as the division of labour bringing about complex social relations. These classical theories of social change relied heavily for causal explanation on the interaction between ideas and material factors. Social change originating in one sphere, such as the economic system, interacts with other spheres, which in turn prompt further adaptations in the initial sphere.

In modern times stress has been laid on the idea of society having moved to a post capitalist and post industrial stage of development. The writings of Dahrendorf and Bell typify this view and they, along with others, subscribe to an implicit idea of social change following some linear ascent, noted amongst classical theorists. Another example derives from T.B. Bottomore who is seeking the origins of social change outlined a different model[3]. He distinguished between change occurring from outside a particular society (exogenous) and within society (endogenous). The latter type of change (endogenous) may be further sub-divided into episodic and patterned. The episodic refers to unpredictable changes, such as the one-off influence of charismatic leaders, revolutions, natural disasters and wars. Their impact on society may be sudden but the effects profound and long lasting. Patterned changes, as the term suggests, are more predictable outcomes of existing institutions and modes of operation in society. Chief amongst these are the workings of the economic system and the effects of scientific knowledge and technological innovation. These are seen to shape and determine society by their relentless capacity to change. Clearly these elements of the forces of production, as Marx termed them, are never static. Education as the organised means for developing knowledge, training manpower and the transmission of culture has grown to occupy an integral role in this process. At least that view accords with the structural-functionalist perspective on society in general and the eductional system in particular. Thus education is seen as a service agency enabling society to function more efficiently through the supply of knowledge and skilled workers. By these means the economic infrastructure evolves into higher forms of sophistication, founded on scientific and technical knowledge and skills. The wealth generated permeates through to the institutions of society and allows for a wider distribution of the benefits of economic growth. Education is an inseparable part of the rational social order, logically determined by this consensus perspective on society and underpinned by a model of social change that puts onus on the transforming power of the forces and values of production. It should be noted that this analysis gives recognition to the significance of ideas an social values combined with the productive outcomes of science and technology – idealist and materialist views of society.

Neither the perspectives on education and social change have much place for conflict, except on a minor scale. This more critical perspective comes from the radicals whose thoughts derive from the classical theories of Marx and Weber[4].

For Weber education is closely linked to status groups in society. The level and type of education received provides a kind of membership card qualifying for a particular status group. More specifically, a status group is formed around a shared social position, largely determined by economic factors but also held together by participation in a common culture (language, clothing style, manners, tastes and interests, opinions and values, etc.). Membership of a status group provides a sense of identity and belonging. Status groups then distinguish themselves from others by an evaluative yardstick, usually implying some moral judgement, such as 'high brow', 'sophisticated', 'respectable', 'devotion', 'integrity' or lesser qualities than these.

Conflict arises between status groups through competition for scarce social goods which are highly valued – wealth, power and prestige. Some status groups are more successful than others in obtaining these social goods. This triggers off conflicts between other status groups who are seen to be in competition and who want to avoid being dominated and controlled. Many of these inter-status group rivalries take place in organisations, especially in the economic sphere where the struggle for wealth is concentrated. The problem for high level status groups is to maintain their advantage over others. An important asset for dominant status groups is control over the thoughts and values of their organisations and subordinate members.

The role education plays in all this is focussed on the drafting of people into status groups on the basis of academic achievement and type of schooling. In this view education may be compared to a complex organisation reflecting the status hierarchies of society. Thus education is made up of different levels of learning both in the acquisition of vocational and practical skills and the transmission of specific cultural values. These levels reflect the status levels within social organisations of all kinds. The education system supplies manpower and new recruits to existing status groups in society. Education, then, by reinforcing the status hierarchies of society fosters the struggle for scarce goods in the form of wealth, power and prestige. This invariably leads to social conflict, sometimes expressed in overt struggles for power between political and economic groups. It is just as likely that the education system is so adept at socialising people into the different sub-cultures as to minimise conflicts of interests. This idea of cultural hegemony is closely allied with neo-Marxist views on education. Attention now turns to this perspective.

Marx made little direct reference to education but his writings have been interpreted and related to the role it plays in society. The starting points are the exploitive nature of capitalist economy and the social relations of production which concentrates power in the hands of the owners of capital. The unequal social relations of production (the class structure) is upheld by institutional arrangements in the superstructure of society. The educational system in this respect, through the processes of selection and the dissemination of knowledge, reflects the hierarchial relations of society and reproduces the conditions necessary to sustain it by allowing dominant groups to legitimise their position and their versions of social order.

This interpretation, which resembles a rigid form of Marxism in emphasising a close fit between infrastructure and superstructure, is quite like the technological determinist model outlined previously. It differs in the following respects. The class bias built into the education system is reflected in the division between mental and manual labour. In the former a more favoured higher education sector caters for the elite minority who are equipped with high level occupational skills. The majority of the population are provided with an education preparing them for manual labour and relatively low level mental skills, neither of which command high level rewards or much power. This aspect of education concerned with the reproduction of skills is reinforced by the ideological function of legitimising failure. This occurs through the equality of opportunity theme which in addition to providing chances for the most able to achieve mobility through education enables the rest to reconcile their relative failure by coming to terms with their own lack of effort or brainpower. This emphasis on individual explanations of failure obscures the

110

problems of experiencing real equality of opportunity through education in a society with deep seated economic and political inequality.

Two themes have been noted in these critical appraisals of education from the conflict perspective. The first is that capitalism reproduces itself in the physical sense by applying knowledge and skilled labour to the productive process. Second, to maintain the relations of production in such a way as to compound the position of dominant groups ideological control needs to be exercised. In both ways education plays an important role and is therefore implicated in the conflicts of interests that arise from a class based and unequal society founded on a capitalist political economy. With these ideas as a background it is useful to identify the thoughts of leading exponents of the conflict approach applied to education in general and the implications of their ideas to adult education in particular.

The ideology of equality of opportunity while promoting the success of a few leaves the majority alienated from education and this state of mind continues through the adult life. This is the interpretation of Westwood following the analysis of Althusser, Bourdieu, Bowles and Gintis and Gramsci[5]. It explains the predominance of middle class participants in adult education, particularly in those activities concerned with liberal and intellectual subjects and learning for leisure and recreation purposes. This leads to the view that adult education reinforces or at least is unable to remedy the class bias built into the earlier stages of education through the selection and control functions.

This general conclusion upon the nature of adult education owes much to the ideas of the various writers noted above. Althusser, for example, has refined the concept of Ideological State Apparatus, of which the educational system is a key agent, reproducing labour through the reproduction of skills and the reproduction of ideology. The reference to the ideology of equality of opportunity has already been noted as a way in which the state exercises control over people's minds and values. Equality in this respect may be seen as a safety valve, giving the impression of wide opportunities which are really more myth than reality.

The myth of equality of opportunity concealing deep seated class inequality and alienation from education has been analysed by Bourdieu, the French sociologist. His depiction of the way cultural capital is transmitted through society by the educational system illustrates the ways in which the ideas of dominant groups pervade the curriculum. Those children of dominant groups have an inherent advantage and are more able to acquire and apply the cultural capital of the curriculum. They then possess the academic means to gain access to the economic capital of society through their entry into the occupational structure. Those unable to acquire the requisite cultural capital are not in a position to compete for access to economic capital.

Where this relates to adult education is in explaining the motives for middle class participation. The interpretation offered is that middle class people are aware of the significance of possessing cultural capital as a resource underpinning their position in the economy and their self perceived competence. To maintain their higher status position they need to replenish their stocks of knowledge and skills (cultural capital) through adult education.

The ideas of Bowles and Gintis also implicitly explain the alientating influence of education on lower class status groups. They describe the educational system as bureaucratic, hierarchical and based on domination and control. These are seen as normal features of a system akin to large scale industrial organisations producing knowledge and training its members. The selection process in particular operates as a reward system for success and, conversely, a disincentive for failure. Whether by design or accident the educational system reproduces the class structure and its inherent rewards and alienation. The thesis of Bowles and Gintis is that the form of education rather than its specific content broadly corresponds to the social relations of production in the class structure. This idea accords with the concept of the hidden curriculum whereupon people in education learn by experience the hierarchical nature of social relations and their position in the class structure. In applying the correspondence theory to adult education it may be conjectured that different providing agencies cater for different class and culture groups. This is more readily observed in vocational education for adults where different institutions provide levels of work related qualifications corresponding to the occupational hierarchy and catering for the needs of different social classes. In this respect a good deal of MSC sponsored adult training shemes are designed to produce a pool of labour, mainly at the lower end of the skill levels, for those whose earlier education was insufficient for secure employment and career opportunities.

The writers in the neo-Marxist framework have put forward rather academic analysis of the nature of the education system in the class society. It should be recalled that originally Marx advocated political action arising from class consciousness of oppression and the power of group solidarity − class for itself. Two latter day activists have something to contribute towards our understanding of political action and education − Antonio Gramsci and Paulo Freire. Both have something very specific to apply to adult education and its relationship to the working class[6].

Gramsci was a revolutionary leader who had a short and tragic life under the Fascist dictatorship of Mussolini's Italy. A revolutionary in this context means using conscious reflection upon real life conditions and possessing a determination to change them through political action invariably involving violent conflict with the forces of oppression. This conforms to the precept by Marx that theory and practice are the backbones of revolutionary change.

Gramsci was critical of traditional working class leadership for operating within the institutional framework of capitalist society while ostensibly seeking its overthrow. The problem was that by the sheer force of what Gramsci termed the cultural hegemony of the ruling class they had the power to determine what ideas constituted commonsense amongst the majority of people. The effect was to isolate radical opposition as a form of deviation from the commonsense values and operations of society. Thus militant trade unionism and extreme left wing political parties were derided through the hegemony of the capitalist class who could call upon the apparent consensus of opinion to muffle such opposition. To avoid such isolation and derision the trade union movement simply organised workers into wage earners, selling their labour rather than forming into a radical opposition to capitalism. This explains the relative success of organised means for containing industrial conflict and the continuing acceptance of capital-labour contractual relations.

Using the concept of hegemony Gramsci regarded the State not only as an auxiliary organiser of the forces of capitalist production but as a form of educator using its propaganda powers, channelled through the educational system and other institutional means of communication, to disseminate the ideas and values of the ruling class.

As a revolutionary Gramsci considered what effective form of opposition could be mounted against the cultural hegemony of the ruling class. He argued for a grass roots form of workers' political education which would provide the seeds of thoughts as the basis of a continual ideological struggle and political action. It was essential that the form of education would be independent of the State and intellectually capable of sustaining a counter hegemony. It needed to look beyond the immediate, individual survival concerns of the working class towards the dictatorship of the proletariat. Gramsci believed that the Communist Party could provide the ideological leadership and support an educational movement with a close bond to the working class. The agents of this process would be worker intellectuals actively involved with the conditions and aspirations of their class and particular occupational groups and communities. Gramsci was never able to realise his visionary ideas but the essence of what he believed has been a source of inspiration for the work of Paulo Freire.

Like Gramsci the writings of Freire are concerned with cultural action with an explicit political aim to counteract the forms of domination experienced by oppressed groups in society. His main focus on the process of social change is the individual, by means of what he terms the humanisation of man. For Freire the oppressed are incomplete human beings, being held captive by the economic, political and cultural domination of their oppressors. These forms of hegemony ensures that the consciousness of the oppressed is alienated and not liberated. One of the agents of oppression is the educational system whose reliance on methods of learning that stifle the free flow of ideas and the raising of consciousness perpetuates the alienation of the subordinate groups in society. Freire is particularly critical of the 'banking concept' of education whose insistence on the storing of knowledge rather than its use as a means of cultural dialogue reinforces a culture of silence amongst those receiving instruction. They are prevented by such an experience of education from examining their circumstances and needs, which is what Gramsci urged as the basis of revolutionary action.

Freire's theory of social change through the awakened consciousness of the oppressed relies on cultural struggle and education, animated by revolutionary leaders (akin to Weber's charismatic leadership as a form of authority). This process of change pivots around political action in the more general guise of what Freire calls cultural action for freedom. It has already been noted that the radical model of adult education, in the context of community development for the disadvantaged and working class, has received much inspiration from Freire's concepts and vision. His thinking provides a practical guide to cultural action by proposing a two stage process of liberation pedagogy – first, the focus on enabling the oppressed to perceive the conditions and causes of their subjection, and second, through the destruction of myths created by the oppressor's new ideas for radical change emerge.

The strength of these conflict perspectives is in their critical approach to the relationship between education and society. Unlike the consensus approaches described earlier the role of education is not taken for granted. By focussing on such issues as the persistence of inequality and the ways in which economic, political and cultural domination is maintained the nature of education takes on a different complexion. It is seen as a means of sustaining social inequality. The alienating effects of education as an experience goes a long way to explain the irrelevance of adult education to large sections of the working classes. Conversely the middle class bias of adult education is more clearly seen as a continuation of earlier advantages conferred on these more privileged groups for whom education corresponds more closely to their cultural backgrounds. Finally these critical appraisals of education provide an insight into the potential for social change arising through a radical, educationally directed class consciousness leading to political action and personal liberation. Certainly this is the optimistic view of S. Westwood whose article succinctly explores many of the perspectives described in this chapter. Westwood's article acknowledges the diversity of adult education and unlike many of the theorists she cites, who project a monolithic structure, she is able to point to activities, many of them innovative, that constitute the beginnings of a counter cultural hegemony along the lines envisaged by Marx, Gramsci and Freire.

SUMMARY OF PART ONE

The introductory chapter stressed the value of having an awareness of the many social theory perspectives that relate to different ideas, possible policy options and practices in adult education. The line taken was that as adult education operated within a wider social context an understanding of the leading ideas about how they related to each other provided intellectual stimulus and insight as well as the basis of rational thought for policy making and practice. No particular social theory perspective has been favoured. Instead the purpose has been to show the diversity of ideas both within adult education, social welfare, community development, education and society that make all these areas of social relations so thought provoking and challenging. All these theory perspectives have been outlined so as to provide an introductory guide to students and practitioners.

The other chapters have sought to portray rather general insights into key concepts and theories. More detailed study would be necessary to understand their richness and complexity fully. Nonetheless these general and holistic interpretations allow connections to be made between adult education and its social context. This chapter simply draws together the central lines of thought and concludes this main section of the book.

A tight definition of adult education has been avoided. Instead an elastic meaning has been recommended to reflect the diverse range of workers and institutions regarding themselves as concerned with the education of adults. This trend appears to reflect an increasing recognition of the usefulness of adult education in a wide variety of situations where learning is involved. In particular, adult education is closely involved with social problems and the needs of relatively disadvantaged groups. But in a more general way too adult education is seen to have universal relevance to individuals throughout all aspects and stages of their lives. Thus the meaning of adult education consciously adopted spans all kinds of formal and non-formal kinds of provision, ranging from vocational to community based learning of a very informal nature. Moreover in a general way this approach embraces the more formal continuing or recurrent education, which is often pitched at professional training and retraining, taking place under the auspices of the higher education sector. Essentially the view favoured is that adult education is an endless and seamless activity and admits to no tight boundary defining its meaning. The term adult education seems to reflect this sense better than any other term.

With regard to the development of adult education from an historical perspective the main theme has sprung from the term dynamic movement. This best reflects the way in which adult education has developed in response to some perceived social need, manifested through the requirements of individuals, groups and whole classes for educational provision. Hence the umbrella theme of adult education and the search for social relevance in a changing society. This particularly reflects three constant themes in adult education for citizenship, social well-being and social welfare. Certainly adult education with a social dimension provides the rationale for this book to explore theories and concepts from social welfare and educational policy and sociology, as they too address themselves to the social problems of individuals, groups, communities and society in general.

The social relevance theme has been expressed in different ways and by clear stages. Historians have delineated the stages of adult education for literacy and salvation; vocation and work; civilisation and higher learning; leisure and recreation; and education for participation. This theme has taken off along several tributaries such as working class political education through the trade unions, political parties and latterly through 'grass roots' social action in neighbourhoods and communities, often related to specific social groups by class, age, sex and so forth. Thus adult education has always had a very purposeful image being associated with spiritual, cultural, economic and political issues and values over the past two centuries. Over that time span adult education has developed a rich tradition and diverse network of institutions providing a wide range of learning activities.

An underlying theme from the history of adult education is the idea of helping people adjust to social change, often experienced initially at the personal level, arising from wider based changes in the economy and social structure. The early history was characterised by social elitism as the more powerful groups in society used adult education as a form of social control, directing their energies towards solving problems arising from the impact of a changing industrial and urbanised society. Latterly the theme has been biased towards enabling adults to gain greater control over their own lives, whether at the personal level or as members of groups and communities. The evolution from elitism to a self-directed democracy of participating learners, by no means complete, is characteristic of the changing nature of adult education, mirroring some significant changes in society. Another way of expressing this change is to identify the trend in adult education from reformist ideas of social change to much more radical views. Again this tendency must not be seen as either/or but rather as strands of development. Moreover adult education is still concerned with activities such as leisure and work training that do not easily fit into any preconceived idea of reformism or radicalism. Nonetheless these two themes emerge as very strong purposes and give a dynamic impetus to adult education as a movement of ideas and actions in a changing society.

As described earlier the social relevance theme, especially where it relates to social problems, has ebbed and flowed around major reports on adult education. This is the case with the 1919 Report and the 1973 Russell and 1974 Alexander Reports. These confirmed the adult education with a social dimension theme, in contrast to the 1944 Act which made more of learning for leisure and recreation. It was noted, though, that the centre of gravity in adult education has shifted from the wider social welfare and community development interest to a more specific concern with employment and work training following the massive impact of the MSC. To complete the historical review it was also noted that new ideas and social prescriptions have led to the search for a more embracing term that would reflect the ideas that education is lifelong, continuous and permanent, necessarily recurrent with changing social and economic circumstances both at the individual and societal level.

From this overview of meaning, purpose and development in adult education four distinct ideologies and models of provision exist side by side. The point was made that these ideologies represent underpinning value perspectives as the basis of policy and practice and reflecting beliefs about the nature of the relationship between adult education and society. Nonetheless for all these divergences of ideology it was argued that adult education is still characterised by the unifying search for social relevance through a social problem focus. It was boldly suggested that adult education has made use of three central ideas of social organisation – liberty, equality and fraternity which can be freely translated into ideas of individuation and personal development; democratic citizenship; social reform and justice; community involvement. These ideas portray adult education as fired by romantic idealism, reinforced by voluntaryism, liberal and open minded approaches to learning.

In surveying the broad and diverse field of adult education four main perspectives emerge. One is the recreational model which emphasises leisure time learning and has a limited commitment to wider social purposes. Two is the work training model and is primarily about economic purposes. Together they represent what may be called the conventional approach to adult education. Three is the liberal progressive model and has the longest history. Four is the radical model and provides a strong set of alternative ideas on the nature of adult education in society. In addition to reflecting differences of social purpose the four models diverge on approaches to knowledge, organisation, teaching and learning and the curriculum. They also differ with respect to the role of public expenditure in support of their activities, although they have little control over this matter. These differences have already been detailed and are not fully repeated here.

There are some features of the relationship between the models and society, however, that warrant repetition.

i.   The Recreation-Leisure model has adopted a 'needs meeting' approach to provision and stresses the importance of leisure and learning as enhancing individual and thereby social well-being. There is a trend away from public expenditure on provision to self-financing.

ii.   The Work-Training model interprets social purpose mostly in terms of economic needs through the acquisition of job skills. Needs are almost exclusively determined by experts and prevailing economic and political contingencies. Provision is largely financed by public expenditure.

iii.   The Liberal-Progressive model has two standpoints – knowledge for its own sake and knowledge as power to change society. With the latter standpoint the route to social improvement is through the intellectual development of individuals. There is a belief in social progress, hence the tag progressive and an emphasis on social reform through adult education. Implicit is the idea of education for democratic citizenship and participation, fostering the pluralist society through a broad consensus of values. These ideas have influenced compensatory and 'second chance' policies directed towards disadvantaged

117

individuals in society. Public expenditure on provision has high priority to adherents of this model.

The Liberal-Progressive position is characterised by a certain romantic idealism with learning as a key to personal and social change; education of the whole person through culturally valued knowledge; and social progress through reforming ideas.

iv. The Radical model takes issue with the romanticism of the liberal-progressive on several counts and in the milder version regards education as a key to revolutionary social change, without the violence. Education is not a neutral activity. Instead the purpose of adult education is action or praxis. The approach to need is on the basis of participant involvement and self determination. Public expenditure is seen as a first line duty of the State welfare system of which adult education is an integral part.

Each model of adult education represents not only an ideal-type but also a speculation about their different approaches to the social theories reviewed in subsequent chapters. What this conclusion does is to suggest connecting links between the models and the various theories. The idea is that in an ideal professional world adult educators faced with the tasks of forming policies and making practical provision would consult and debate these theoretical perspectives in order to line up the options and make decisions. The real world is different, of course, and there is much to be said for pragmatic decision making not unduly influenced by competing and complex theories. Furthermore theories are not absolutes but trains of thought and susceptible to revision in the light of experience. Nevertheless the point of this book is to relate theory to practice in a general way, not debate its value. Theory has already been claimed as a hallmark of professionalism in adult education.

Instead of repeating the nature of these various social theory perspectives only their titles will be used again. The real piece of speculative thought lies in connecting these social theory perspectives to the three major ideological positions in adult education. The word speculative could not be more heavily underlined. The main reason is that the everyday world of policymaking and practice in adult education is largely influenced by crisis, giving rise to contingency responses, and pragmatism, stemming from custom and practice and the inherent tendencies of organisation to be conservative in their habits of thought. The other reason is that pure theories only exist on paper and in the mind. Their practical application is inevitably subject to distortion if only because adherents to any theory see so many ways of interpreting and doing things. Therefore it is better to regard the connections between ideology and theory as directions of thought, not a detailed map. Finally it would assist understanding if these ideas were presented in diagrammatic form. Reference is made first to a summary account of ideologies of social purpose and the three models of adult education. This is followed by the possible links between adult education ideology and the wider context of social theory concepts and perspectives presented in the previous chapters in more detailed form.

Such perspectives attach significance to the numbers of adult students as a yardstick of progress and enable a shift of emphasis away from the idea of residual, mopping-up actions by a loosely federated body of adult education services to a system of provision where returning to study is a normal process. Adult students thus embody the principle of education as part of life and not just preparation for it.

This might be termed the ideal realm of discussion, where education is regarded as an investment in human capital and a means of realising social and personal goals. Such thinking could not have fallen upon harder times. Educational policy at the pragmatic level, however, will doubtless continue, as is the tradition of British politics and administration. For example, the implications of demographic change, with a predicted shortfall in demand for places by school-leavers, have led to discussion about the recomposition of the student body in higher education. Hence 'Model E' was one of the proposals for student recruitment policies in the 1990s, seeking to take up the spare capacity by providing more places for mature students, especially from working class backgrounds. This type of proposal should appeal both to administrators and to progressives seeking more equality in the system of higher education but the wrangles over equality or excellence look like persisting for a long time to determine access policies and consideration of credit schemes, teaching methods, assessment procedures and the like.

The second broad heading is descriptive studies of adult students and learners usually of a practical kind. Thus the body of participation studies in adult education fall into this category. The long history of self educated men and women recorded through auto-biographical and biographical accounts would also be included. So too would descriptions of the characteristics of adult students as these are often useful for training adult educators as teachers and administrators. Together these descriptive accounts fit alongside other studies depicting the process of becoming an adult student, their academic and personal adjustment, performance at examinations compared with conventional-age students, and subsequent careers. Such studies are drawn from the entire field of post-school education, in institutions of adult, further and higher education as well as different modes of learning typical of participation in non-formal and informal educative activities.

The third broad area is of theoretical studies, which is the centrepoint of this book. These theoretical contributions are mainly drawn from sociological studies upon other subjects than adult students but their ideas are applicable. The value of theory in respect to adult student studies is that they provide a disciplined framework of ideas elucidating the complex processes of why and how adults turn to formal learning and become students.

The remainder of this chapter will follow the direction of each area of adult student studies in the same sequence, selectively illustrating lines of thought and examples of the literature. Before beginning the section on theory perspectives the essence of social action theory in sociology will be presented. Attention turns now to the ideal realm of adult student studies as this area fits more closely to the holistic sociological perspectives of the previous chapters.

123

As outined in the brief description of the ideal realm adult students have been discussed in relation to major educational and social goals. Some elaboration is in order.

Adult students have occupied three historical phases in their relationship to higher education, particularly universities, which has traditionally been the fountain head for adults returning to study and formal learning. The earliest and longest historical phase, from the last century through to the Second World War, regarded adult students as exceptional and rare entrants to the highest levels of education. Entry to universities was tight and those who made it were truly the testaments to perseverance and survival over many years of sweated learning and hardship. This was the era of the self-educated and there is a small and lucid literature about them. Their efforts no doubt contributed to the idea of the heroic age of adult education, where the whole movement had to struggle to gain acceptance and survive the rigours of a harsh political, economic and cultural climate.

The second and briefest phase was during the immediate post-war years leading into the period of expansion into the early 1970s. This was the era of manpower shortages in the teaching profession and expanding sections of the welfare services and industry. Older people were seen as suitable for re-training, often on the basis of their maturity and experience in other walks of life. The easing of acess opportunities and the proven worth of admitting older people into higher education from the period of demobilisation after the war probably paved the way for adult students thereafter.

The third phase takes off from the very much leaner years of the cutbacks in public expenditure seriously affecting education and other welfare services. This has continued to be the era of restriction and the expansionist ideals of the 1960s have fallen away. In spite of this the themes of continuing, recurrent and lifelong learning have managed to convey a sense of optimism and policies for future expansion. If these materialise in a concrete form adult students will be critical yardsticks of progress from vision to policy and practice. In the meantime adult students have been viewed in a more limited way, as gap fillers arising from the projected shortfalls in demand for higher education places from the conventional age entry group. Hence the earlier reference to the since abandoned 'Model E' by the last Labour government for adult/mature student places. The spirit of these proposals still have an existence, albeit a shadowy one, in the minds of policy-makers.

Throughout the post war years traditional adult education, rather than the further and higher education sectors, have maintained an almost evangelical commitment to the idea of adult rights to educational opportunity and the expansion of provision across all sectors and forms of learning. Within adult education there has been no doubt about the need to expand opportunities, clear away administrative obstacles and generally smooth the communication channels so that serious learning is both attractive and relevant to adult lives. Ideas and policy options are not the problem, simply the lack of resources.

From this ideal and rather lofty perspective adult educators, like many others, look back on the workings of the mainstream system of compulsory child and youth education. Some of the problems of adult education, in terms of its marginality politically and economically, stem from the over-concentration of status and resources on what is called the 'front-end' model. Undoubtedly the major debates in political and educational circles is about child and youth education and training, the latter more in terms of contingency action in response to unemployment and economic recession.

The problem with education is its failure to deliver to the twin 'gods' of economic efficiency and social justice. More concretely, education has been shown to be wasteful of ability and divisive by class, sex and race. In an earlier chapter some theoretical explanations from differing sociological perspectives were used to highlight the causes of these failures. In a more ordinary way these problems bear revisiting briefly as they form an important background perspective on adult students returning to education.

From an ideal perspective education is seen as a vehicle for social progress and change. This idea was translated by post war social architects in two ways. First there was the belief that investment in education meant that more people could be trained to occupy increasingly complex jobs. This was seen as a direct contribution towards economic growth, which was generally held to be a necessary means for sustaining post war affluence and adjusting the political economy to the loss of the colonies. In any case, a changing economy needed higher level skills to maintain any semblance of competitiveness in a shrinking world market.

The second educational 'god' of social justice, translated into the theme of equality of opportunity, linked to the economic growth ideal by offering a solution to the need for more people to train for skilled jobs. The social elites who had traditionally used education as a means to a good living could not reproduce themselves in sufficient numbers to meet the manpower requirements of the modernising economy. This could only be done by recruiting from 'below', as it were, intelligent and hardworking children from working class backgrounds. There was more to the equality theme than a crude utilitarianism. The appeal of social justice goes wider to encompass ideals of natural rights and legitimate claims on welfare benefits of any kind. These are seen as matters of human dignity and worth irrespective of social background.

Behind these ideals lay even more grand designs for the future of society. Together they represent an imaginary pact between the parties to the political consensus of the 'golden age' of the liberal social democratic era, which has since been vanquished by a more extreme political ideology. The prescriptions of the open society were designed to encourage a greater commitment to social mobility through meritocratic achievement, at the workplace and through education. Meritocracy means an agreed system of differential rewards, status and power, seen to be fair and reasonable and providing more to those whose positions in society carried more weight and responsibility. With regard to education meritocracy implied, for adult education, a commitment to learning as a lifelong process, properly institutionalised and offering flexible access to a variety of opportunities for all. These ideas are embodied in the spirit of the major reports on adult education and their advocacy of a comprehensive, community based service, continuous with the front-end model of educational provision. Reality proved otherwise and some of the reasons for the demise of education as a significant force for change are outlined below.

The central problem of education is the wastage of talent and underachievement, unearthed by a series of studies and reports on different levels of the education system in the 1960s[2]. These studies showed that there was a large pool of untapped ability, as measured by intelligence tests, amongst the adult population. Their abilities had gone undetected or had not developed during their school careers. Either way a great deal of sociological attention was directed towards explaining the social influences on learning and achievement in education.

The major factor identified by research studies was the influence of social class background as a determinant of success[3]. Social class as a research concept used in the context of these studies was regarded as a multi-dimensional variable. Thus social class referred to economic and cultural factors, both operating in complex ways to influence learning and achievement motivation.

Social class exerted an influence in several ways. Economically it determined 'life chances' and levels of living such as housing conditions, family income and residency in different types of neighbourhoods. The latter often determined the state of the schools attended with poorer neighbourhoods having poorly equipped and staffed schools, in keeping with similarly inadequate cultural and environmental facilities in the immediate surroundings. Social class in this sense expressed the connection between economic and cultural factors, with the former setting limits on the latter. This shows up clearly in studies of class sub-cultures and family life where class affected personal attitudes and values. The lower the social class the more limited the cultural horizons, reducing ambition and motivation to a 'getting by' strategy rather than an aspiring and achieving one. There were exceptions to this general rule, as adult education continually testifies, but the weight of the research evidence was convincing. For the exceptionally bright and ambitious their struggle was to sustain the considerable effort required to climb up the ladder of individual success from a lower position on the rungs than their middle class counterparts.

Social class is not the only explanation of wastage and under-achievement and much research has been focussed on the role of education in rejection and reducing motivation by complex psychological processes. Studies have suggested that achievement is influenced by such elusive factors as the general atmosphere of the school, teacher-pupil relationships, teacher expectations and the learner's self image. Moreover the organisation of learning; through the content of the curriculum, teaching methods, provision of learning resources, timetabling, ability grouping and so forth have all been identified as having a bearing on achievement motivation. The important point to grasp is the complexity of factors affecting educational attainment. Social class is a major element although its influence on learning and attainment is difficult to determine without the need to indicate all the other factors involved which may not be directly related to social class.

The bearing of these findings on adult education works in two ways. First it offers a package of explanations of non-participation. An earlier chapter dealt with this area of knowledge with regard to the influence of social class and sub-cultural values and lifestyles on attitudes towards adult education. Another chapter, by emphasising the awareness in adult education of the need to innovate more relevant forms of provision for working class adults, implicitly acknowledged the negative effects of early educational experiences and the normal desire not to return to the ethos of school life. The lessons of all this are mostly felt in the organisation of adult education provision.

The second lesson of these findings transpires through descriptive and auto-biographical accounts of adult students. Certainly with biographical research into the backgounds of adults returning to learning the significance of early educational experiences and social background is paramount in explaining why and how they embark upon formal study leading to university degree courses or similar activities involving a considerable amount of personal change. Rather less directly, accounts of the characteristics of adult students usually imply some reference to prior education and how this affects attitudes towards learning and the self. This often emerges as a problem with learning and study skills, rusted over after a long absence from education. Similarly the past experience of school life may be more inclined towards relative failure than modest success, manifesting as a lack of self-confidence, underestimation of intellectual ability and the fear of failure. These and other things pose questions about the best ways of teaching adults and enabling them to learn, not only effectively but happily.

The ideal realm of adult student studies with its predominant focus on the themes of economic efficiency, equality of opportunity and the problems of wastage and social class influences on learning and achievement links to the backgrounds of adult students in another way through the theme of 'second chance' adult education. Historically adult education has provided opportunities for people to return to learning and overcome early failures, and for some the chance to go on to higher education. Adult education is not the only influence at work. Autobiographical accounts of successful people from previous socially disadvantaged backgrounds highlight the importance of meeting particular people at critical times in their lives. Their influence awakened deep seated needs, tapped latent abilities and showed the various routes and directions to take out of the limitations of the disadvantaged background of restricted language, impoverished culture, slum conditions and low self-confidence. But the road to university and successful careers has to include a great deal of hard learning as an adult. For some the route is by self-directed study. For others it is by a variety of formal routes – the WEA, university extension, vocational/technical training, education through the armed services and so on. Even the rather casual and informal learning typical of clubs and other voluntary associations have provided a starting point for more serious learning. Similarly, the accounts of adult students testify to the stimulus effect of informal discussion, media programmes, cultural activity and recreation in setting off or reinforcing the desire to learn more and achieve long term personal goals. To regard all this as adult education is a matter of personal interpretation but it is undoubtedly significant as learning experiences leading to formal study. An elastic view of adult education would embrace these ideas about learning and personal change under the theme of the 'second chance'.

Specifically, the idea of the second chance has several facets[4]. Historically adult education has provided a first chance for some to learn in the absence of child education. The organisation of Sunday schools for adults to learn to read and write expresses this idea. In modern times second chance refers to the provision of learning opportunities for those whose early education was marred by a lack of success for a variety of reasons – personality and temperament, social background limitations, selection errors and other aspects of educational administration and organisation. The best way of characterising this idea of second chance is to refer to such adult students as late developers. A book on this theme used another term, 'Breakthrough', to express how some adults made up for a poor start at the school stage by later efforts and achievements as an adult. Another category are more aptly described as 'drop-outs' insofar as they never made use of their opportunities after a fairly good start at school but after leaving had second thoughts and returned to formal learning with renewed vigour. A final category are those who did well at school and established themselves in reasonable jobs and careers only to seek new avenues later. Education in this context provides the second chance for a change of career or lifestyle.

The idea of the second chance is both an idealistic and practical expression of vision and thought in adult education, with both a long historical strand and contemporary relevance. It provides a remedy for the failings of the educational system and the restrictions of class inequality while at the same time forging a functional link between the sectors of education –school to higher education. Second chance adult education has direct personal meaning to adults seeking to overcome their own sense of under-achievement or as a means of redirecting their lives along new avenues of learning, vocation and lifestyle. Like so many other ideas in adult education it is best regarded as an elastic meaning, conveying and reflecting the diverse motives, needs and characteristics of adult students as well as the complex relationship between education, society and the individual.

Finally, the idea of 'second chance' should quite easily be incorporated into the principles of continuing or recurrent education because adults require access to learning opportunities that are easy to secure and approach, with a curriculum that is diverse in terms of subject range and learning methods. Adults seeking second chances to achieve educationally also need a system that is flexible in the manner of its presentation and delivery which also upholds the principles of equity and democratic participation in decision making, particularly in those sensitive areas of learning and administration where tutors and students interact with each other. These ideas once more express the elastic nature of the second chance ideal in adult education as well as its practical and personal dimensions.

Turning to the second area of adult student studies reference has already been made in passing to some examples of the literature[5]. The key area to comprehend are those studies which focus, partially or wholly, on the reasons why adults return to learning and how they do so. There are many descriptive accounts. The biographical studies of the self-educated, for instance, focus on their character traits which is comprised of a mixture of puritan virtue, non-deferential attitudes, a certain awkwardness, aloofness and a rather narrow outlook on life, often fixed by religious zeal, political radicalism, ambition and an abiding thirst for knowledge for its own sake. It should be apparent that no one adult could possibly represent all those complex behaviour patterns but together they portray them as rather exceptional people, albeit of a past era.

In more contemporary accounts on the 'breakthrough' theme they are described as people of determination and ambition, tenacious and clear sighted in their pursuit of personal goals. Ability is seen as an unfolding process arising from the awakening impact of mental stimulus, good personal guidance and examples set by mentors, blended with a certain amount of good luck. From unpromising social origins the 'breakthroughs' took advantage of second chance education in adult life to become prominent political and trade union leaders, academics, writers and businessmen. The routes to their success for this atypical group were diverse, ranging from the influence of significant others, ambitious mothers, positive influences at school and work, army life, involvement in local associations and the charisma of certain teachers. At the same time this process of self determination created some stresses with estrangement from relatives, work strain and an inner psychological struggle to succeed. The solitary nature of the climb up the ladder of success has been noted by at least one writer as producing a conflict of values between the culture of the working class with its ideas of solidarity and of the middle class with its ideal of individualism[6]. This can produce a rather rootless person, marginal to class and community origins and an uneasy member of a new class. More on that theme later.

It would be possible to continue with other descriptions of adult/mature students but as summaries of these appear elsewhere there is little purpose to be served. However, it is useful to outline a theoretical model, used for research purposes, giving a conceptual framework to the 'how' and 'why' focus. This model combines descriptive survey methods with focussed interviews based around self-reported biographical accounts of the process of becoming an adult/mature student. Although the model was used on mature students in university it has general applicability in locating the sources of influence and the educational routes taken towards higher forms of learning[7].

Following a typical progress in a personal career it is possible to identify overlapping stages from the home and family to different school levels and then to work, community and post school education. Each of these stages represented by social institutions (family, school, work, etc.) can be examined from three related perspectives – structural, cultural and relational. These are best presented under these simplified headings and selected items.

STRUCTURAL	CULTURAL	RELATIONAL
(meaning aspects of social orgnisation)	*(meaning attitudes, values and behaviour)*	*(meaning aspects of social relations and interaction)*
eg	*eg*	*eg*
1. Social class of family 2. Type of schooling 3. Work experience 4. Social mobility 5. Achieved social class	1. Self perceived values of home, school and neighbourhood 2. Workplace culture 3. Leisure activities 4. Community activities	1. Peer influence 2. Parent influence 3. Teacher influence 4. Significant others
providing demographic data used to chart personal status and change	providing qualitative data on perceptions and experiences affecting achievement motivation	providing qualitative data on perceptions and experiences affecting achievement motivation

The model is simpler than it appears. Each item provides a focal point for questions about why and how an adult changes from being a relative underachiever during the school/child stage to someone with the motivation, tenacity and educational achievement record sufficient for progress to a university degree as an adult. The only reasonably reliable way into this metamorphosis is to chart the progress by common measures of social status and self perceived autobiography, which tells the story as the teller thought and felt it happened. This is not the final word on accuracy, of course, for storytelling is difficult without some embroidery. Yet it is better than an outsider's interpretation. Moreover the model is not rigid and elements can be modified and replaced according to the specific requirements of the research project. The value of the model is in providing a reasonably systematic framework for the analysis of the process of becoming an adult/mature student. It provides a means of organising the various studies of this aspect of adult/mature student biographies and descriptive backgrounds, many of which are partial and somewhat scattered across the literature.

To make sense of many of the theoretical studies of adult students some general appreciation of the sociological perspectives upon which they are based is necessary. These fall under the micro-sociological theory perspectives often referred to as social action or interactionist theories. A rather more general introduction is required before defining this aspect of sociology.

There are two kinds of sociology applied to adult student studies. The first is the descriptive empirical used in participation research, often with little theoretical basis but practically useful for administrative and policymaking purposes. The second is theoretical sociology comprising both 'holistic' and social action perspectives. Holistic theories are used to discuss wider social issues such as equality of opportunity, the problem of underachievement and the role of adult education in providing 'second chances' to overcome earlier set-backs to attainment. Social action theories are used to more closely understand the processes of becoming and being an adult student.

Whatever perspective is used very little of this sociology can claim to be unique to adult student studies. Most of the studies have adapted and applied sociological ideas and methods from a variety of sources. Moreover the borderline between sociology and psychology is very blurred in examining the complex biographies of adults finding their way into education and making progress academically, intellectually and vocationally. This is because most adults go through a demanding process of personal change affecting their identity, social relationships, social roles and values. These changes go far wider than a single focus on education and learning can comprehend. Similarly, a narrow sociological focus would miss much of significance about adult students as people as well as learners.

The theoretical perspectives within sociology used from this point is drawn mainly from the social action or interactionist approaches. Like systems theory there are several perspectives but at this juncture it is necessary to outline its general meaning first.

Systems theory interprets social relations in terms of society as a whole (such as the problem of underachievement and the relationship between social class and equality of opportunity in society), seeking sound generalisations about social behaviour in macroscopic ways. Social action theory takes a predominantly microscopic, individually focussed perspective on social relations. This approach can dovetail quite comfortably with the larger scale generalisations of systems theory even though its starting point is the everyday interactions of people. This will emerge later in some of the theories to be illustrated.

Whereas the systems approach, by taking a global view emphasising social structure (institutions and roles, norms and values), regards these influences as 'out there' beyond the individual's control, the social action approach pays attention to the particular aspects of social relations and interaction stemming from what goes on 'inside' the heads of individuals. The essential point is that what goes on inside the minds of individuals is usually meaningful to them. This remains the case even though individuals vary enormously in their perceptions, experiences and interpretations of the society around them. This contrasts quite markedly with the view of society as something given and handed down through cultural transmission and socialisation which is passively assimilated and incorporated into social behaviour through role playing and observance of norms and values. In the social action perspective society is constructed by the meaningful actions of individuals giving rise to considerable variations of behaviour and at the same time broad patterns of social relations forming the framework of norms and values underpinning social order. These broad patterns are continuously made and re-made according to the changing nature of individual interpretations of reality. These are as many and varied as the diversity of individual experiences and perceptions.

It would appear that the systems and social action perspectives present an either/or view of social relations. This need not be the case for even the most determinist perspective is bound to acknowledge the importance of individual variation and subjectivity. This view still gives prominence to social structure as setting the goals and means of social behaviour and relationships of individuals, while at the same time noting subjective interpretation and action, especially in a diverse and complex society. This means that the individual is not a puppet but a perceiving, thinking, feeling person with the capacity to make particular adjustments and terms with the 'outside world' leading to different ways of achieving goals within a broad framework of social rules of conduct, norms and values. This suggests the idea of common and consensual values typical of functionalist theory. It also applies to social situations where conformity to societal norms and values are enforced by fear and repression, for it can be observed that people find ways of 'working the system' by guile and small acts of individual deviousness. These personal strategies provide a few crumbs of comfort and enable the individual to live with a social world mostly beyond personal control and making.

This rather generalised connection between the determinism of systems theory and the subjectivity and variability of individual behaviour in the social action approach reduces the latter to a rather residual position. Other views of social action theory gives individual subjective meaning theoretical priority. In explaining this further some background on the ideas of the founding writers on this sociological perspective is useful.

The ideas of Weber are the starting point for social action theories. Weber presented four ideal types of individual social action – traditional (bound by custom), affectual (motivated by emotion) and two forms of rational action defined in terms of subjective meaning and interpretation. These were called, respectively zweckrational and wertrational. The former refers to instrumental actions where the individual calculates the means and utility of achieving personal goals. The idea of instrumental adjustment applied to adult students is an example of the zweckrational kind of social action. This will be examined fully later. The latter wertrational kind of social action is more concerned with a personal goal as an end in itself. This might be compared to the pursuit of knowledge and a love of learning as an ideal state of mind, conferring no particular economic or social benefits. Liberal adult education upholds this interpretation of learning and individual behaviour in a pure and ideal sense. Adult students pursuing established personal interests or embarking upon new subjects out of interest personifies this form of social action and educational ideal.

A conceptual development from Weber's ideas is the school of symbolic interactionism derived from the writings of two American sociologists, C. Cooley (1864-1929) and G.M. Mead (1863-1931)[8]. Both writers focussed their attention on interaction between individuals and members of small groups. Weber was more concerned to explain the 'fit' between the individual and social structure. This line of thought can be traced through to the positivism of modern day systems theories and the demands of objective analysis by the conventions of empirical research. Symbolic interactionism was begun as a conceptual means of understanding the effects of subjective meanings of social reality on individual social interaction. The problem of this and related perspectives is to link their insights back into macroscopic and holistic theories of society.

The specific contribution of symbolic interactionism is in stressing the partial independence from society of individual subjective experiences. At the heart of this theory is the idea that there is a critical difference between animal and human behaviour because the latter possesses a mind which provides the capacity to choose from a variety of possible courses of action. Self consciousness and identity is the key feature of human behaviour and this is mediated through complex symbols of communication such as language. People use language to convey thoughts and feelings to others and these serve to communicate the uniqueness of the self and interpretations of the external world. Mind is an integral part of our nature and it is the basis of social interaction through language and action. As well as acting upon external influences the mind generates self-directed action and at the same time reflects upon the effects of those actions upon others and the self.

These insights took sociology into a far less deterministic direction and posed a challenge to orthodox research methods. The problem with systems theories is their deterministic view of social relations which reduces social behaviour to a simple response mechanism. Theories of society founded upon such a view uphold a rigid research methodology which although technically correct overlook the highly individual nature of behaviour and the way experiences, thoughts and feelings determine from the 'inside', as it were, interactions with society. The individual variability of social behaviour clashes with the idea of positivist sociology which uses the assumptions and methods of the natural sciences to uncover general laws of social behaviour. The assumption of this approach is that laws of cause and effect in human affairs are as given as the behaviour of animals and matter. Such an approach has great problems dealing with individual variation in social behaviour and weakens the empirical validity of holistic interpretations of social relations and society.

Social action theories adopt a phenomenological approach, meaning research starts from the perceived meanings and subsequent actions of the subjects of sociological inquiry. It is their self-consciousness and internal logic that is important as a guide to social interaction and behaviour, not that imposed by the researcher bent on fitting data to an existing theory of society. The phenomenologist examines the self-reported insights and understandings of their research subjects rather than cause and effect relationships. The latter is useful for large scale research of populations where it is desirable to chart social trends, such as the take-up of educational and welfare services by different social groups. The phenomenological approach is better suited to smaller scale research projects where it is important to know what people were thinking and feeling and how this affected their behaviour. There is no absolute measure of this kind of phenomena. The exactitude of the natural sciences is unobtainable. Instead reliance is placed on sensible interpretation and intuition regarding meaning and social behaviour. Such an approach is useful in biographical research on adult students especially in charting their progress into full time study from unpromising beginnings involving considerable personal change and the working out of complex goals, values and relationships. The idea of an educational 'career' outlined previously where adults return to serious study after a school career of relative underachievement is an example of this kind of research. The framework is only a sketch map giving a general direction which has to be detailed by the highly personal accounts of individual adult students.

After this brief digression into research methodology it is necessary to return to the main task of outlining the branches of social action perspectives. Essentially they are alike and the distinctions between them are of degree only. Symbolic interactionism by emphasising the use of symbols such as language in communication and interaction deals with the processes that relate individual actions to the broader framework of society through role relationships and socialisation into norms and values. Phenomenology is concerned with examining the assumptions and recipe knowledge of everyday life as a means of understanding the meanings behind social interaction. The guiding idea is that everyday knowledge represents a store of meanings upon which social actions are based. These social actions are not random but logically constructed into meanings by the individual. Through time and experience many meanings become common property and typical knowledge providing a useful structure to many social actions. This is referred to as the life-world.

Phenomenological sociology owes much to the work of A. Schutz (1899-1959)[9]. He argued that people arrive at their version of meaning as a basis of action from two related processes. The first is that social action is governed by internal motives which refers to future goals to be attained by interaction with others. This happens through role playing and relationships with social institutions, such as adult education. The second area of meaningful action derives from reflection upon personal needs and the history of the self that has led the individual to act in certain ways. For the most part the social actions that follow are based on worked out personal meanings deeply related to personal identity and self-knowledge. From that basis social interaction is a meaningful process of negotiation with others involving personal strategies of behaviour to reach personal goals. In this process it helps to have clear sighted goals, determination, ability and sufficient power to promote an individual view of reality. This characterises the biographies of people who make successful changes to their lives and amongst these are many adult students.

Finally there is ethnomethodology which is more concerned with the rules people invent for themselves to solve problems and accomplish practical goals in a rational way – (people's methods' in the literal meaning of ethnomethodology – a term invented by H. Garfinkel (b.1917)[10]. Like the other social action perspectives there is a critical view of the impositions of systems theory taken for granted assumptions about social life and the rigidities of positivist research methods.

Ethnomethodology starts from the idea that social life is orderly simply because people are constantly at work trying to make sense of their world to others and convince them of their meaning of everyday reality. This leads to common agreements as to the meanings of everyday life which become both taken for granted, recipe knowledge and at the same time endlessly open to re-intepretation as a means of keeping in contact with others. The problem for those experiencing personal change and movement between different groups, each with their own cultural meanings, is to learn the rules of the game with each individual, group and institutional encounter. Adult students in making their way through educational and social worlds have to learn to adapt to others and invent their own rules of survival. This is more than just learning the subject matter of a course. It is essentially about the nuances of cultural worlds.

In sum social action perspectives hold some key ideas in common. The first is that social interaction is meaningful to those involved and comprise a large number of mutual agreements underpinning the expectations of social roles and relationships. These agreements are based on common meanings mediated through language and non-verbal communication. Moreover such meanings are not fixed but fluid and responsive to change. These changes are brought about by individual actions and the complex process of negotiating an acceptance of the self by others. The rules of everyday living are carved out of such exchanges involving give and take and the nuances of social learning. This kind of sociology starts with the idea of the individual self and how the self-concept is developed from the multitude of interactions with others. Because we are both acting and reflecting beings we define ourselves in relation to how others regard us – the idea of the 'looking glass self'. At the same time we have some power to persuade others of our definition of reality. Hence the idea of the negotiated self. The social context in which the individual operates provides a variable means of expressing the complex levels of the self and the possible varieties of social interaction. The social world for many is tight and restrictive with norms and values imposed on individual behaviour from above-authority systems typical of formal organisations and totalitarian political regimes. Indeed every group imposes some restrictions on individuality. Yet for all that, there is usually some leeway whereupon the individual can explore a niche which is personally comfortable and meaningful. The use of these extreme images of a deterministic social context is deliberate and demonstrates the significance of the self as a focus of sociological interest.

It is not really necessary to grasp the details of these perspectives to appreciate their general value as an insight into individual behaviour and social interaction. Holistic sociological theory by itself is too generalised and superficially at least treats individuals like puppets or cogs of a complex social mechanism. The particular value of social action perspectives is in providing an insight into adult students which starts from their views and experiences and the uniqueness of individual behaviour. This certainly does not rule out the observation of patterns of behaviour, like the relationship between social background and participation in adult education. Nor does it diminish the importance of such themes as social inequality and its relationship to educational opportunity and achievement. And in interpreting the role of education in society, conventional, liberal and radical ideal type perspectives are made more meaningful by understanding different political ideologies and consensus and conflict models of society. But for those seeking a microscopic perspective of adult students before enlarging the focus it is useful to appreciate the main ideas of social action perspectives.

With these ideas as a background it is easier to proceed to those adult student studies which have either borrowed sociological theories or generated them. Two examples deal with the concept of social role and these will be outlined first. Attention then turns to two general sociological concepts that can be applied to adult student studies. These are the concepts of status passage and marginality, neither of which have been much used in empirical research although their potential application is considerable. Finally the theory section is rounded off by outlining the major contribution of sociological perspectives to adult students which brings into account many ideas and concepts touched on elsewhere.

The first selected illustration of theoretical studies of adult students/learners is from the American developmental psychologist R.J. Havighurst. His paper 'Changing Status and Roles During the Adult Life Cycle: Significance for Adult Education' combines psychological and sociological insights and provides a forerunner for optimistic scenarios for the future educational system devised on the ideas of lifelong learning[11].

Predicting the future, Havighurst argued that education was changing from a preparatory system to a lifelong, continuous one designed to meet learning needs throughout the life cycle. This was a significant contribution to the critical appraisal of the limitations of the 'front-end' model and the relevance of the continuing education model for a rapidly changing society. It also challenged the traditional view of education as a storehouse of knowledge, rather than an instrument of learning, which in a changing society was better suited to the need for retraining and the acquisition of adaptive social and economic skills, ideas and values.

The kinds of learning required embraces both instrumental and expressive, that is, practical and vocational for future purposes and the intrinsic benefits of learning for its own sake, related to immediate needs and interests. Both forms of learning are necessary throughout the life cycle and at each phase and stage of adult development. Havighurst conceived of the life cycle as a series of sequentially related developmental stages, generally linked to age groupings and changing roles. Each stage is characterised by dominant concerns which require both instrumental and expressive learning to achieve competence at these developmental tasks. The concept of developmental tasks comprises three forces – biological changes of the ageing process, demands and expectations of social roles taken on during adulthood and personal aspirations and goals.

With regard to social roles Havighurst argued that throughout life adults took on commitments to others and to the self and these are mediated through the major roles of worker, parent, spouse, neighbour, friend and so on. At different stages of the life cycle some roles were predominant concerns and in an increasingly complex society required new learning and adaptive attitudes to rise to the challenges they posed – being a competent worker or well informed citizen, for instance.

Closely linked to these social roles is the self. There is a normal desire to want to perform well at social roles for these are often the basis upon which the self is judged and accepted by others as competent, reliable, hardworking and so on. Furthermore the self in progressing through the stages of life is faced with developmental tasks of an individually challenging kind. In adult life these can be focussed on establishing oneself as an acceptable, competent person; exerting and asserting oneself; taking and maintaining responsibility; changing roles successfully; handling the zenith phase of career and life; preparing to disengage and making the most of disengagement in all spheres of one's life. Developmental psychologists have labelled these phases as the achievement of identity (personal and occupational); intimacy with others; generativity (giving oneself fully and successfully in various spheres of life); and the final phase of integrity, which is a view of one's life as worthwhile.

Havighurst is at pains to point out that these ideas are not to be regarded as fixed and pre-determined to fit particular ages and stages, but rather as guidelines of thought and a broad conceptual framework for direction in the life cycle. Moreover Havighurst acknowledges the culturally specific nature of these ideas which accord more with the middle class ideal than the real life circumstances of relatively disadvantaged groups and other ethnic groupings.

The self-acknowledged limitations of Havighurst's ideas need no further discussion. Nonetheless the broad scope of his framework is useful. It provides insight into two related processes that explain adult involvement in education and learning. The first is the idea of changing roles and status positions during the life cycle. The second is the pursuit of education and learning for deep seated personal reasons connected with psychological states of mind, such as self-esteem, confidence and feeling valued through doing things that are regarded as socially worthwhile.

These ideas present themselves strongly and clearly in the popularity of education for women. Many are in the process of handling quite complex social roles, such as spouse, parent, homemaker and at the same time seeking a satisfying work role or career, which confers personal and economic independence. Moreover the world of work provides recognition and status in a way that being a home based person does not. This relates to the deep seated psychological needs referred to earlier. Work has traditionally provided a sense of self-worth for men and now women are seeking the same opportunities. Whereas child bearing and rearing meets some needs it no longer embraces them all, if it ever did.

Both men and women in adult education are often aware of the several levels of purpose behind their desire for learning, often involving considerable personal change and some conflict with the expectations and demands of others. At one level are the instrumental motives associated with learning vocational skills. These can be accompanied by a recognition of the value of learning for its own sake. Just as likely is the awareness that learning involves the self in different challenges going beyond the acquisition of knowledge to the realms of self-confidence and self-esteem. More than that learning is a means of self-assertion and personal competence at aspects of life that continually demand being in command of oneself. Certainly many occupations pose that challenge but so do the complex areas of inter-personal relations in the community, home and family life. Finally many adult students regard themselves as in the process of self-directed personal change having ramifications on social roles, social status, interactions and relations with others, and a far reaching appraisal and reorganisation of personal values and behaviour.

At this point the insights of social action sociology has much to offer in terms of the subjective meanings adults attach to learning activities and involvement in education. The work of Havighurst assumes that adults seek education as a form of adjustment to society 'out there', through learning new skills, attitudes and other competencies. This is probably the case but the ways in which adults make such adjustments are varied and very personal. This means that the form or way these adjustments are made are essentially voluntary, guided by inner needs and volitions and subjectively meaningful on a very individual basis. Therefore it would be an error to assume a uniform and deterministic relationship between adults and education. Each contract is an individual one reflecting different stages, dominant concerns and needs. Each contract between an adult and education, even tenuous ones, represents a significant personal gesture which exposes the individual to self needs, part of which is related to changing roles and status and part concerned with the particular challenges to the self which are asocial and unique.

In the light of these observations the implications for adult education are for an individually orientated, learner centred service, as far as practicable tailored to individual needs and variations. This is indeed the way in which adult education has responded to a changing world, except perhaps for the conventional, work training approach. This may be because much of the recent growth in that form of provision stems from political contingencies dealing with the massive problems of unemployment and training. Furthermore such provision is directed from outside the normal circles of adult eucation thought and practice.

Another, more recent study also presents a theoretical perspective on the concept of social role applied to the adult student. G. Harries-Jenkins in his article 'The Role of the Adult Student' starts from the standpoint of a critical appraisal of the conventional use of the sociological concept in adult education and argues for the analytical value of the social action/interactionist perspective [1][2].

Running through adult education, in keeping with other branches of institutionalised education, is the notion of the good student. In the attainment orientated world of education where knowledge and excellence are valued the 'good student' represents an ideal state. The idea of a good student with its regard for achievement, excellence and conformity to the values of the educators is heavily prescribed by the latter on the former. The role of the student becomes a stereotype of deterministic values and normative expectations. The expected behaviour of the good student, therefore, is an ideal vision. This way of thinking is most overt in the conventional wisdom of liberal adult education with its traditional homage to academic and intellectual excellence and ideal of civilised cultural values founded upon a reverence for knowledge and learning. But even in the utilitarian world of training the good student is one who demonstrates competencies in the various skills taught.

In the voluntary world of adult education the student role is marginal to the other interests and commitments of most participants. Educational activity as a student or learner is a minor role and adults do not invest themselves significantly. Therefore adult students do not submit themselves to the prescriptions of tutors as readily. This is a generalisation for it is clear that how adults perceive the values and expectations of tutors depends upon their commitment to the student role and making a success of it. The previous descriptions of adult students underline the seriousness of their commitment, in terms of the efforts they make and the extent to which their sense of self-esteem and identity as a peson is involved. Thus it needs to be borne in mind that there are different kinds of adult students in degree of commitment and involvement. For many the student role is a minor activity whereas for some it is a matter of intense importance, for all kinds of instrumental and expressive reasons, and is a major undertaking.

The point of Harries-Jenkins' argument is to shift attention away from the systems theory approach to role to a social action perspective. In the systems perspective role is regarded in terms of the closeness of fit between the individual and the norms and values of educational institutions, and society in general. Role is the mediating acting part or social construction that relates the individual to society. This takes place in a pre-determined way through the process of socialisation into norms and values, underpinned by positive and negative sanctions. There is much to be claimed for this rather abstract approach to social relations applied to adult education for it provides an example of society at work. It also provides a means of illustrating the functions of adult education as a sub-system of society; in transmitting culture, socialising into prevailing norms and values, skill training, vocational preparation, regulating ambitions, providing second chance opportunities and so forth.

Nevertheless the perspective is not responsive to individual behaviour and the meanings, significance and complex processes by which adults voluntarily engage in education and learning activities. From the social action perspective the individual negotiates a particular relationship between the self and learning. This view encompasses the complex needs of the individual which are derived from a variety of influences from other roles and social backgrounds. The obvious examples of this idea are socio-economic status, cultural experiences, living environment, family and work roles. Each of these comprise a variety of everyday experiences conferring different kinds of rewards, stimulus, negative feelings. The work role for instance provides economic rewards which may be perceived by the adult as insufficient, or status which is low, authority, power and autonomy which are virtually non-existent. Together they represent a source of alienation and agitation to resolve these conditions by regarding education and qualifications as an escape route to better prospects. Some of the biographies of mature students at university refer to the negative experience of the work role as an incentive to obtain more education. Just as likely, some mature students regarded work experience as a helpful stepping stone to higher education by providing day release, training facilities, personal encouragement and promotion opportunities.

The point is that the work roles of individuals are differently experienced and the relationship with adult education that follows is an individually felt and negotiated contract meeting very particular needs and interests. The social action perspective on the student role provides access to these inner dynamics of thought, feeling and experiences derived from the complexity of an adult's everyday context. In this view the student role is created and experienced by each individual according to their unique backgrounds. This is an altogether more sophisticated view of role than the mechanistic approach of systems theory. The 'fit' between adult education and individuals through the student role is essentially a merging of conventional expectations and prescriptions of the tutor with the uniquely determined needs of the student. This involves, often at a very subtle level, a considerable amount of inter-personal adjustment to each other's expectations. This negotiated process of interaction is compatible with the ideas of student-centred learning, developmental psychology and andragogy.

The other matter of significance arising from a re-appraisal of the concept of the student role is that adult education is regarded in a much broader context. The orthodox approach to the student role prescribes the values of a dominant interest group in education (the liberal idea of scholarship and excellence). This narrows the concept of education. The effect is to exclude a wide range of learning activities taking place in informal, community based settings involving adults with far less acquaintance with formal educational values and practices. Some of this community based learning is geared towards social and political action representing a power struggle between authority and unequal groups. The lofty view of education and the student role discounts such activity as having any learning significance and, indirectly, the alternative values of community, class and group solidarity. The alternative view would have little reverence for the conventional view of the student role and might even regard it as an expression of cultural hegemony of the dominant classes in society.

Related to the idea of changing roles and different ways of perceiving the concept is the idea of social status. This concept is mostly used to refer to a social position, typically in a hierarchy of socio-economic positions or in terms of prestige ranking. Hence the use of the term social status in adult education participation studies to indicate the socio-economic backgrounds of students and non-participants. Similarly social status can be used to refer to the standing of the student role in society. It is difficult to be precise for there are mixed views on the social importance of the student role. As a generalisation it carries only a lowly status. This may be because adults have other major role commitments. It is also poorly rewarded. Grant aid to mature students in higher education, for instance, is barely sufficient to survive economically. At the same time, adults who do become full time students are admired for their courage and determination which suggests some status to be derived from the esteem the role carries. Whatever the particular views the idea of social status is to confer on the student role some standing in society, in just the same way as the role of housewife, tutor and other kinds of workers have status. Moreover a particular social status is not fixed but subject to re-evaluation and change in the eyes of society.

There is another idea of social status, called status passage, which is the focus of this theory section[13]. It is a concept that has been used on other subjects than adult students but it has valuable insights on the process of changing roles and the process of becoming a student.

The process of becoming an adult student, especially on a full time basis, entails movement through social positions which has some effect on personal identity and sense of belonging. Examples of these are the change of status and role from being a housewife or paid worker to being a full time adult student. The movement from one status position to another, involving some change in social prestige, as well as role and personal identity, is termed status passage.

It might be visualised as a corridor or elevator, conveying the person from one social position (made up of roles, relations with others in role sets, personal identity and different kinds of status – economic, prestige and power) to another. An example of the process of status passage would be the public declaration of the intention to marry. This is a signal to others to keep their hands off the bride-to-be; a planning stage for the wedding ceremony, often involving inter-family connections; and observance by the engaged couple of the conventions of fidelity and building up a bottom drawer of household chattels. There is no doubt that the change of status from singlehood to marriage is a major change of status position. Status passage is the in-between stage of moving from one status to the other. It is also a rule bound passage, as the above illustration suggests. Before going further with the application of the concept to adult student studies more explanation about status passage theory is necessary.

The concept of status passage may be seen as a movement between statuses joined together by age (from adolescence to adulthood), social position (fiancé to marriage), organisational position (foreman to manager), and occupational position (worker to unemployed status). These movements may entail locating oneself from, say, a primary involvement in the home and family to an educational institution, or from one part of the social structure (employment) to another (education). The essence of any status is that it is always a temporary position implying some eventual change and exit. The precise nature of the status passage may be associated with various kinds of personal gratification, such as the passage into marriage, child bearing, job promotion or the student role. It may also involve grief, disorientation, and a sense of loss of privilege, influence and power, arising from the death of a partner, leaving a marriage, going to hospital, becoming a student, retirement, etc. The notion of status passage implies a great deal of personal adjustment, learning and change for there is a great deal of new knowledge and experience to comprehend and act upon, such as becoming a student.

Status passages are governed by fairly clear rules concerning when the change of status should be made, by whom and by specified agencies. Thus admission to a course of study is normally prescribed by rules of application and selection. There are prescribed steps to take in order to complete the passage properly. It is one thing to be fired by a burning desire to enter a college or monastery or become a settler in another country and quite another to submit to the processes of selection, personal examination and control by bureaucratic forces. In other words, scheduling, regulation and prescription are integral features of status passage. An umbrella term for these processes is rites of passage.

There are other properties of status passage which may be outlined without discussion. From the standpoint of the individual a passage may be deemed desirable/undesirable, inevitable or not inevitable, reversible, repeatable, experienced alone or with others, consciously or unconsciously entered. Although aware of the passage the person may not be able to communicate with others undergoing the same experience. But this is rare for one of the essential features of a status passage is the commonality of many of the experiences, hence the customs and rules associated with most passages. Status passages differ with regard to the amount of personal control an individual can exert over the transition. Furthermore the clarity of the various elements of a passage (values, norms and sanctions) may be variable in quality and in some cases not easy to understand. The centrality of a particular status passage in a person's life will vary. For some the passage is uneventful or unremarkable, whereas for others it is seen as a major personal event leading to new ideas and life changes. Finally the length of time it takes to go through a status passage will also vary.

It would be possible to discuss each of these properties in relation to adult students but many are self evident and do not require elaboration. There are two general problems of status passage, though, worthy of further explanation, expressed by the terms dislocation and dovetailing. With regard to dislocation the assumption is that the process of shedding and acquiring status positions, such as housewife to student, affects the stability and continuity of personal identity leading to the re-evaluation of self, new relationships and behaviour. The ease with which the transition from one status to another can be made depends upon the prevailing flexibility within an adult's cultural and economic milieu. A rigid social world with tight expectations on role behaviour and relations with others would make the passage to student status fraught with conflict. Emotional problems would probably ensue from a difficult passage, undermining motivation and personal goals. On the other hand, a more open society where personal change was accepted as normal would benefit adults who choose to return to study and give up, temporarily suspend or give less priority to other role commitments.

The part educational institutions play in minimising the dislocating effects of personal change and smoothing the passage to adult student status is significant. This is expressed by the term dovetailing, which is not a sociological term but one used in wood joinery to illustrate a neat fit. In the particular case of adults and education dovetailing refers to various aspects of provision which enable people to fit as comfortably as possible into the new status and role of being a student. Examining the process of interaction more closely questions may be asked about the ways in which the status passage experiences adult students undergo are made smooth or awkward by their relationship with educational personnel such as administrators, tutors, counsellors, resource staff and other students and by the organisational ethos of the institution, like its rules and regulations, facilities, ambience and sense of community. Biographical accounts of adult students' experiences vary and no single picture emerges but the process of induction into educational institutions and the culture of the world of learning certainly bear regular assessment through status passage analysis.

Another concept of relevance to the idea of transition and change, from familiar roles and statuses to being an adult student, is expressed by the term marginality[14]. Like status passage the concept of marginality is best used from a social action perspective, to get close to the experiences of individuals engaged in a process of change deeper and more significant than a change of role and status.

The concept can be applied to adult students insofar as many of them have experienced the feelings and the fact of being between two worlds: the one left behind and the environment and culture of being a full time student. Not all adult students experience such a major transformation of their social worlds and personal lives but many do undergo the 'terror and the ecstasy' of 'being on the edge' and being an 'in-betweener'. It seems as if the majority of adult students experience limited forms of marginality for returning to study is still regarded as a relatively unusual step to take in adulthood because it is taxing economically, socially, intellectually and emotionally.

Marginal people and situations are to be seen all around – vagrants, disabled, exiles, lonely people, isolated people, religious converts giving up their careers to become evangelists, undeclared gays and various kinds of drop-outs from the mainstream norms and values, behaviour and lifestyles of conventional social groups. The common factor for all is that they feel or have felt marginal to these mainstream groups such as family members, friends, workmates, neighbours and others going about their everyday lives at work, recreation and in the home. They are obliged to adopt or choose to adopt different norms, values and lifestyles that temporarily or permanently set them apart from other people. Some become increasingly marginal before they eventually leave their conventional roles and lifestyles. Others continue to move between various social worlds without settling into anyone of them. Most adult students, though, experience marginality for awhile before making a permanent transition to other roles, status positions and lifestyles.

To understand the concept of marginality more fully it is necessary to start with two quite distinct theories of personal development and change.

The first idea is that adult identity is stable and complete as major changes associated with personal development in the adult stage of life have taken place at earlier stages of the child/adolescent phases. This encourages the belief that adults who depart from the normative expectations of behaviour and values are somewhat deviant and exceptional. Behind this view, admittedly extreme, are psychological theories of maturation and development which lay great emphasis on the significant influences of early stages of growth for the subsequent adult personality. Similarly sociological theories within the social systems approach highlight the importance of the socialisation process through the family, education and other aspects of social structure in determining the norms and values underpinning social roles. Primary socialisation is the social process of forming the idea of a mature adult who has undergone a series of natural and unfolding sequences of development. Adult identity is therefore a relatively fixed feature of a person. Change where it occurs is on a minor scale and towards well defined goals, norms and values designed to enhance the stability of the self and society. Everyday behaviour and interactions is guided by familiar, recipe knowledge.

This stark view of adult identity and development is contrasted by another equally extreme one. This view is the core of the marginality idea and is based around the notion that the self is really endlessly prone to inner directed change. This is more the case in a pluralist society where the sources of influence on the personality, identity and social roles are greater. The pluralist society offers choice, not only of consumer goods and lifestyles but also of the kinds of personality to be and kinds of self-selected identities. The social world is made up of many cultures, each in their own way providing stimulating possibilities about the personas to be acted out in society. The self becomes a composite mixture of ideas and in an active and adventurous lifetime personal change in pursuit of what one might become is normal and healthy and not deviant. The essence of this line of thought is to regard life as a challenging drama of opportunities to live and experience, not with a single identity and self but several. These can be played out sequentially, or for some, simultaneously. Of course, this scenario invites everyday problems of the management of the self and personal change. Moreover, learning new roles and identities is an endless task given to trial and error. More immediately, the pursuit of this idea clashes with the orthodox version of reality with its emphasis upon taking on responsibilities and sticking to allotted roles.

These two ideas bring to the forefront opposing versions of social reality. The first is a conservative, deterministic view of life where roles are handed down and learnt in a conforming way. The first view treats the individual like a puppet to be moulded and pulled into shape. At the other extreme is the idea of the inner directed person creating and modifying roles. It is with regard to the latter perspective that the concept of marginality has its place.

The basic premise is that adult change occurs from the effects of secondary socialisation influencing consciousness and personal behaviour. This does not discount the significance of primary socialisation during the child/adolescent phases of development but simply adds to the duration and widening range of influences arising from the experiences of adult life. This view is straightforward enough and makes commonsense of the observation that adult life is not simply the yoke of roles and responsibilities but a long period of potential awareness and response to the rich sources of stimulus and ideas about ways of living.

The second point is that adults often experience marginality in embarking upon personal and role/status change. This means that adults move away from and to the edge of existing social relations in order to make transition to new ones. This is an unsettling process involving the loosening of ties often before new ones can take their place. Such a process is sustained by conscious thought and self-directed reasoning aimed at achieving personal goals, often pitched at some future and distant date. At the same time the feelings and emotions associated with existing social ties and relations run much deeper and are more resistant to change than intellectual rationalisation. Thus the experience of marginality is often quite painful at the feeling and emotion level. Marginality invites ambivalent feelings such as the intellectual stimulus of self selected and directed change on the one hand and the sense of loss and temporary disorientation on the other. These feelings can be covered up with vigorous action concerned with achieving goals but a subsequent reflecting period brings back ambivalent feelings.

To some extent the reactions of others to the person undergoing change and becoming marginal is crucial in handling the situation as a whole and ambivalent feelings in particular. Acceptance by others or indifference and hostility makes all the difference to being marginal and makes the experience anything from soft and easy to hard and conflict or guilt ridden.

Although this area has not been examined fully, imagine the experiences undergone by adult women who deal with their restlessness at the conventional roles of wife and mother and turn to education as a means of personal expression and change. Just a slight move away from the commitments of everyday roles invites criticism and some degree of antagonism from family members who resist such change in defence of their own interests. This immediately places the woman in a marginal situation vis-a-vis primary social relations. This generates for most women in such a situation considerable inner conflict between divided commitments for the self and others and between thought and emotion. Under such circumstances it is hardly surprising that marriages and other long term relationships come under severe strain, compounding the marginality of the person initiating the changes to their own and others' lives. A supportive network of friends and supporters, often making the same changes, acts as a kind of buffer and source of continued determination. Again this support might hasten the sense of marginality with regard to some relationships while enabling the transition to be made to others. This complex area of social interaction warrants more study.

Marginality is not a single meaning and this needs to be made clear[15]. First there is a broad distinction between those in marginal situations who seek to resist change (called passing) and those who proclaim and embrace it (called coming out). As a generalisation, adult students fall under the second category insofar as they may be assumed to seek change, although their means of proclaiming it may require diplomatic handling of social relationships in the family, workmates, friends and so forth.

Amongst the passers-by two groups emerge − convergers (who play down the differences between their situation and the main values, norms and everyday recipe guidelines of social relations) and quietists (whose ambition is to pass unnoticed and find a secure niche in society). Some disabled people may come into either of these categories, depending on their temperaments and experiences of disabled living in society.

With regard to those who have acknowledged their marginality positively some distinction may be made between the utopians (who stand apart from society but seek to change it) and separatists (who assert the superiority of their lifestyle). It is not clear whether adult students comfortably fit either type of marginality status.

In general terms, people in marginal situations comprise those who are reluctant to change, who do so grudgingly and slowly, contrasting with those who seek it positively and rapidly. The former want to minimise personal change and the latter to undertake major transformation of self and lifestyle. The former are more orientated towards the mainstream of society in terms of norms, values and behaviour, whereas the latter are moving away from such a framework towards the off-beat or radically different lifestyle. For some the experience of marginality is involuntary (like being disabled through accident or illness), while for others it is voluntary. Marginality for some is a chosen permanent state, for others an involuntary permanent state and for yet more a temporary experience. On the latter point, some people experience marginality as the incorporation of new layers of identity combined with elements of the former self, while others seek to shed previous selves and all that is entailed through roles, statuses and relationships. Finally, marginality involves a kind of journey away from one social identity to the centre of another via the margins of society for the purposes of attaining higher social status, power and rewards. For others marginality is a lone journey away from the trappings of everyday society towards some deeply felt sense of personal dignity and being true to oneself. It is only necessary to touch upon the complexity of the experience of marginality to realise the importance of social action perspectives as a means of individual biographical analysis of adult students.

Being more specific, it would be useful to identify the particular experiences of marginality undergone by adult students as they make their way from previous roles, norms and values within their social worlds to the point of entry into being an adult student and progressing through a course of study. At those three points in time – making their way into college or university, just about to start a course, and participating during the course – it should be possible to specify whether or what kinds of marginality are experienced. This should be examined in relation to perceptions of the self, family members, friends, work peers, neighbours, fellow students, course tutors and others. In each case what is examined is the effect of change on roles, norms and values which embrace the notions of relationships, status, culture and lifestyle and personal identity. Together these ideas bring into focus the sense of self-worth, personal fears and joys, sense of success and failure and other factors which make a person feel different and sometimes marginal.

By way of summary, the following points relate the idea of marginality to adult students. In a pluralist society the opportunities for personal change through adult education are seemingly greater. Nonetheless the process of change does involve movement away from one way of life into another. The experience of marginality is fairly common although its degree and intensity varies but encompasses feelings of uncertainty and pain as well as stimulus and excitement. This suggests that transition and personal change is not as smooth as the existence of a pluralist society suggests because deeper seated changes in identity are necessary in order to grow away from conventional expectations of behaviour – hence the feelings of ambivalence towards oneself and others at times. The process of becoming marginal and then being incorporated into another self, status or lifestyle entails

146

insecurity as well as positive development as 'letting go' and 'coming out' involves change with one's past.

The final selected example of theoretical studies of adult students is the most complex and embarking, taking into account a range of concepts and research propositions. It is also one of the few examples of theory generated from the study of adult students, as opposed to the application of borrowed concepts and empirical insights. The work in question is by Hopper and Osborn and, although it was published several years ago, its insights are still most valuable [16]. It is proposed to summarise first the essential ideas of theory as advanced by Hopper and Osborn and then to detail the background to their work to provide further explanation.

Reduced to essentials, the theory postulates that adult/mature students illustrate the errors of selection at the school stage, which is when most of the sorting and grading by ability and behaviour takes place. Later as adults they experience a problem of identity, arising from ineffective 'warming-up' and 'cooling-out'. Their return to education springs from the difficulties they have experienced as failures and rejects of the school selection process. The decision to become students, in the wide and varied field of adult, post school education, is prompted by what Hopper and Osborn term 'bridging factors'. These may arise in the shape of supportive individuals, of sponsorship by employers, trade unions and other institutions, or other sources. Indeed, the process of 'instrumental adjustment', the term used for the underpinning motives for becoming adult students, is shown to be very complex. The empirical work of their study and closely related ones go a long way towards substantiating their theory, given that the student sample was quite small. This is a common methodological problem for such studies are usually based on small scale case illustrations of particular institutions and sub-groupings.

Returning to the details of their explanations the first point to make is that Hopper and Osborn succinctly combine 'systems' and 'social action' sociological perspectives backed up by a sound methodology. They also include a useful synoptic history of adult education.

Starting with the perspective on education, this is seen in functional terms with the central tasks of the system being the transmission of culture, socialisation and selection for the occupational structure. Particular emphasis is placed on selection as a process involving various kinds of training. With regard to selection and training there are three preparatory processes blended into the curriculum. One form of training is called career preparation which deals with the acquisition of technical knowledge and skills. These range from basic literacy and numeracy to advanced levels of mechanical and scientific knowledge. These are relevant to a wide range of occupations as well as highly specialised skills.

Status training refers to a range of diffuse skills usually geared to social behaviour and mental attitudes relevant to work life in general, as well as particular occupations, with their cultural norms and values. The teaching profession, for example, has all sorts of explicit and implicit expectations about the social behaviour appropriate to being a teacher, not only at the workplace but in society as a whole.

Mobility training, the third of Hopper and Osborn's types, refers to the inculcation of ambitious attitudes to motivate the desire to achieve and maintain successful job performance. It is also concerned with occupational mobility in the sense of gaining promotion and a diversity of career experiences. All three forms of training are embedded in the teaching-learning process, the curriculum and other aspects of the educational career and are designed to achieve a good functional 'fit' between the preparatory stage of schooling and the occupational structure of the economy. Furthermore the functional efficiency of training preparation is also concerned with socialisation and control as a means of maintaining order in society.

The second dimension of the selection process is the idea of educational routes. These routes through the educational system are best seen as links between specific kinds of knowledge and certification, leading to different job and status levels in society. The design of the 1944 Education Act was for a three part route structure – grammar, technical and modern – each geared to different knowledge and skills in a hierarchy of esteem corresponding to the existing division of labour and class structure. Moreover within each major route further sub-divisions took place on the basis of ability and performance tests, ranging from the slow and remedial to fast and advanced levels. It should be noted that this is an 'ideal type' design with many variations in practice owing to the relative independence of local education authorities and individual schools to modify the system.

The important idea is that progress through the selective routes of the educational system is based on the principle of selection (warming up) or rejection (cooling-out). Warming up means support and encouragement to go further and higher through the selective process. Cooling out represents the process by which school performance is not considered sufficiently high enough to progress further. Both selection and rejection act as a form of social control by regulating ambition and setting limits to achievement. 'High flyers' in the school selection process personify the effects of continual warming up whereas remedial students represent the cooling out process in operation.

There is nothing controversial about this process of selection, given that the sorting and grading is done on a fair basis. This begs the question of the fairness and accuracy of intelligence tests and the deeply implicit cultural bias of such measures. Leaving that aside, if such selection is efficient nobody has grounds to dispute the results. Expressed more formally, when educational selection is efficient people are likely to possess clear goals, status consistent with ability and relatively satisfied work role expectations. The passage between school and work, childhood to adulthood is relatively smooth and straightforward. Those 'high flyers' at school would, therefore, find themselves as a consequence of continuous warming-up in good jobs, offering career opportunities and above average status and rewards. Just as consistently, those whose school careers are marked by poor performance and subsequent cooling-out enter the labour market with low expectations and equally limited prospects for employment and satisfying work. Both groups, although having very different prospects, nonetheless recognise that the process of educational selection reflected their ability and performance and they got their just deserts.

The real issues start when the selection process is not efficient. This means two things. First the selection process would be experienced as initial selection followed by rejection, for whatever reasons. Second, selection could start off with rejection followed by subsequent selection. Expressed simply, some start off their school careers doing well but fade later, while others get progressively better after a poor beginning. The most obvious illustrations are those who do so well that they get transferred to a grammar from a secondary modern school or do so badly that they go the other way. With the arrival of comprehensive schools and the deferment of eleven-plus selection the sorting and grading or warming-up and cooling-out process now takes place within schools. In that regard the selection and rejection process may be measured by streaming or ability groupings, even from individual records of school performance. Whichever way school selection is viewed the process is mixed rather than consistent and straightforward. This generates a variety of self-perceptions and subsequent behavioural dispositions in adult life arising from an inefficient selection experience.

Hopper and Osborn go on to identify several states of mind including a sense of relative deprivation with regard to job rewards and status, ambivalent feelings towards such goals as well as society in general and the self in particular, marginality in various settings and personal value conflict. Their return to education in adult life is a means of coping with being a selection error. This is called instrumental adjustment and is seen as a legitimate way of coming to terms with feeling less than adequate in a competitive labour market and an achievement orientated society.

More specifically, relative deprivation means comparing oneself with particular groups, usually better placed in terms of socio-economic status and types of occupations. The comparative activity is the basis of perceived inequality and a sense of being wronged. It is usually related to a negative evaluation of oneself in relation to others' wealth, status, power, personal attributes, educational background, abilities and lifestyles. From this comparative and relatively deprived perspective feelings of marginality emerge because what others possess the adult lacks and this compounds the sense of isolation. The sense of relative deprivation is made more acute by comparing oneself unfavourably with normative reference groups from when the individual takes his or her everyday standards.

Given that the attainment of personally valued goals are made more difficult with a lack of appropriate educational credentials adults may well experience some ambivalence about the pursuit of career ambitions, higher status and material rewards. This provides a rationalisation for the possibility of failure. With such prospect ambivalence turns on the self with the idea of luck holding the balance between success or failure. The same view may be held towards society in general as well as the specific goals of career mobility and success. Luck is not a quantifiable meaning but its use in explanations of everyday events and significant changes is commonplace and cannot be ignored.

Marginality arises as a consequence of being an educational selection error. The adult has not come to terms with the situation and feels estranged from the membership reference group to which he is compelled to belong, while at the same time being a nonmember of the normative reference group to which he aspires but cannot join without the right credentials. This puts the adult in an in-between situation marginal to both his membership and normative reference group.

It is not surprising that these states of mind produce inner conflict about the meaning and value of chosen personal goals. Nonetheless, adult students are characterised by resilience and determination to succeed. There is, of course, a natural wastage rate in this process of becoming an adult student and coping with the psychological and social situation encountered on the way. But for those that keep going returning to education is a means of instrumental adjustment, in the sense of being a practical way of coping with early rejection and feeling unfulfilled both as a worker and a person.

The return to education is a result of two key factors – personality and what Hopper and Osborn term 'bridging factors'. Personality amounts to the intensity of achievement motivation rediscovered in adult life which is geared towards status goals, especially through employment and career success. Such self-expression is generally acceptable as a social and personal goal even though the process of getting there is often open to criticism by others, hence the earlier references to the problems of status passage and feelings of marginality. Bridging factors refer to the wide array of means by which the adult student obtains support and encouragement, directly or indirectly from other people, employers, union activities, church membership, cultural interests and so forth. Studies of bridging factors demonstrate the diversity and complexity of such influences on personality and instrumental adjustment, both as an underpinning motive and process of returning to education as an adult.

It is interesting to note the position of adult education in this analysis of educational selection. Starting first with a view of adult students, they are seen as people who have struggled to improve their prospects in life through career opportunities. They are portrayed as being rather discontented with their lot, as determined by their early educational experiences which they perceive as having dismissed them prematurely and erroneously. In adult life they are dissatisfied with their work experience and, more generally, out of step with their social world. Altogether the conditions that adults have to transcend in order to improve their life chances are seen as restrictive, dead-end experiences compounding the sense of underachievement and lack of opportunity.

The key to all this is the significance of educational achievement as a determinant of occupational opportunities which is a principal means of allocating people to economic and status positions in a stratified and unequal society. Against these backgrounds adult education has been a small but vital element in the struggle for equality of educational and social opportunities. Hence the theme of adult education as a second chance to succeed academically and improve life chances. This assigns to adult education the role of a rearguard rescue service. Another scenario is to assign adult education the task of extending educational opportunities, a view in keeping with the ideas of continuing, lifelong education.

Returning to the main lines of analysis, Hopper and Osborn put forward six propositions about adult students that are built upon their theoretical exposition. These deal with the social and educational backgrounds of adult students and the consequent effects these experiences have on their self-concept and relationships with others, employment and society in general. The propositions are empirically examined in their work and a kindred study conducted at the same time provides a fair measure of support for their findings, though the biographical accounts of the process of becoming a student produces an even more complex picture of individual variations[17]. Yet their main point, that the profiles of adult student corresponds to lower middle class social class backgrounds and a history of near success at school, somewhat modifies the idea that mature students at university, for instance, are all working class 'breakthroughs' and 'late developers' from socially disadvantaged backgrounds. Some are but many more adult students are representative of a sub-grouping who are neither real successes or outright failures educationally and occupationally and the prospects for improved life chances require far less effort than those whose backgrounds are more extreme. The problem with Hopper and Osborn's analysis is that not enough recognition is given to the multiple obstacles to early achievement which arise from the inequalities in social and educational opportunities that large numbers of adults met during their schooldays. To be fair, the authors implicitly note the adverse effects of wider social and educational conditions on motivation and attainment, but their main focus is narrowed to the processes of selection and control, rendering their theory only a partial explanation.

This section of the book has focussed on the adult student and learner using micro type sociological perspectives to highlight the process of becoming and being a returner to formal education. Once more, detailed accounts of theory and research have been put aside in order to focus more generally on an overview of ideas as an introduction to adult student studies, mainly from a sociological angle. The principal difference between section one and two of this book is that whereas the former presents a variety of often opposing views and perspectives the latter is far less given to controversy and is more focussed on researchable ideas. The significant message of this part of the book is that no matter what ideological perspective on adult education is favoured as a background to policy and practice without students ideas barely get off the ground.

NOTES AND REFERENCES

Chapter One

1.a.   The standard reference for the complete range of adult education topics is the latest edition of 'A Select Bibiliography of Adult Continuing Education in Great Britain', edited by J.E. Thomas and J.H. Davies and published by the National Institute of Adult Continuing Education (NIACE) 1984. The select bibliography is published every ten years and the latest edition includes works published to the end of the year 1981. It is also necessary to consult earlier editions, particularly 1974.

b.   The NIACE have also published an equally useful set of reviews of research and resource materials covering a wide span of topics which include computer print-outs as an addition to the annotated reviews.

c.   Several Departments of Adult Education, like the University of Nottingham, regularly publish books, monographs and various papers on adult education theory and practice, research reports and annotated bibliographical guides to the literature on selected disciplines.

d.   My own choice is clearly selective but the best general histories of adult education are, J.F.C. Harrison, 'Learning and Living 1790-1960', Routledge and Kegan Paul, London, 1961; T. Kelly, 'A History of Adult Education in Great Britain', University of Liverpool, second edition, 1970.

e.   In more recent times the contemporary history of adult education is contained in the major reports of the 1970s and ensuing commentaries —see the 1984 Select Bibliography, pp 13-16.

f.   For clear and lucid accounts of the structure and organisation of adult education consult the following —B. Jennings, 'Adult Education in Britain: Its Organisation and Structure', The University of Hull, Department of Adult Education, 1981; D. Legge, 'The Education of Adults in Britain', Open University Press, 1982; A. Stock, 'Adult Education in Great Britain', NIACE, 1980.

g.   For a critical analysis of organisation in adult education see G. Mee and H. Wiltshire, 'Structure and Performance in Adult Education', Longman, 1978; K. Percy et al., 'Post Initial Education in the North West of England: A Survey of Provision, ACACE, 1983.

h.   The philosophical perspective in adult education is well expressed through the writings of K.H. Lawson, 'Philosophical Concepts and Values in Adult Education', 1st Edition, 1975; and 'Analysis and Ideology —Conceptual Essays on the Education of Adults, 1982; both published by the University of Nottingham, Department of Adult

Education; R.W.K. Paterson, 'Values, Education and the Adult', Routledge and Kegan Paul, 1979.

i. For various psychological approaches consult the 'Psychology of Adult Education' section in the 1984 Select Bibliography, pp 94-101.

j. Policy perspectives and advocacy in adult continuing education are contained in the major reports cited in the Select Bibliography and the important documents published by the Advisory Council for Adult and Continuing Education ACACE, especially 'Continuing Education: from Policies to Practice', 1982; and 'Protecting the Future for Adult Education', 1981.

2. For example, ACACE, 'Adults: Their Educational Experiences and Needs', 1982; B. Elsey et al., 'Volunteers in Adult Education', ACACE, 1983; B. Elsey and M. Gibbs, 'Voluntary Tutors in Adult Literacy', University of Nottingham, Department of Adult Education, Working Papers in the Education of Adults, No.3, 1981; NIACE, 'Adequacy of Provision', Adult Education Journal, Vol.42, No.6, March 1970 (whole issue).

Chapter Two

1. See, for instance, the discussion on meaning by P. Jarvis, 'Adult and Continuing Education: Theory and Practice', Croom Helm, London, 1983; and for a mainly American perspective G.G. Darkenwald and S.B. Merriam, 'Adult Education: Foundations of Practice', Harper and Row, New York, 1982. For a distinctively British view see the famous '1919 Report', properly known as 'The Final and Interim Reports of the Adult Education Committee of the Ministry of Reconstruction 1918 and 1919'. Full text and commentary reprinted by University of Nottingham, Department of Adult Education, 1980. A particularly wide view of adult education is by P. Bergevin, 'A Philosophy for Adult Education', the Seabury Press, New York, 1967. Another approach to definition and meaning is through taxonomies of adult education. See, for instance, J. Lowe, 'Adult Education: A Critical Survey', Michael Joseph, London, 1970.

2. Other writers in addition to Harrison and Kelly are cited in the 1984 Select Bibliography. For a worldwide history of adult education through the biographies of adult educators in many countries consult 'The International Biography of Adult Education', edited by J.E. Thomas and B. Elsey, University of Nottingham, Department of Adult Education, 1985.

3. Unpublished paper entitled 'The Historical Evolution of Adult Education in Great Britain', no date.

4. The Russell Report properly titled is 'Adult Education: a Plan for Development', Department of Education and Science (DES), HMSO publication, 1973.

5.   The Alexander Report properly titled is 'Adult Education: The Challenge of Change', Scottish Education Department, HMSO, 1975.

6.   The history, origins and development of the Manpower Services Commssion (MSC) has yet to be fully documented especially with regard to its considerable impact on the educational system arising from its central emphasis upon work related and economic skill training.

7.   P. Jarvis op cit

8.   There is a good account in Darkenwald and Merriam, chapter 2. The critical appraisal of liberal adult education from a radical standpoint is expressed throughout the very stimulating book edited by J.L. Thompson, 'Adult Education for a Change', Hutchinson, 1980, especially the foreword by K. Jackson and J. Thompson's introduction. Many of the writings of H.C. Wiltshire and K.H. Lawson succinctly express both the conventional and liberal perspectives – see Select Bibliography for details. The radical perspective benefits from a lucid comparative treatment in J.E. Thomas, 'Radical Adult Education: Theory and Practice', University of Nottingham, Department of Adult Education, 1982.

9.   See the two articles arising from my MA thesis, 'Leisure and Learning in Voluntary Organisations', University of Liverpool, 1973, entitled 'Voluntary Organisations and Informal Adult Education', Adult Education Journal, Vol.46, No.6, 1974, pp 391-396; and 'Adult Education and the Expressive Functions of Volunary Organisations, 'The Vocational Aspect of Education, Vol.27, No.68, 1975, pp 91-101.

10.   H.C. Wiltshire, 'The Great Tradition', Adult Education Journal, Vol.29, 1956-7.

11.   I. Illich, 'Deschooling Society', Calder and Boyars, London, 1971. See also the reference to Illich in the International Biography, pp 278-280 by P. Lund.

12.   P. Freire, 'Education: The Practice of Freedom', Writers and Readers Publishing Cooperative, 1976, and 'Pedagogy of the Oppressed', Penguin, Harmondsworth, 1972. See also the reference to Freire in the International Biography, pp 183-185 by D. Thompson.

Chapter Three

1.   There are several general histories of the welfare state, notably, M.Bruce, 'The Coming of the Welfare State', Batsford, London, 1968; D. Fraser, 'The Evolution of the British Welfare State: A History of Social Policy Since the Industrial Revolution', Macmillan, London, 1973; P. Gregg, 'The Welfare State: An Economic and Social History of Great Britain 1945 to Present Day', Harrap, London, 1967; T.H. Marshall, 'Social Policy', Hutchinson, London, 1975, revised edition.

2.   The Beveridge Report properly titled, 'Social Insurance and Allied Services' (Cmnd 6404) HMSO, London, 1942.

3.   R.M. Titmuss, 'Commitment to Welfare', Allen and Unwin, London, 1968. For the concept of diswelfare see pp 62-64.

4.   For further analysis and discussion on the meaning of social welfare see W.A. Robson, 'Welfare State and Welfare Society', Allen and Unwin, London, 1976; R.M. Titmuss, 'Commitment to Welfare', 1968, 'Essays on the Welfare State', 2nd edition, Unwin University Books, London, 1963; and 'Social Policy: An Introduction', edited by B. Abel-Smith and T. Titmuss, Allen and Unwin, London, 1974.

5.   I am indebted to a most stimulating article by I. Gough, 'The Crisis of the British Welfare State', International Journal of Health Services, Vol.13, No.3, 1983, pp 459-477, written from a Marxist perspective, and to T.H. Marshall, 'Citizenship and Social Class' in 'Sociology and the Crossroads', Heinemann, London, 1963, pp 67-127.

6.   For further analysis and discussion see R. Mishra, 'The Welfare State in Crisis', Wheatsheaf Books, Harvester Press, UK, 1984.

7.   See R. Pinker, 'Social Theory and Social Policy', Heinemann, London, 1971; 'The Idea of Welfare', Heinemann, London, 1975, for detailed explanations of the three models of social welfare.

Chapter Four

1.   P. Clyne, 'The Disadvantaged Adult', Longman, London, 1972.

2.   A most comprehensive modern treatment of poverty and social policy is by P. Townsend, 'Poverty in the United Kingdom', Penguin, Hammondsworth, 1979.

3.   F. Field, 'Inequality in Britain: Freedom, Welfare and the State', Fontana, London, 1981.

4.   P. Townsend, op.cit., and (editor) 'The Concept of Poverty', Heinemann, London, 1970. See also his article, 'Poverty as Relative Deprivation: Resources and Style of Living' in D. Wedderburn (ed), 'Poverty, Inequality and Class Structure', Cambridge University Press, 1974.

5.   British profiles of the disadvantaged are implicit in P. Clyne op.cit. and various official reports on aspects of the social work services, such as the 'Seebohm Report', properly known as 'Report of the Committee on Local Authority and Allied Personal Social Services', (Cmnd 3703), HMSO, London, 1968. See also K. Coates and R. Silburn, 'Poverty: The Forgotten Englishman', Penguin, Hammondsworth, London, 1972; and

M.L. Rutter and N. Madge, 'Cycles of Disadvantage', Heinemann, London, 1976. For data specifically relevant to adult education the most useful publication is American, D. Anderson and J.A. Niemi, 'Adult Education and the Disadvantaged Adult', Occasional Papers, No.22, Syracuse University, New York, 1970. A useful British addition is the policy document published by the ACACE, 'A Strategy for the Basic Education of Adults', 1979.

6. The starting point for understanding equality as a concept and ideal is the classic by R.H. Tawney, 'Equality', 4th edition, Allen and Unwin, London, 1964. See also B. Goodwin, 'Using Political Ideas', Wiley, London, 1982; J. Le Grand, 'The Strategy of Equality', Allen and Unwin, London, 1982, especially part 1; and where it relates to education, H. Entwistle, 'Class, Culture and Education', Methuen, London, 1978, especially chapter 1.

7. For a summary see I. Reid, 'Social Class Differences in Britain', Open Books, London, 1977.

8. The radical adult education approach to the disadvantaged is well argued by J. Thompson (ed) op.cit. in her chapter entitled 'Adult Education and the Disadvantaged', pp 83-108.

Chapter Five

1. An apt illustration is the study by J. Daines, B. Elsey and M. Gibbs, 'Changes in Student Participation in Adult Education', University of Nottingham, Department of Adult Education, Working Paper No.4, 1982, which embraces many elements typical of participation, descriptive survey research with policy and practice implications.

2. ACACE op.cit., 1982.

3. NIACE op.cit., 1970.

4. For instance, J. Lowe, op.cit. and B. Elsey, op.cit. (1973 MA thesis), and for an American perspective see J.W.C. Johnstone and R.J. Rivera, 'Volunteers for Learning', Aldine, Chicago, 1965.

5. Johnstone and Rivera op.cit. and J. Trenaman, 'Communication and Comprehension', Longman, London, 1967, and particularly, 'Education in the Adult Population', Part 1, in Adult Education Journal, Vol.30, 1957-8, pp 216-224, which deals with attitudes to opportunities for education by adults.

6. A useful introduction is by K. Roberts, 'The Working Class', Longman, London, 1978. A collection of studies is in J. Klein, 'Samples from English Cultures, Vol.1, Routledge and Kegan Paul, 1965, conveying the variety of working class sub-cultures. A

more specific treatment is available, for example, in a study of a mining community, by F. Henriques, et al., 'Coal is Our Life', Eyre and Spottiswoode, London, 1956. Along these lines it is important to read the classic by R. Hoggart, 'The Uses of Literacy', Chatto and Windus, London, 1957. An American example is by A.K. Cohen and H.M. Hodges, 'Characteristics of the Lower Blue Collar Class', Social Problems, Vol.10, No.3, 1966. In all cases it is necessary to refer to the bibliographies for further reading.

7. See the useful summary article by J. Klein, 'The Parents of Schoolchildren', in M. Craft (ed), 'Linking Home and School', Longman, London, 1967, on such classifications of working class culture and sub-groupings.

8. J. Klein op.cit. See also D. Lockwood, 'Sources of Variation in Working Class Images of Society', The Sociological Review, Vol.14, No.3, 1966.

9. This idea is vividly described in R. Hoggart, op.cit.

10. The model shown in the text is a modified version of an interesting American study by M.J. Lundberg, 'The Incomplete Adult: social class constraints on personality development', Greenwood Press, Westport, 1974.

11. R. Hoggart op.cit.

12. See for example, L. Rainwater, 'The American Working Class', in S. Tax (ed), 'Anthropological Backgrounds of Adult Education', CSLEA, Chicago, 1968.

13. J. Clarke (ed), 'Working Class Culture: Studies in History and Theory', Hutchinson, London, 1979.

14. F. Parkin, 'Class Inequality and Political Order', Paladin Books, London, 1972.

15. Reference group theory is explained in sociological dictionaries and some textbooks. An example is N. Abercrombie, S. Hill and B.S. Turner, 'Dictionary of Sociology' Penguin, Harmondsworth, 1984. An extended treatment of the concept is in W.G. Runciman, 'Relative Deprivation and Social Justice', Routledge and Kegan Paul, London, 1966.

16. The theory is throughly outlined and examined in J. Goldthorpe, D. Lockwood, et al., 'The Affluent Worker in the Class Structure', Cambridge University Press, 1969.

17. H. Rodman, 'The Lower Class Value Stretch', Social Forces Journal, Vol.42, 1963, pp 205-215.

Chapter Six

1. See the useful philosophical treatments of the concept by R. Plant, 'Community and

Ideology', Routledge and Kegan Paul, London, 1974; and R.A. Nisbet, 'The Quest for Community', Oxford University Press, 1953.

2. F. Toennies, 'Community and Association', Routledge and Kegan Paul, London, 1955, English translation.

3. R. Frankenberg, 'Communities in Britain', Penguin, Hammondsworth, 1966.

4. G.A. Hillery, 'Definitions of Community: Areas of Agreement', Rural Sociology, Vol.20, No.2, June 1955, pp 111-123.

5. R. Armstrong, 'New Directions for Community Education', Community Development Journal, Vol.12, No.2, 12 April 1977, pp 75-84.

6. R.E. Pahl, 'Patterns of Urban Life', Longman, London, 1970, chapter 7, pp 100-113.

7. M. Stacey, 'The Myth of Community Studies', British Journal of Sociology, Vol.20, 1969, pp 134-147.

8. A.H. Thornton and F.J. Bayliss, 'Adult Education and the Industrial Commuity', NIACE, London, 1965.

9. The 1984 Select Bibliography has a section on community education which also covers some readings in community development, pp 129-137. See also the section on 'Community Development and Welfare Rights' in the bibliography by T. Blacksone, 'Social Policy and Administration in Britain', Frances Pinter, London, 1975.

10. I am indebted to the useful summary provided in the PhD thesis of J. Wallis, 'Community Schools: theory and practice', University of Nottingham, 1983.

11. The Plowden Report properly titled, 'Children and Their Primary Schools', Vol.1, Report of the Central Advisory Council for Education (England), HMSO, London, 1967.

12. The Skeffington Report properly titled, 'People and Planning', HMSO, 1969.

13. See the Scarman Report, properly titled, 'The Brixton Disorders', (Cmnd 8427), HMSO, 1981.

14. I am indebted to an excellent paper by R. Ashcroft, 'The School as a Base for Community Development', in Centre for Research and Innovation, 'School and Community', OECD°HMSO, 1975.

15. Adapted from Community Development Project Final Report, Part 1, 'Coventry and Hillfields: prosperity and the persistence of inequality', March 1975.

16. For the Keele project see R. Shaw and L. West, 'Class Dismissed?', Adult Education Journal, Vol.44, No.6, March 1972, pp 353-358; and R. Shaw's earlier article which began a debate on the role of the WEA in working class commuities, 'Universities and the WEA: Myths and Reality', Adult Education Journal, Vo.44, No.1, May 1971, pp 7-13. See also related articles by others defending the WEA in the 1984 Select Bibliography, pp 26-28. The summary account of the Southampton project is by P. Fordham et al., 'Learning Networks in Adult Education', Routledge and Kegan Paul, London, 1979. For inner London and the idea of outreach adult education see M. Newman, 'The Poor Cousin −A Study of Adult Education', Allen and Unwin, London, 1979. For the WEA in Liverpool see T. Lovett, 'Adult Education Community Development and the Working Class', Ward Lock, London, 1975, reprinted by the Department of Adult Education, University of Nottingham, 1982. T. Lovett, 'Community Development −A Network Approach', Adult Education Journal, Vol.46, No.3, September 1973, pp 157-165. For the university involvement in Liverpool see articles written by R. Ashcroft and/or K. Jackson. For example, K. Jackson, 'Adult Education and Community Development', Studies in Adult Education, Vol.2, 1970, pp 156-179. K. Jackson, 'The Marginality of Community Development −Implications for Adult Education', International Review of Community Development, Summer 1973. K. Jackson and R. Ashcroft, 'Adult Education, Deprivation and Community Development −A Critique', Nuffield Teacher Inquiry, University of York, 1972. R. Ashcroft and K. Jackson, 'Adult Education and Social Action' in D. Jones and M. Mayo (eds), Community Work One, Routledge and Kegan Paul, London, 1974. For a good summary see T. Lovett, 'Adult Education and Community Action', Croom Helm, London, 1983.

17. K. Jackson op.cit., 1973, 'The Marginality of Community Development −Implications for Adult Education'.

Chapter Seven

1.   My own preferred list includes the following texts −E.C. Cuff and G.C.F. Payne (eds), 'Perspectives in Sociology', Allen and Unwin, London, 1979; D. Berry, 'Central Ideas in Sociology', Constable, London, 1974; T.B. Bottomore, ' Sociology: A Guide to Problems and Literature', Allen and Unwin, London, 1971 and 1984 editions; C.H. Brown, 'Understanding Society: An Introduction to Sociological Theory', John Murray, London, 1979; D. Lee and H. Newby, 'The Problem of Sociology', Hutchinson, London, 1983; P.L. Berger and B. Berger, 'Sociology: A Biographical Approach', Penguin, Harmondsworth, 1976; T. Campbell, 'Seven Theories of Human Society', Clarendon Press, Oxford, 1981. Each of these introductory texts have extensive bibliographies which should be consulted especially in dealing with key concepts and the ideas of major contributors to the discipline.

2.   The best introduction to these concepts is in P. Cohen, 'Modern Social Theory', Heinemann, London, 1968. The concepts are lucidly discussed in relation to adult education in J.E. Thomas, 'Radical Adult Education: Theory and Practice', Department of Adult Education, University of Nottingham, 1982; and J.E. Thomas and G. Harries-

Jenkins, 'Adult Education and Social Change', Studies in Adult Education, Vol.7, No.1, 1975, pp 1-15.

3. See the condensed illustrated outline in Cuff and Payne op.cit. and, of course, extended treatment by T. Parsons in his various publications.

4. J. Goldthorpe and D. Lockwood, 'The Affluent Works in the Class Structure', Cambridge University Press, 1969.

Chapter Eight

1. The sociology of education extends much wider than systems theory. Useful introductory texts are O. Banks, 'The Sociology of Education', Batsford, London, 1968; H. Entwistle, 'Class, Culture and Education', Methuen, London, 1978. Systems theory applied to education is discussed in two key articles – R. Collins, 'Functional and Conflict Theories of Educational Stratification', American Sociological Review, Vol.36, 1971, pp 1002-1019; J.C. Jacob, 'Thoeries of Social and Educational Inequality: From Dichotomy to Typology', British Journal of Sociology of Education, Vol.2, No.1, 1981, pp 71-89.

2. D. Bell, 'The Coming of Post Industrial Society', Heinemann, London, 1974.

3. T.B. Bottomore op.cit., chapters 17 and 18, especially pp 308-310.

4. There are many introductions to Marx and Weber. Two easily read ones are by D. McLellan (on Marx) and D.G. MacRae (on Weber) in the Fontana/Collins series 1975 and 1974 respectively. Quite the best guide to radical sociological theory applied to adult education is by S. Westwood, 'Adult Education and the Sociology of Education: An Exploration', pp 31-44 in J. Thompson (ed) op.cit.

5. S. Westwood op.cit. see her references to the works of the authors cited.

6. There is a short biography of Gramsci in the International Biography pp 210-212 by C. Nisi and V. Mascia. See also S. Westwood's bibliography. Friere also appears in the International Biography pp 183-185 by D. Thompson which also includes a short biography.

Other References

T. Husen, 'The School in Question', Oxford University Press, 1979.

J. Demaine, 'Contemporary Theories in the Sociology of Education', Macmillan, London, 1981.

Sociology of the Adult Student

1. There is a section on Mature Students compiled by the writer in the 1984 Select Bibliography, pp 87-90. Some of the material in this section of the book has been adapted

from an earlier article by the writer entitled 'Mature Students' Experiences of University', Studies in Adult Education, Vol.14, 1982, pp 69-77.

2.   For example, in Secondary Education the Newson Report/Central Advisory Council for Education (England), 'Half our Future', HMSO, London, 1963; for Further Education the Crowther Report/Central Advisory Council for Education (England), '15 to 18', HMSO, London, 1959; for Higher Education the Robbins Report, 'Committee on Higher Education', HMSO, London, 1963.

3.   See for instance the Robbins Report findings illustrated and discussed in O. Banks op.cit. pp 53-65. See also T. Husen, 'Social Influences on Educational Attainment', OECD, Paris, 1975; and A. Griffiths, 'Some Recent British Research on the Social Determinants of Education: An Annotated Bibliography', Institute of Education, University of Leeds, 1971.

4.   There is a good discussion in E. and E. Hutchinson, 'Learning Later: Fresh Horizons in English Adult Education', Routledge and Kegan Paul, London, 1979.

5.   There is a summary account in the writer's PhD thesis, 'The Social and Educational Backgrounds of Mature Students at University', University of Nottingham, 1978.

6.   R. Williams, 'Culture and Society 1780-1950', Penguin, Chatto and Windus, London, 1958, pp 331-332.

7.   B. Elsey, PhD thesis, op.cit.

8.   See for example reference to their ideas in N. Abercrombie (et al) op cit.

9.   A Schutz, 'On Phenomenology and Social Relations: selected writings', Chicago University Press, 1970.

10. H. Garfinkel, 'Studies in Ethnomethodology', Prentice-Hall, 1967.

11. R.J. Havinghurst, 'Changing Status and Roles During the Adult Life Cycle: Significance for Adult Education', in Sociological Backgrounds of Adult Education, edited by H.W. Burns, CSLEA, New York, 1963, pp 17-38.

12. G. Harries-Jenkins, 'The Role of the Adult Student', International Journal of Lifelong Education, Vol.1, No.1, pp 19-39.

13. The best treatment of status passage theory in general terms is by B.G. Glaser and A.L. Strauss, 'Status Passage', Routledge and Kegan Paul, London, 1971.

14. The best treatment of marginality theory is by F. Musgrove, 'Margins of the Mind', Methuen, London, 1977.

15. See pp 17-19 of Musgrove's book.

16. E. Hopper and M. Osborn, 'Adult Students — Education, Selection and Social Control', Francis Pinter, London, 1975.

17. B. Elsey, PhD thesis, op.cit.

SELECTED BIBLIOGRAPHY

Abel-Smith, B. and Titmuss, T. 'Social Policy: An Introduction', Allen and Unwin, London, 1974.

Advisory Council Adult and Continuing Education (ACACE) 'A Strategy for the Basic Education of Adults', Leicester, 1979.

ACACE 'Protecting the Future for Adult Education', 1981.

ACACE 'Continuing Education: From Policies to Practice', 1982.

ACACE 'Adults: Their Educational Experiences and Needs', 1982.

Alexander Report 'Adult Education: The Challenge of Change', Scottish Education Department, HMSO, 1975.

Anderson, D. and Niemi, J.A. 'Adult Education and the Disadvantaged Adult', Occasional Papers, No.22, Syracuse University, New York, 1970.

Armstrong, P. 'The −Needs Meeting− Ideology in Liberal Adult Education', International Journal of Lifelong Education, Vol.1, No.4, 1982 ,pp 293-321.

Armstrong, R. 'New Directions for Community Education', Community Development Journal, Vol.12, No.2, 12 April 1977, pp 75-84.

Ashcroft, R. 'The School as a Base for Community Development', in 'School and Community', Centre for Research and Innovation, OECD/HMSO, 1975.

Ashcroft, R. and Jackson, K. 'Adult Education and Social Action', in Jones, D. and Mayo, M. (eds), Community Work One, Routledge and Kegan Paul, London, 1974.

Banks, O. 'The Sociology of Education', Batsford, London, 1968.

Bell, C. and Newby, H. 'Community Studies: An Introduction to the Sociology of the Local Community', Allen and Unwin, London, 1971.

Bell, D. 'The Coming of Post Industrial Society', Heinemann, London, 1974.

Berger, P. and Berger, B. 'Sociology: A Biographical Approach', Penguin, Harmondsworth, 1976.

Bergevin, P. 'A Philosophy for Adult Education', The Seabury Press, New York, 1967.

Berry, D. 'Central Ideas in Sociology', Constable, London, 1974.

Beveridge Report 'Social Insurance and Allied Services' (Cmnd 6404), HMSO, London, 1942.

Blackstone, T. 'Social Policy and Administration in Britain: A Bibliography', Frances Pinter, London, 1975.

Blackstone, T. and Mortimore, J. 'Disadvantage and Education', Heinemann, London, 1982.

Bottomore, T.B. 'Sociology: A Guide to Problems and Literature', Allen and Unwin, London, 1971.

Brown, C.H. 'Understanding Society: An Introduction to Sociological Theory', John Murray, London, 1979.

Bruce, M. 'The Coming of the Welfare State', Batsford, London, 1968.

Campbell, T. 'Seven Theories of Human Society', Clarendon Press, Oxford, 1981.

Clyne, P. 'The Disadvantaged Adult', Longman, London, 1972.

Coates, K. and Silburn, R. 'Poverty: The Forgotten Englishman', Penguin, Harmondsworth, 1972.

Cohen, A.K. and Hodges, H.M. 'Characteristics of the Lower Blue Collar Class', Social Problems, Vol.10, No.3, 1966, pp 303-334.

Cohen, P. 'Modern Social Theory, Heinemann, London, 1968.

Collins, R. 'Functional and Conflict Theories of Educational Stratification', American Sociological Review, Vol.36, 1971, pp 1002-1019.

Craft, M. (ed) 'Linking Home and School', Longman, London, 1967.

Crowther Report '15 to 18', HMSO, 1959.

Cuff, E.C. and Payne, G.C.F. (eds) 'Perspectives in Sociology', George Allen and Unwin, London, 1979 and 1984 editions.

Daines, J., Elsey, B. and Gibbs, M. 'Changes in Student Participation in Adult Education', University of Nottingham, Department of Adult Education, Working Paper No.4, 1982.

Darkenwald, G.G. and Merriam, S.B. 'Adult Education: Foundations of Practice', Harper and Row, New York, 1982.

Demaine, J. 'Contemporary Theories in the Sociology of Education', Macmillan, London, 1981.

Elsey, B. MA Thesis, 'Leisure and Learning in Voluntary Organisations', University of Liverpool, 1973.

Elsey, B. 'Voluntary Organisations and Informal Adult Education', Adult Education Journal, Vol.46, No.6, 1974, pp 391-396.

Elsey, B. 'Adult Education and the Expressive Functions of Voluntary Organisations', The Vocational Aspect of Education, Vol.27, No.68, 1975, pp 91-101.

Elsey, B. PhD Thesis, 'The Social and Educational Backgrounds of Mature Students at University', University of Nottingham, 1978.

Elsey, B. and Gibbs, M. 'Voluntary Tutors in Adult Literacy', University of Nottingham, Department of Adult Education, Working Papers in the Education of Adults, No.3, 1981.

Elsey, B., Hall, D., Hughes, I. and Laplace, C. 'Volunteers in Adult Education', ACACE, 1983.

Entwistle, H. 'Class, Culture and Education', Methuen, London, 1978.

Field, F. 'Inequality in Britain: Freedom, Welfare and the State', Fontana, London, 1981.

Fordham, P. et al. 'Learning Networks in Adult Education', Routledge and Kegan Paul, London, 1979.

Frankenberg, R. 'Communities in Britain', Penguin, Harmondsworth, 1966.

Fraser, D. 'The Evolution of the British Welfare State: A History of Social Policy Since the Industrial Revolution', Macmillan, London, 1973.

Freire, P. 'Pedagogy of the Oppressed', Penguin, Harmondsworth, 1972.

Freire, P. 'Education: The Practice of Freedom', Writer and Readers Publishing Cooperative, 1976.

Gamble, A. 'Britain in Decline', Macmillan, London, 1981.

Garfinkel, H. 'Studies in Enthnomethodology', Prentice-Hall, Englewood-Cliffs, 1967.

George, V. and Wilding, P. 'Ideology and Social Welfare', Routledge and Kegan Paul, London, 1976.

Ginsburg, N. 'Class, Capital and Social Policy', Macmillan, London, 1979.

Glaser, G.B. and Strauss, A.L. 'Status Passage', Routledge and Kegan Paul, London, 1971.

Goldthorpe, J., Lockwood, D. et al. 'The Affluent Worker in the Class Structure', Cambridge University Press, 1969.

Goodwin, B. ' Using Political Ideas', Wiley, London, 1982.

Gough, I. 'The Crisis of the British Welfare State', International Journal of Health Services, Vol.13, No.3, 1983, pp 459-477.

Gregg, P. 'The Welfare State: An Economic and Social History of Great Britain 1945 to Present Day', Harrap, London, 1967.

Griffiths, A. 'Some Recent British Research on the Social Determinants of Education: An Annotated Bibliography', Institute of Education, University of Leeds, 1971.

Harries-Jenkins, G. 'The Role of the Adult Student', International Journal of Lifelong Education, Vol.1, No.1, 1982, pp 19-39.

Harrison, J.F.C. 'Learning and Living 1790-1960', Routledge and Kegan Paul, London, 1961.

Havighurst, R.J. 'Changing Status and Roles During the Adult Life Cycle: Significance for Adult Education', in 'Sociological Backgrounds of Adult Education', (ed) Burns, H.W., CSLEA, New York, 1963, pp 17-38.

Henriques, F. et al. 'Coal is Our Life', Eyre and Spottiswoode, London, 1956.

Hillery, G.A. 'Definitions of Community: Areas of Agreement', Rural Sociology, Vol.20, No.2, June 1955, pp 111-123.

Hoggart, R. 'The Uses of Literacy', Chatto and Windus, London, 1957.

Hopper, E. and Osborn, M. 'Adult Students −Education, Selection and Social Control', Francis Pinter, London, 1975.

Hostler, J. 'The Aims of Adult Education', Department of Adult and Higher Education, University of Manchester, 1981.

Husen, T. 'Social Influences on Educational Attainment', OECD, Paris, 1975.

Husen, T. 'The School in Question', Oxford University Press, 1979.

Hutchinson, E. and Hutchinson, E. 'Learning Later: Fresh Horizons in English Adult Education', Routledge and Kegan Paul, London, 1979.

Illich, I. 'Deschooling Society', Calder and Boyars, London, 1971.

Jackson, K. 'Adult Education and Community Development', Studies in Adult Education, Vol.2, 1970, pp 156-179.

Jackson, K. and Ashcroft, R. 'Adult Education, Deprivation and Community Development −A Critique', Nuffield Teacher Inquiry, University of York, 1972.

Jackson, K. 'The Marginality of Community Development −Implications for Adult Education', International Review of Community Development, Summer 1973.

Jackson, K. Foreword in Thompson, J.L. 'Adult Education for a Change', Hutchinson, London, 1980.

Jacob, J.C. 'Theories of Social and Educational Inequality: From Dichotomy to Typology', British Journal of Sociology of Education, Vol.2, No.1, 1981, pp 71-89.

Jarvis, P. 'Adult and Continuing Education: Theory and Practice', Croom Helm, UK, 1983.

Jennings, B. 'Adult Education in Britain: Its Organisation and Structure', The University of Hull, Department of Adult Education, 1981.

Johnstone, J.W.C. and Rivera, R.J. 'Volunteers for Learning: A study of the educational pursuits of American Adults', Aldine, Chicago, 1965.

Jones, D. and Mayo, M. (eds) 'Community Work One', Routledge and Kegan Paul, London, 1974.

Kelly, T. 'A History of Adult Education in Great Britain', University of Liverpool, second edition, 1970.

Kelly, T. 'The Historical Evolution of Adult Education in Great Britain', University of Liverpool, undated.

Klein, J. 'Samples from English Cultures', Vol.1, Routledge and Kegan Paul, London, 1965.

Klein, J. 'The Parents of Schoolchildren', in Craft, M. (ed) 'Linking Home and School', Longman, London, 1967.

Lawson, K.H. 'Philosophical Concepts and Values in Adult Education', University of Nottingham, Department of Adult Education, 1975.

Lawson, K.H. 'Analysis and Ideology – Conceptual Essays on the Education of Adults', University of Nottingham, Department of Adult Education, 1982.

Lee, D. and Newby, H. 'The Problem of Sociology', Hutchinson, London, 1983.

Legge, D. 'The Education of Adults in Britain', Open University Press, 1982.

Le Grand, J. 'The Strategy of Equality;, Allen and Unwin, London, 1982.

London, J. 'The Influence of Social Class Behaviour Upon Adult Education Participation', Adult Education (USA), Vol.20, No.3, 1970.

Lovett, T. 'Community Development – A Network Approach', Adult Education Journal, Vol.46, No.3, September 1973.

Lovett, T. 'Adult Education and Community Action', Croom Helm, UK, 1983.

Lowe, J. 'Adult Education: A Critical Survey', Michael Joseph, London, 1970.

Lund, P. Biography of Illich, I. in 'International Biography', 1985.

Lundberg, M.J. 'The Incomplete Adult: social class constraints on personality development', Greenwood Press, Westport, 1974.

MacRae, D.G. 'Weber', Fontana/Collins, London, 1974.

Marshall, T.H. 'Citizenship and Social Class' in 'Sociology at the Crossroads', Heinemann, London, 1963.

Marshall, T.H. 'Social Policy', Hutchinson, London, 1975.

McLellan, D. 'Marx', Fontana/Collins, London, 1975.

Mee, G. and Wiltshire, H.C. 'Structure and Performance in Adult Education, Longman, London, 1978.

Mishra, R. 'The Welfare State in Crisis', Wheatsheaf Books, Harvester Press, UK, 1984.

Musgrove, F. 'Margins of the Mind', Methuen, London, 1977.

National Institute of Adult Education (NIAE) 'Adequacy of Provision', Adult Education Journal, Vol.42, No.6, March 1970.

National Institute of Adult Continuing Education (NIACE) Reviews of Research in Adult Education (Series).

Newman, M. 'The Poor Cousin – A Study of Adult Education', Allen and Unwin, London, 1979.

Newsom Report 'Half Our Future', HMSO, London, 1963.

Nisbet, R.A. 'The Quest for Community', Oxford University Press, 1953.

Nisi, C. and Mascia, V. Biography of Gramsci in 'International Biography', 1985.

Pahl, R.E. 'Patterns of Urban Life', Longman, London, 1970.

Parkin, F. 'Class Inequality and Political Order', Paladin Books, London, 1972.

Paterson, R.W.K. 'Values, Education and the Adult', Routledge and Kegan Paul, 1979.

Percy, K. et al. 'Post Initial Education in the North West of England: A Survey of Provision', ACACE, 1983.

Pinker, R. 'Social Theory and Social Policy', Heinemann, London, 1971.

Pinker, R. 'The Idea of Welfare', Heinemann, London, 1975.

Plant, R. 'Community and Ideology', Routledge and Kegan Paul, London, 1974.

Plowden Report 'Children and Their Primary Schools', Vol.1, HMSO, London, 1967.

Rainwater, L. 'The American Working Class' in 'Anthropological Backgrounds of Adult Education', Tax, W. (ed), CSLEA, Chicago, 1968.

Reid, I. 'Social Class Differences in Britain', Open Books, London, 1977.

1919 Report 'The Final and Interim Reports of the Adult Education Committee of the Ministry of Reconstruction 1918 and 1919', full text and commentary reprinted by University of Nottingham, Department of Adult Education, 1980.

Robbins Report 'Committee on Higher Education', HMSO, London, 1963.

Roberts, K. 'The Working Class', Longman, London, 1978.

Robson, W.A. 'Welfare State and Welfare Society', Allen and Unwin, London, 1976.

Rodman, H. 'The Lower Class Value Stretch', Social Forces Journal, Vo.42, 1963, pp 205-215.

Runciman, W.G. 'Relative Deprivation and Social Justice', Routledge and Kegan Paul, London, 1966.

Russell Report 'Adult Education: A Plan for Development', Department of Education and Science (DES), HMSO, 1973.

Rutter, M.L. and Madge, N. 'Cycles of Disadvantage', Heineman, London, 1976.

Scarman Report 'The Brixton Disorders' (Cmnd 8427), HMSO, London, 1981.

Schutz, A. 'On Phenomenology and Social Relations: selected writings', Chicago University Press, 1970.

Seebohm Report 'Report of the Committee on Local Authority and Allied Personal Social Services' (Cmnd 3703), HMSO, London, 1968.

Shaw, R. 'Universities and the WEA: Myths and Reality', Adult Education Journal, Vol.44, No.1, May 1971.

Shaw, R. and West, L. 'Class Dismissed?', Adult Education Journal, Vol.44, No.6, March 1972.

Skeffington Report 'People and Planning', Report of Committee on Public Participation in Planning, Ministry of Housing and Local Government, HMSO, 1969.

Stacey, M. 'The Myth of Community Studies', British Journal of Sociology, Vol.20, 1969, pp 134-147.

Stock, A. 'Adult Education in Great Britain', NIAE, 1980.

Tawney, R.H. 'Equality', 4th Edition, Allen and Unwin, London, 1964.

Thomas, J.E. and Harries-Jenkins, G. 'Adult Education and Social Change', Studies in Adult Education, Vol.7, No.1, 1975.

Thomas, J.E. 'Radical Adult Education: Theory and Practice', University of Nottingham, Department of Adult Education, 1982.

Thomas, J.E. and Davies, J.H. 'A Select Bibliography of Adult Continuing Education', NIACE, 1984.

Thomas, J.E. and Elsey, B. (eds) 'The International Biography of Adult Education', University of Nottingham, Department of Adult Education, 1985.

Thompson, D. Biography of Freire in 'International Biography', 1985.

Thompson, J.L. 'Adult Education for a Change', Hutchinson, London, 1980.

Thornton, A.H. and Bayliss, F.J. 'Adult Education and the Industrial Community', NIAE, London, 1965.

Titmuss, R. 'Essays on the Welfare State', Unwin University Books, London, 1963.

Titmuss, R. 'Commitment to Welfare', Unwin University Books, London, 1968.

Toennies, F. 'Community and Association', Routledge and Kegan Paul, London, 1955.

Townsend, P. (ed) 'The Concept of Poverty', Heinemann, London, 1970.

Townsend, P. 'Poverty in the United Kingdom', Penguin, Harmondsworth, 1979.

Trenaman, J. 'Education in the Adult Population', Adult Education Journal, Vol.30, 1957/8.

Trenaman, J. 'Communication and Comprehension', Longman, London, 1967.

Wallis, J. Phd Thesis 'Community Schools: theory and practice', University of Nottingham, 1983.

Wedderburn, D. (ed) 'Poverty, Inequality and Class Structure', Cambridge University Press, 1974.

Westergaard, J. and Resler, H. 'Class in a Capitalist Society', Heinemann, London, 1975.

Westwood, S. 'Adult Education and the Sociology of Education: An Exploration' in Thompson, J.L. 'Adult Education for a Change', 1980.

Williams, R. 'Culture and Society 1780-1950', Chalto and Windus, London, 1958.

Wiltshire, H.C. 'The Great Tradition', Adult Education Journal, Vol.29, 1956/7.

INDEX

169